Change Your Reality and You Change Your Life

6 Dimensions of Healing
- Handbook -

Change Your Reality and You Change Your Life.

Gayle Maree with Allan Herring

6DimensionsofHealing.com

Six Dimensions of Healing

Copyright © 2017 by Gayle Maree and Allan Herring

ISBN: 978-06480140-2-7

All rights reserved. No part of the book may be reproduced by any mechanical, photographic or electronic process, or in the form of a photographic recording; nor may it be stored in a retrieval system, transmitted, or otherwise be copied for public or private use – other than for "fair use" as brief quotations embodied in articles and reviews – without written permission of the copyright holder.

The authors of this book do not dispense medical advice or prescribe the use of any technique as a form of treatment for physical or medical problems without the advice of a physician, either directly, or indirectly. It is the intent of the authors only to offer information of a general nature to help you in your quest for physical, emotional and spiritual well-being. In the event you use any of the information in this book for yourself, which is your constitutional right, the authors assume no responsibility for your actions.

6 Dimensions of Healing™ and 6D Healing™ are registered trademarks.

Printed on acid-free paper.

2017

First Edition

Change Your Reality and You Change Your Life

Dedication

In appreciation of all our loving friends and family,
Both physical and non-physical.

In the words of William Ernest Henley (*Invictus*, 1849-1903)
I am the master of my fate,
I am the captain of my soul.

Six Dimensions of Healing

Change Your Reality and You Change Your Life

🌀 *For Your Protection* 🌀

This handbook will awaken information that has lain dormant for many years within, which can benefit your life and the life of those around you. Reading this handbook will not make you a 6D Healing Practitioner or 6 Dimensions of Healing Facilitator. It will not make you knowledgeable to teach 6 Dimensions of Healing or allow you to represent yourself to others as a 6D Healing Practitioner or 6 Dimensions of Healing Facilitator. Successful completion of the course 6D Healing Practitioner or 6 Dimensions of Healing Facilitator taught by Gayle Maree or Allan Herring is a requirement for these qualifications.

Presently Gayle Maree and Allan Herring are the only authorized and qualified instructors for 6D Healing and 6 Dimensions of Healing. In the future a list of instructors can be found on the 6DimensionsofHealing.com website. You can contact 6D Healing and 6 Dimensions of Healing at the email and phone numbers found on the website which will be the most recent information available.

For your protection, please contact us at **info@6DHealing.com**, prior to attending any seminar that proposes to offer training in Six Dimensions of Healing as a facilitator, practitioner or instructor, taught by anyone other than Gayle Maree or Allan Herring. We will let you know if that instructor is qualified to teach 6 Dimensions of Healing.

To find out more about becoming more self aware in Six Dimensions of Healing, to attend a workshop or to become a teaching assistant or mentor, contact us at info@6DHealing.com or the contact information on our website at 6DimensionsofHealing.com. We look forward to your comments and inquiries.

FOREWORD

Gayle Maree

"I learned this, at least, by my experiment: that if one advances confidently in the direction of his dreams, and endeavors to live the life which he has imagined, he will meet with success unexpected in common hours."

Henry David Thoreau (1854), *Walden*

From the time I was young, I remember that if I hurt myself, I would put my hands on the affected area and the pain would go away. I thought that was what everyone did. I didn't want anyone to touch me or talk to me; I would just turn my focus inward. As I got older and found that I did the same when I was giving birth, I realized that the healing truly lay inward. Not in what you could do, but where you could send your focus.

In our natural therapies practices, we used the same techniques on all our clients but found that no matter how much pain we could help to eliminate, our clients had a choice as to whether it was gone completely, or whether the pain returned. It seemed that the combination of physical alignment *and* emotional transition was the transformation people were searching for, without knowing it.

Counseling came naturally to me, as I was always standing up for the underdog at school and then becoming the target. I lost count of the number of times I talked my way out of a fight, and it was always by showing a different perspective, long enough to get me to safety anyway. What I didn't like about counseling was that it was a method that dealt with the past by dredging up the past over and over, until it became numb. I knew from experience that focusing on the past created more of what you didn't like about it. After years of writing and moving in a different direction, I came up with a process I called 'Emotional Life Coaching'. I was experienced and talented in the direction of the emotions, and understood you didn't need to go looking in the past to find what was going wrong in the present, as what was happening now would provide you with the tools you needed to move forward. It has been my experience that others can often see your life more clearly illustrated than you do, and so Emotional Coaching has been a very effective method that has helped many people.

There has always been a drive within me to empower people, as I had experienced the amazing effect of confidence when other people had uplifted me throughout my life. I wasn't drawn toward success in the usual sense of the word; but rather to fulfillment and happiness, and somehow I knew money was going to come with that.

I experienced much refining of my life. It was a process I taught, so knowing that I enjoyed helping people find a new perspective changed my focus. The love of empowering people, added to the focus. Needing my own time alone and wanting acknowledgment for what I did seemed conflicting, yet I added them to my list. This was the process I used, and when the refinement was complete for now, I allowed opportunities to present themselves over the years. My husband and I came across *The Law of Attraction: The Basics of the Teachings of Abraham* by Esther and Jerry Hicks (2006), a book that changed my life. It was so simple and succinct, yet many people I introduced it to could not understand the philosophy. So, we started to simplify the teachings.

We had the opportunity to live in the USA for fourteen months in 2013. Taking two children with us, we sold up everything in Australia, and enjoyed the adventure in Palm Desert (east of LA) where we met some truly wonderful people. We gained a large following of people wanting to make sense of their lives and this helped us redefine, yet again, what we wanted from life. We had expanded beyond whom we had dreamed of becoming, and now had a new adventurous platform from which to create a bigger and better life.

Allan Herring

My life changed in an instant. Not really an instant though, as mine has been a life in progress for, well, a lifetime. Probably several lifetimes. This 'instant' moment was like the next piece of a jigsaw falling into place. You know – when you find that small piece of the large jigsaw with colors and tabs that link to so many others; it is like a pathway. Well this was the journey of meeting my life partner and knowing from the first moment that she was the one I had been waiting for.

It was a Friday afternoon, a rainy day late in April. It was a day of change, but I was unaware of the full impact it would have on me. There was going to be change anyway; it was that kind of atmosphere. That was to be the day our souls met again. It really was instant. Our paths had unknowingly crossed many times during this life, but not connected until then. The stars were now lining up. Was this a healing time? Most definitely.

The meeting place was a personal-growth workshop. We both had a 'knowing' that we needed to be at the workshop that weekend. Physically, I felt pretty good; I was strong, healthy and vibrant. I felt I knew my strengths and weaknesses. Having this physical strength in my corner was a major asset, because I could tap into the memory of how things were supposed to feel when everything was working (or not working, for that matter). That was my mood map – with its emotional, mental, and spiritual dimensions. To be truthful, I wasn't even aware of the latter two dimensions at the time. Suffice it to say, I was looking for change in a big way.

The workshop itself was life changing. Our eyes met a few times that weekend. We even sat down for lunch together. There were indicators of attraction, but the defining moment came when we embraced. That happened during the workshop, and there were many other people to embrace, but when Gayle and I held each other, I knew. It was the feeling of belonging, felt for the first time in my life, but I still recognized it as true. It was the feeling of coming home, of ease, of all being well with the world. There was no past or future; there was only now. The moment. They say you know when you meet the right person, and I have to agree.

All Six Dimensions of healing washed through my being like a beautiful wave of emotion. My mind was alert, my senses piqued, I saw everything only with the light of love, which gave me an optimistic outlook for the future. I now had clarity. There was a new and exciting vision of how I wanted to live my life. By Sunday afternoon, the alignment of the emotional, spiritual and mental side had started to bridge the vast gap, giving me a sense of balance and purpose for many years to come. Of course, at the time, I was unaware of the changes that would unfold. My life changed over those couple of days as I became aware that I wanted to be the person I was put on this earth to be. I didn't know exactly what that would look like, but was inspired by my newfound love to move towards a new 'me'. To help heal my spirit, I had met an amazing woman. Gayle helped me place my life into a perspective that I could understand and grow with. It still is an amazing work in progress.

There was a major impasse, a turning point with all lights blazing, and I recognized it. I still do – again, and again, and again.

Six Dimensions of Healing

Contents

Introduction to the Six Dimensions — 1
The Role of Source Energy — 3
What is Reality? — 5
Have a plan — 6

Dimension - Physical — 9
A Robust Body is a Healthy Body — 11
Your Body, Your Choice — 17
Enjoy your Body — 30
Activity Enjoyment Scale — 35
Food Consciousness — 39
Dynamic Posture — 46
Create Your Piece of Paradise — 49

Dimension - Mental — 57
You Create Your Own Reality — 59
Fairness Vs. Worthiness — 63
Universal Truth — 65
Benefits of Self-talk — 70
Overriding the Cells of your Body — 76
Create Your Own Story — 81
The Lost World of Imagination — 86
Cleaning up Stress — 93
Methods of Relaxation — 97
Sympathy and Compassion — 108
Role Model or Anti-Role Model — 111
Opportunities for Growth — 115
The Determining Factor — 117

Dimension - Emotional — **125**

Connection and Contrast — 127
Your Mood Map — 133
Every Subject is Really Two Subjects — 135
Mood Barometer — 141
The Game of Triangles — 144
We Teach only by Example — 150
Resistance is Your Friend — 151
Emotional Baggage — 156
Shortcut to Manifestation — 160
5 Easy Steps to Change your Life — 166
Giving Up is Good — 169

Dimension – Attitude — **173**

What is Attitude Anyway? — 175
Right and Wrong Decisions — 179
Finding Inspired Answers — 183
Your Perspective is Important — 187
Become the Person you Love — 192
Desires, Goals and Dreams — 194
Our Journey Spans Lifetimes — 197
Sharing Energy — 201

Dimension - Vibration — **203**

When to Take Action — 205
90% Rule — 207
Find your Direction by Feeling your Way — 209
Expanding Vibration — 210
The Five Steps of Manifestation — 215
Master your Mood Changes — 219
The Importance of Clarity — 223
Vibrational Awareness — 226
How we attract people — 227

A New Understanding of Communication	231
The Power in Your Present Moment	241
New Patterns for the Future	245

Dimension – Intention   253

Set your intentions!	255
The Parent Trap	258
Relationships	264
Transforming Your Relationships	268
Pretending to be Polite	271
Manifesting Negative or Positive	273
Choose your Master wisely	274
Look where you are going	278
Changing Patterns of Behavior	280
Old Habit Patterns	282
Free Yourself from Fear, Anxiety, Stress & Tension	284
Releasing Pain through Acknowledgement	287
How Unconditional is your Giving?	290
The Benefits of Feeling Great!	293

You and Your Purpose in Life   297

In Conclusion - Keep It Simple	300
Journey through Time	301
Interview	303

Glossary   307

Bibliography   309

Six Dimensions of Healing

Introduction to the Six Dimensions

What if you were given the opportunity to expand and grow in directions that were uncharted? What if you were offered a journey of freedom, love, money, health and travel? What if you could take a map on your journey so there would always be accurate and consistent guidance, so that you could not get lost, and what if you knew there was no risk because you couldn't fail? Would you take the opportunity for fun and adventure? Would the journey be worth the peaks and troughs? Knowing there was no risk and you were guided with a detailed map, would you take the opportunity?

The answer, of course, is 'yes', as that is what you enthusiastically embraced. Just breathing life into this physical body of yours began a sense of fun and adventure that would always stir excitement in the soul, and excitement was always a beacon towards the path of your joy. Becoming physical gave you an opportunity to grow beyond who you were when you were born, and it presented continuous opportunities for manifesting the joy within you. Your willingness to come forth on this leading edge of creation was celebrated by those who were physical and non-physical. It was never a punishment, or a series of lessons.

You were aware that any risks were only apparent risks, and that you would gather new beliefs and understandings from experience, that would mold your journey. These new beliefs, whether real or perceived, would become the veil over your reality; you would perceive life through this mantle and then decide what worked for you and what didn't. There was no wrong or right path, and you were never to feel alone, as you always had a map and loving guidance.

Your map was built-in; it took the form of a Mood Map, so that when you felt good you knew you were on track. When you didn't, you knew it was up to you to change something. It was a simple but effective plan, because your emotions are the connection to your soul, which is always guiding your path.

When you became focused in a direction unwanted which is commonly known as being stuck, there would come a nudge or bump in the road, and there would be those willing to come into your life and offer another perspective. You weren't always going to recognize them as divine helpers, but they weren't after recognition. There would be time for thanks further down the track. Meditation and sleep were to be your reset buttons, places from which you could emotionally start again. Immersing yourself in nature was to be a means of rejuvenation for your soul, as you were then amongst 'connected' beings.

Never did you once think you could get lost, or that others could control your path. Not for a moment did you think it wasn't worth the journey, because you always knew it was. You chose to come forth into this body to experience the expansion through joy that your choices would provide and in so doing, would help all mankind. Every footprint you made upon this earth was changing the fabric of your design. You knew you were never going to be the same person ever again, as every contrast and experience was expanding the knowledge and emotion of your inner being. You knew your path would connect with those of others, and that it would inspire them to expand and grow, as we are all in this together.

You are a Divine being who came to enjoy life by sorting through life's experiences to decide what you would give your attention to, thereby inviting into your reality, and what not to invite. You chose this noble pursuit for yourself, for your non-physical family, and for those to come. The Earth is a much better place since you have been here, and every thought you ever think is alive and searching for an opportunity to grow. Constant thought and emotion are what puts the eternalness into Eternity.

The Role of Source Energy

We are one with all creation, and because of this, we are never separated from that which is our Divine Being. When we were born, only part of our Divine Being came forth into this our physical body; the remainder stayed in non-physical dimension, so that we could be guided by broader perspective, which always remained in the light of clarity. When we are aligned with our Divine Being, Inner Guidance, Source Energy, or the Higher Self part of us (call it what you will), we are connected with the fullness of who we are, and we feel joy and appreciation. Everyone experiences connection to the wholeness of their being, *sometimes*. It allows infinite knowledge and clarity. This is where inspired ideas come from; it is the place of ease and flow, and is the most desired pathway for living a joyful life. When we are out of alignment with our connection with Source Energy, we feel tension as the movement away from our Source Being causes emotional, and eventually, physical pain.

The reason we usually don't remember much about the fullness of who we really are, is that our soul has had many experiences from which to draw that may not enhance our present journey of expansion and growth. Many lifetimes of experiences filled with joy and pain could become overwhelming, and if we remembered them all, we would get stuck in the detail. In any case, life isn't about the situations; it is always about the emotions. We have come to this lifetime with a clear memory, and particular areas of growth dominant within us. We attract opportunities for growth like a magnet, so there is no need for us to look for expansion, as it will inevitably occur through the choices we make. It is desirable, but not a requirement, that this growth should take place in an atmosphere of fun, and the choice is always ours.

Our Mood Map will guide us through our emotions to connect with our Source, but we will always feel much better when connected, and will feel tension the farther our mood is from our Higher Self. This is the guidance of Source Energy, and it will always take the moral high ground, so when we feel discomfort, this is an indicator that our opinion differs from that of the Source.

What is Reality?

What is happening and how you're feeling about life right now is reality. It's referred to as 'your' reality, as every person on the planet has a different reality. An interlude from the time you're born to the time you die is called *life*, which is made up of a continual series of realities. These join together to become memories. A memory can be either an ally or an adversary, but all have a place in the creation of who we are becoming.

Nobody else's thoughts or actions create your reality. Instead, your reality is the direct reflection of the thoughts *you* think and the emotions *you* feel. When you feel a particular way because of what another is doing or has said, the emotion affects your reality. When your mood is lowered in response to another person's actions, it is commonly referred to as someone else's fault. It's easy to see how you can mistake your response to what another has done for what *you* have chosen, but always, *you* get to choose how you think and feel, and nobody can take that away from you. What *you* think and feel creates your reality.

Reality is made up of moods and is influenced by perception. Every time you think a thought, it adds to the stream of thoughts and emotions that are already actively becoming a reality. When you think a thought that's in opposition to how you feel, there is a fork in the road of emotions, and it influences your reality in another direction, wanted or unwanted. Realities are flexible and organic. They bend and move constantly, often before you are even aware of them. However, realities don't have a mind of their own. The creating belongs to *you*.

How long does it take to change your reality?

You can change your reality instantly by changing a thought, as the thought you are thinking in the here and now has the potential to become your future. However, it takes twenty-one days to create a new habit with new and effective patterns of thought. It may take a while for you to decide what your new path is to be, so thirty days is a reasonable time to be conscious of change in your life. This happens through your creating new mood patterns, new understandings, and new awareness. As you become more acutely aware of changing thoughts and emotions, there will come a time when you will change your thought, feel the emotion, and immediately be aware of the reality being created.

Have a plan

This handbook is about providing simple tools to move toward a life you love; they will serve you immensely when you're ready. It is designed to be a self-empowering book. Rather than tell people what they should or should not be doing, we offer knowledge, maps and the understanding of guidance for finding your own joyful path. We understand that self-empowerment is the true path to fulfillment, so it is our intention to provide as much information as we can for the seeker of love and abundance. In our workshops, we guide people to develop their own plans, as nobody else in the world knows better than they do, what dreams lie dormant. A plan isn't a dreary task like a budget, it's a 'looking forward to life and creating something special' type of feeling. As you read through the *Six Dimensions of Healing*, be aware of two things: that which resonates, and that which has resistance. Both will serve you.

When something you read resonates, it will feel comfortable and 'aha', as you already *know* it to be true. That feeling is confirming what you already know, and it is a building block for who you'll become, as this knowledge forms the foundations of your future. When you read something that you have an emotional reaction to - the subjects or suggestions that annoy or anger you, these are closed paths of resistance. Look at any blockages you find, and ask yourself if they're affecting your life, and if so, in which way? Bringing an awareness to these points of resistance will help you understand how big a part they play in your life. Even these are beneficial as they act as subjects of contrast, and contrast leads to clarity. Acknowledgement is sometimes all they need. You can't remove blocks, but you can make peace with them and lessen their effect on your life. Subjects of resistance will serve to help you understand what you do and don't want. If you meet resistance, just choose another mood.

Your plan becomes a written statement about the person you are and who you want to become, clarified into a few simple sentences. If you need more suggestions with this, look for the 6Dimensions of Healing Workbook or visit our website: 6DimensionsofHealing.com.

Everything you need to become the person you want to be is present within you. Including the inspiration, the dream, the means and the fun. This book is a tool for unlocking inspiration in the direction of your dreams. Some of the topics in the 'Six Dimensions of Healing' will be enlightening, and others will be confronting as they motivate you to create another pathway. Each time you read the *Six Dimensions of Healing* you will gain something different as your moods are the filter for all of your perceptions. Therefore, as you change your mood you create a different reality.

Look forward to an inspired reality and creating new and wonderful dreams.

For more information about forming your plan, see *New Patterns For the Future,* in the *Vibration chapter,* p.247.

Physical Dimension

Six Dimensions of Healing

A Robust Body is a Healthy Body

Being robust is to be healthy and fit enough so that, no matter what happens, your body can deal with it. This doesn't refer to extreme fitness or extreme dieting; it is about creating a pattern of health, a pattern that is practiced and becomes your default pattern.

Each of us has our own idea of what health is. To one it may be about being fit and vegetarian, to another it could be about minimizing pain. This is all determined by your history, as you have already created your own pattern of health. What you need to decide is whether that pattern you have developed, usually by default, is working for you or not. It is no coincidence that you have a pain in your knee like the one that your father experienced, or have tendencies to worry and depression just like your mother did. These were patterns you adopted a very long time ago. What you didn't understand, as these patterns were being formed, was that they were going to become your default patterns. They were going to become etched into your body just as they were etched into your parents' bodies. The medical fraternity calls it 'heredity'; we call it 'patterning'.

Everything is changeable. When you know you have created something that you don't want, you can then choose whether you want to change it, or not. Some of you may be wondering why this is even a question. If you have a pattern adopted from your parents that is detrimental to your health, surely you would want to change it, right? But this is not always so. Not everyone is interested in changing to a healthy lifestyle. There are many reasons for this, and they can range vastly from person to person.

A forty-year-old male client came in to see us and spoke about the line of depression in his family. It extended to his mother, father, grandmother and so on. He was nonchalant about what he termed as his 'hereditary depression', as he felt he couldn't do anything about it. When I explained to him that he may have adopted depressive behavior from his parents, as that was his environment in his growing up, he was surprised. I suggested that it may be worth his while to bring about some change in his thinking patterns, and his response was quite surprising. After we spoke together, I realized *he actually didn't want to change;* he just wanted to let people know he had an excuse for his behavior. When I tried to take that away from him, it was like removing his safety blanket and it is suffice to say, we never saw him again. There are many reasons people hold on to an illness or debilitating disease, and we all need to respect where they are on their journey of life.

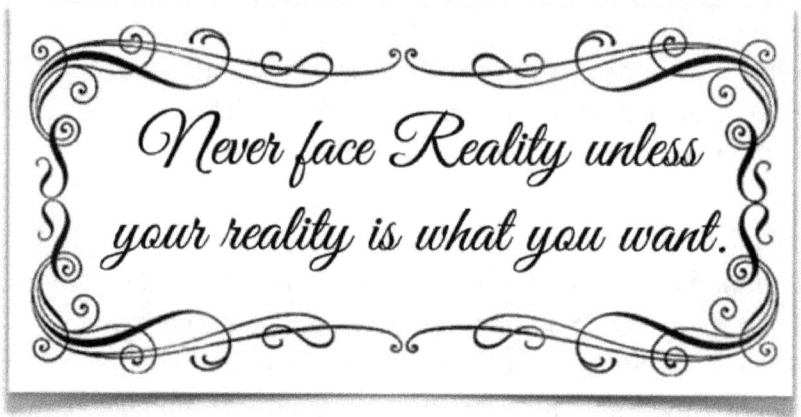

It may be a current reality that pain is in your life, or you don't have any money, but never face reality, unless your reality is what you want.

Change Your Reality and You Change Your Life

For those of you who *do* want to create patterns that serve you and your body well, this may be a good time to reflect on the default patterns that were created in your childhood. You don't need to travel back in time, for these as any past debilitating patterns will display in your present life. Since most people adopt the patterns of their parents, it stands to reason that those thought patterns have been established for generations. Now that you don't live with your parents any more, you are able to see your parents' relationship from an outside perspective, which can give you an insight into the patterns you have adopted. By observing how they created bliss or attracted illness, and what patterns influenced their health, you can gain an insight into your own patterns.

Rebecca grew up in a household in the sixties that was what she described as 'ordinary'. She had parents who were still married, a sister, a dog, and lived in a suburban house. Her father worked and her mother stayed home. Although Rebecca was exposed to outside influences with school and activities, her main influence was the family unit. Rebecca admits she had always found it difficult to make friends. People didn't take to her very kindly as she spoke her mind. She looks back and describes herself from the past as self-centered and abrasive.

Nobody told Rebecca to change her ways; she came to that conclusion because she wanted something different. Rebecca wanted to be friends with people; she wanted to see the best in them and she wanted to feel good about it.

When Rebecca was asked to look at how her parents related to one another and their friends, she was shocked at the resemblance between their behavior and hers. She had used the template her mother displayed for making friends and could clearly see, now that she no longer lived at home, that the tools her mother had displayed were the same ones she used. Rebecca also realized that the tools her mother used didn't even work for her mother, as she too had challenges with being friendly.

This acknowledgement of where her tools were adopted from was empowering for Rebecca as she could now look for another Role Model to adopt new patterns from. She knew what she wanted, and looked for people that displayed those traits comfortably. The change was instant as Rebecca had created a better feeling mood and moved forward onto a new path, where she was optimistic of her new reality.

This is not a criticism of anyone's parents but an observation, as many people have patterns that disrupt their lives, and are usually unaware of them. It's a topic we address in our workshops; it's uplifting and very empowering.

Patterns of Robustness

Developing strong patterns for your body gives you robustness, and the stronger the pattern, the more it sets itself up as a default pattern for later use. A default pattern of robustness benefits you when you are feeling under the weather, have a cold or flu, an injury, or are in a stressful situation, as the physical body can deal with a situation like losing a wallet quickly and effectively. Your body will automatically reach for its default pattern of response. The body will always follow what your mind thinks, and so you need to have a reservoir of robust patterns of response to deal with any situation that arises.

These responses are building a platform of health to deal with situations in a comfortable manner. The platform is created when a habit pattern is established. It's the *processing* rather than the situation that is important, and it's built up over a period of time. The time to start developing healthy patterns is right now, when you are already feeling good. Feeling present in your body, and clear in your mind are the foundations of a robust pattern. That is the time to emphasize what you are enjoying and how wonderful it feels.

Building a pattern is a conscious creative process, and is strengthened by choosing positive self-talk. You can do this by:

- *Creating a mantra.* This is a short statement that is repeated constantly. The power of a mantra is in the focus. You are moving your focus from a busy mind to a consciously focused pattern of thought. Choose a mantra that feels joyful to move your vibration in the desired direction.

  Some examples are "I create my own reality and I can do anything." Or "Life loves me." Maybe a Sanskrit mantra "Om Namah Shivaya" which translates as: "I bow to Shiva (the supreme deity of transformation who represents the truest, highest self)."

- *Using a journal*, morning, or evening, to appreciate what you have now. Write *lists of notes* about what you have appreciated recently. Time spent in appreciation will reap great rewards by feeling appreciative.

- *Starting new patterns* when you are feeling healthy. It's much more difficult to find the feeling of health when affected by disease. You have already built the momentum of what you don't want. Instead, use the moments that you feel great to write lists of appreciation and immerse yourself in the joy of creation so that you are developing a pattern of robustness.

A pattern of robustness processes your thoughts in a way that helps your body respond with a more favorable outcome. When your mind processes naturally, your body can respond favorably with less tension than in situations that would otherwise be stressful.

1. Jenny was a client who was always rushed and busy. This is not necessarily a bad thing, as many people can handle a lot of tasks at once. It's when the mind is busy and they start to feel they cannot cope that they begin to spiral out of control. Jenny was always too busy to meditate, and worked in a manner that was *reactive* to situations, trying to manage them *after* they would occur. She frowned more than she smiled, and thought that everyone's life was the same as hers.

2. Neville was similar, in that he too led a busy life. However, he really enjoyed being busy, and took on projects he enjoyed. He was always involved in the community, worked hard, and still had time for his family. Exercise and meditation were a priority for him. He knew that his mind reflected his life, and that a balanced mind led to a healthy and a balanced lifestyle. So, you see, Neville was building a pattern of robustness.

When you look at these situations from the outside, it's easy to see which person will cope with physical, emotional and mental stress better. Jenny is a walking time bomb, and is unlikely to cope with added stress. However, Neville will find that he processes naturally, and will be able to choose the direction in which he responds. This will empower him, and so, he will be the one who will find growth just another step up on the ladder.

Your Body, Your Choice

The term, Physical Dimensions, encompasses *both the inside and outside* of the body. It represents your health, as what you think and how you feel presents itself in your body.

The cells within your body have a cellular membrane which functions similarly to a nervous system. This membrane has a form of intelligence, as it is able to see, hear, feel and interpret messages from the body. Your cell's membrane has the ability to make functioning decisions. Receptors on the surface of the cell receive information from chemical sources throughout the body, which they communicate to the nucleus. The genes inside the nucleus of the cell are then given directions on which proteins in the body to synthesize for the cell to function in accordance with the information received by the membrane. Each of the trillions of cells in your body communicates with the others through the proteins, which regulate the function of your body.

Your cells can only follow one direction at a time, which creates a positive balanced response or a negative survival response. (Lipton, 2006)

All of your cells are controlled by their inner environment, which is determined by your thoughts and emotions. Your cells chemically eavesdrop on what you think, and how you feel.

Science has only just started to understand the complexity of the wisdom of the cells.

Breathing happens unconsciously and yet synthesis is performed in perfect harmony with every organ throughout the body. It's a constant miracle, yet this organic marvel of a physical body is taken for granted by most, until it is no longer working properly. When the body has broken down, many people visit our clinic and complain their body is worn out, or they would like a replacement. In some ways, you can liken the human body to a car. Service it regularly, give it a polish, add some love and care, and your car will last a long time. If you malnourish it by running it into the ground, having a few accidents or giving it dirty fuel, eventually you can expect trouble.

It is common for people to neglect their bodies and then wonder why they aren't working properly. They feed them dirty fuel in the form of depleting thoughts, and wonder why the performance is slow. It doesn't make sense that the body would be at fault, as each cell in your body constantly replaces itself. Some cells replenish themselves more often than others, but you really have a brand-new body every few years. Cells take no lunch breaks or holidays, and perform well on good fuel that comes in the form of care and nurturing. For the cells of your body to be balanced and healthy, the fuel required is self-love.

Of the thirty-seven trillion cells (approximately) in your body, two trillion cells are replaced each day. Your body has a wonderful capacity for renewal built-in for free. Yet many people believe it is inevitable that their bodies will break down as they age. They expect to have arthritis after the age of 50, or they anticipate that their bones will become brittle. Most expect to become much more sedentary. If

Change Your Reality and You Change Your Life

forebears have experienced an ailment or disability, others in the family expect to suffer the same fate. This becomes a self-fulfilling prophecy.

The effects of aging can also become an excuse. Many people have cited 'getting older' as the reason for pain or lack of movement. They use that as an excuse not to exercise, or look after their bodies. It may seem illogical that someone would choose aging as an excuse over poor health, but sometimes it is disguised as the path of least resistance. It's not a conscious choice, of course. Nobody gets up in the morning and states with conviction, "I think I will feel old and weary today." Yet, that's the story they're telling themselves and the world when they wake up and say, "Oh, my knee hurts and my bones creak. I hate getting old."

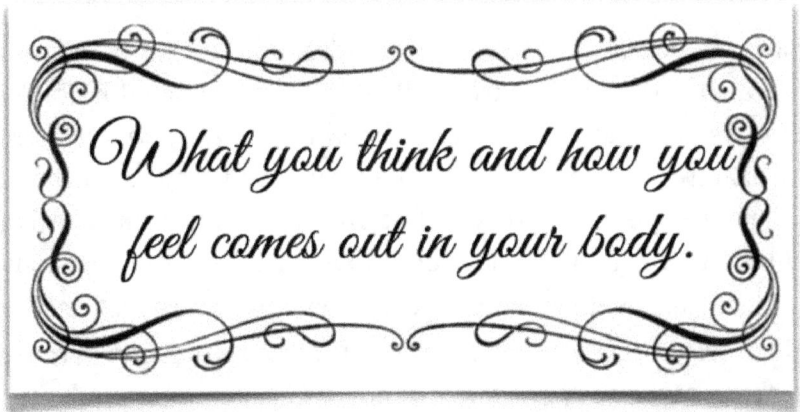

What you think and how you feel comes out in your body.

As the thought patterns of aches and pains continue, their emotions begin to influence the chemical makeup of the body that the cells adhere to.

Each cell in your body knows exactly where it should be, and what it should be doing for optimum health, but all are directed by your thoughts and emotions. If there was no interference by your emotions, your cells would function beautifully and your body would feel great. When you are feeling happy, your body produces whatever it needs to maintain perfect balance. Your mind is working in harmony with your body.

All moods affect your cells, and thirty-seven trillion is a big family to be responsible for. If a pain in the knee creates the thought program that something is wrong with your knee, the cells will make sure there is something wrong with your knee for as long as the pattern remains. The cells' healthy operating system will be overridden by your story and they will perform to the expectations your mood patterns have created. This is the story of your body, one that you've created without any knowledge or wisdom. It is how you redesign your own physical reality.

If you're wondering if the cells' eavesdropping is a good idea or not, the advantage of the capacity for the cells to be affected in this way is that just as you create illness, *so too can you create healing*. There are many examples of people being told they have no hope for their body and their life, yet they proceed to turn themselves around to become so much fitter, healthier, and more robust than they were as teenagers. This is all due to their ability to get out of the way of the cells' healing system. **When you make a conscious choice to expect something other than what is already present in your body, you are changing your reality.**

A beautiful woman I had the pleasure of meeting had recently experienced a brain tumor. It couldn't be operated on because of its delicate position, and the doctors gave her little hope of survival. She looked at the patterns of thought she had been creating, and decided she would find a way of allowing the cells do what they do best – heal. Twelve months later, with meditation and a pattern of consciously choosing her thoughts, her scans showed the tumor had not merely reduced significantly; it had nearly disappeared. To this day, she is tumor-free and feeling great. Telling her story was a way of inspiring people to heal themselves. It is, indeed, a wonderful parable.

Your body doesn't seek much attention; it only asks that you appreciate it, and allow it to recuperate regularly. The recuperation your body needs is the ability to move into the intelligence of its own cells without your interference, and this can be achieved through meditation, appreciation, enjoyment and fun. The body responds to your moods, so being aware of the thoughts you think regularly will help you to change patterns. When you are aware you don't feel good, changing your mood will assist your health. The body will respond quickly to changing emotions, so when there is an ailment you would like to help on its way, your imagination is the greatest tool of creation.

Your body has an amazing capacity for self-healing, as each and every cell boasts infinite intelligence in its connection to Source Energy. Just like you, each of your cells was created from Source and still remains Source Energy, unless you interrupt this pattern. When your mood is buoyant, your body is balanced, as you are working in unison with the cells' infinite intelligence. When your mood is cheerless you are out of balance and not on the same frequency as infinite intelligence, so your cells don't operate in optimum harmony. The wheel of a bicycle works exceptionally well until a stick in the spoke interrupts the pattern of movement, then disaster strikes. The same happens with the cells of your body. They can only flow in one direction at a time and the direction is influenced by your thoughts. Simply believing you're going to get a cold each winter, or hay fever in spring, can change the direction of naturally healthy cells. Cells are never without influence and they receive their information from your mood to determine how to synthesize proteins. You are the person who determines which path they take.

If you're standing on the verge, which represents illness, and wanting to reach the farther side of the canyon, which is health, sometimes a *bridge* is needed. This can come in the form of products such as vitamins, supplements, or prescription drugs, a friend's encouragement or even a psychologist. When the other side of the canyon is reached and health is obtained, it's often attributed to the bridge, but the supplements and medicine would not work as well without your help. You are the springboard for the bridge in your life, and until you decide you want something different, and are able move your mood to a place of relief, all the medicine and advice in the world will be of little help. The true springboard for the bridge to be effective is the belief in yourself. It changes your reality from one of circumstantial living, where your emotions are in response to what is observed, to one of self-empowerment, where emotions are *chosen*, no matter what is happening around you. Either way, your cells respond according to your mood.

People have often said that when they're in pain or going through a crisis, they feel very alone. It doesn't matter who's with them and how supportive their network is; they can still feel alone. There will always be the feeling of loneliness when you aren't connected with Source Energy. You can't completely disconnect because it is the broader, non-physical part of you, but you can 'pinch yourself off' so well that you *do feel* alone. This has nothing to do with the people around you; it has only to do with the lack of connection between you and your Higher Self. Self-empowerment is the opposite. It means feeling tuned in to how you feel, and knowing that no matter what happens, everything is OK.

After birthing three children, I got to know my body and how it responded to the different tests I would have when pregnant. One of these was a test for low hemoglobin, or iron count. Hospital staff would often say I was anemic, and put me on iron supplements. During the pregnancy of my fourth child, I was walking one morning, and I asked my body to change my iron or hemoglobin level to above ten, and move my blood pressure to the normal range, as it was usually low. It's not that I felt tired or depleted, but in this way I could still choose to go through the birthing suite with the midwives. I just liked the freedom it provided. That afternoon, I had tests as usual, and the readings had changed to a 'normal' range in both blood pressure and hemoglobin. I was delighted, the midwives were happy and we went on our merry way. Later the same afternoon, I started to feel a bit jittery, as if I had eaten a bag of sugar; my body felt strange, and it was only then that I realized what had happened. I immediately thanked my body, and asked it to return to balance, realizing that 'normal' for me was different from other people's 'normal'. It surely was an interesting experience, and one that gave me a great understanding of how the mind could drive the patterning of the cells in my body.

It helped me to understand why in the course of some tribal rites in Africa, young men can eat poison whilst in a trance, and yet not become affected by it. The Shaman would take the young men away for a couple of days and places them in a hypnotic trance. They are fed poisonous plants, yet they are unaffected by the poison. The

Shaman is careful to remove all traces of the poison from their bodies or mouths before bringing them out of the trance. If they have known they have eaten poison, they will die, so strong is their belief. Instead, their bodies process the poison as ours would an apple.

Structural Integrity

Structural integrity is the mark of a body that is feeling strong, healthy and fit, with energy to burn.

The physical integrity of your frame often comes down to the jobs you are performing each day. We call it 'vocational posture'. Every profession has a posture. Driving a truck, sitting at a desk, house painting, or sitting at a computer. Whether you are waitressing or baking cakes all day, your body will develop habit patterns from the posture most used.

When your body is slumped over a computer during the day, the upper back will follow the posture most used and develop a pattern. These patterns can lead to symptoms that are unconnected with the back and shoulders, but will be directly associated with poor posture. Restricting the blood flow from your spine can affect every aspect of your body, from your eyes to your toes. You may be satisfied that you get plenty of exercise, but because you are bent over a counter most of the day, you may not know that shortness of breath is associated with poor posture in the mid-thoracic area, and that a pattern is created from standing in poor posture for long periods of time. When your job is driving a truck and your wallet is sitting in your back pocket, it won't be long before lower back pain develops from the uneven position of your hips in the truck, which, in turn, is exacerbated by the lack of muscle-tone in the stomach, as when you sit down you usually turn your stomach muscles off.

Think now about how your job is affecting your health, and how you can make changes that affect your well-being. It is in understanding what you do every day, and how this affects your body, that change is created.

Maintaining a feeling of good health and robustness goes hand in hand with a healthy well-aligned spine. The chart on the next page is an indicator of the spinal misalignment and its effects on the physical body.

Six Dimensions of Healing

Effects of Spinal Misalignment

Spine	Nerve Supply	Relationship
C1	Blood supply to the Head, Scalp, Pituitary Gland, Brain, Inner and Middle Ear, Bones of the Face, Nervous System	Headaches inc. migraines - High Blood Pressure - Dizziness - Chronic Fatigue - Insomnia - Nervous Breakdown
C2	Eyes, Ears, Tongue, Sinuses, Forehead, Tongue, Mastoid Bones	Sinus Trouble - Allergies - Ear aches - Hearing Difficulties - Vision Problems - Fainting spells, Crossed Eyes
C3	Cheeks, Facial Bones and Nerves, Teeth, Outer Ear	Neuralgia - Eczema - Acne - Tooth Ache
C4	Mouth, Lips, Nose, Eustachian Tube	Runny Nose - Hearing Loss - Adenoids - Hay Fever - Catarrh
C5	Vocal Chords, Pharynx, Neck and Glands	Laryngitis - Hoarseness - Sore Throat
C6	Tonsils, Neck Muscles, Shoulders	Tonsillitis - Arm Pain - Rigid Neck - Persistent Cough - Croup
C7	Thyroid Gland, Shoulder Bursa, Elbows	Colds - Bursitis - Thyroid Imbalance
T1	Fingers, Wrists, Hands, Forearms, Esophagus, Trachea	Shortness of Breath or Breathing Difficulties - Asthma - Lower Arm and Hand Pain
T2	Heart, Coronary Arteries	Chest Pain - Heart Conditions
T3	Lungs, Pleura, Bronchial Tubes, Chest	Congestion - Pneumonia - Pleurisy - Bronchitis
T4	Gallbladder	Gall Stones - Gall bladder conditions - Shingles - Jaundice
T5	Liver, Blood, Solar Plexus	Poor Circulation - Low Blood Pressure - Liver Conditions - Arthritis - Fever
T6	Stomach	Heartburn - Indigestion - Dyspepsia - Nervousness
T7	Pancreas, Duodenum	Gastritis - Ulcers
T8	Spleen	Lowered Resistance
T9	Adrenal Glands	Allergies - Hives
T10	Kidneys	Kidney Stones - Kidney Problems - Fatigue - Hardening Arteries - Nephritis
T11	Kidneys, Ureters	Pimples - Acne - Boils - Eczema - Skin Conditions
T12	Lymph Circulation, Small Intestines	Rheumatism - Wind Pains - Some Sterility
L1	Large Intestines, Inguinal Rings	Diarrhea - Colitis - Hernia - Constipation
L2	Abdomen, Appendix, Thighs	Varicose Veins - Leg Pains - Cramps
L3	Knees, Uterus, Bladder, Sex Organs	Knee Pain - Menstrual Problems - Miscarriage - Impotency - Bed Wetting
L4	Lower Back, Prostate Gland, Sciatic Nerve	Back Pain - Urination Infrequency and Difficulties - Sciatica
L5	Lower Legs, Feet, Ankles	Leg Pain - Sore Feet - Constipation - Swollen Ankles - Cold Feet - Weakness in the Legs - Leg Cramps
Sacrum	Buttocks, Hip Bones	Hip Pain - Back Pain - Sacroiliac Conditions - Spinal Curvature
Coccyx	Rectum, Anus	Tail Bone Pain from sitting - Hemorrhoids - Itching

Your muscles are trained by the posture you have adopted, and this can often cause pain and compound to cause side effects seemingly unrelated. For instance, when you have a sore foot, and start limping, it is very likely that, because your muscles are trying to protect you from the pain already present in the foot, they will cause a misalignment on the opposite side of the body due to the limp. Many people live with this pain and yet, in most cases, it can be simply remedied. When you have learned to accept a constant pain threshold as normal, it is a strong message to your cells for more pain. This message of pain can be changed.

Looking at the chart above, you will notice there is a vertebra to influence every part of your body. Back pain is not necessarily the symptom of a misalignment; there are many other factors involved. When you are not enjoying completing the tax return for example, there is a tendency for the neck to experience pain. It is not the fault of your back that you are in pain, it is an indicator of imbalance. The complex system shown in the chart can be used to remedy a situation that might otherwise have sought invasive corrections. The spine is really the central point of your physical body; it brings everything together in a beautiful harmony of blood, bones, movement, and warmth. Its integral structure is crucial to your health and well-being.

Stretching and suppleness

The movement representing a bent arm snow angel has been a savior for me. For over twenty years I have found this exercise to be of immense value. Shown to me by a physiotherapist during a dancing class, it retrains the muscles in the upper back. When poor posture results from the daily chores of computer work, cooking or bookwork, nursing a baby, fixing the car, or in fact any activity that calls for the body to adopt a bent position for prolonged periods of time, the muscles train themselves to accommodate that bending position. In a way, this is the muscles' defense mechanism. They form a pattern from the position you use most often to protect the body by developing strength in the frequently adopted position. You are communicating to the cells in your muscles the position you want to retain by your pattern of posture. You only notice how efficient your muscles have been operating when you try and straighten up.

Pain indicates the muscles have created a new default pattern. Just as you create default patterns, so do your cells and the cells of your muscles create default patterns by the communication you provide. Doing, saying or thinking the same things repeatedly, creates default patterns. The bent arm snow angel movement retrains the muscles by communicating a different posture to your cells. This exercise is nothing short of miraculous, as it retrains the muscles into adopting an upright posture. I have used it after the birth of all of my children, and when I have been cooking or working on the computer, and feel myself involuntarily bending forward. It is a stretch used against a wall; you place your back with bent arms against the wall with your elbows shoulder height and the slide your hands upward as far as they go. It's a simple exercise and the benefits are evident very quickly.

There are stretches for retraining muscles all over the body and we will include them on the website, www.6DimensionsofHealing.com and in the Six Dimensions of Healing Workbook. When you integrate favorite movements into your everyday life you won't even realize you are exercising.

Suppleness is different from stretching. Suppleness is what a baby has when it moves its big toe into its mouth without even a moment of difficulty. Now nobody is suggesting that you can still suck your big toe, but it would be good to bend and reach those hard to get at places when you drop your television remote control down the side of the lounge chair, and what about getting up and down stairs effortlessly?

A feeling of ease and flow in the body with each movement is evidence that suppleness is present. Suppleness keeps pain and creaking joints at bay. The aim is to be able to stretch and reach all the difficult cupboards, and move with a grace that defies age. It is a relaxation of the muscles achieved by movement. Physical activity increases suppleness, and that helps the body feel youthful for a very long time.

I recently had an elderly client come to visit me. She owed her youthfulness to working on the farm, which was her home. Only in the past year had she given away breaking in horses and decided instead that dogs were presently more her size. Movement has been the savior of her body for well over ninety-five years.

Another elderly woman came in for an appointment. Her lower back was causing severe pain, and she was in tears not only because of the pain but also because this ailment was hindering the freedom she loved. There are certain movement exercises that are effective for people in pain, and even though she was in her nineties, she was by far the supplest person we had seen that day. Her body was relaxed, and there was no shortening of the muscles that you see, even in much younger people. She responded beautifully, and the pain dissipated after she had integrated those movements into her daily life. Suppleness is not necessarily related to age, but rather to movement and is pivotal in healing temporary physical disabilities and pain quickly.

Aged, retired farmers are common clients in a country clinic. Many ex-farmers think they are experiencing pain because of the hard work they used to do on the farm in the past. The truth is that many are having trouble now because of their current *inactivity*, not their past activity. When they were living on the farm, their NEA* was high. Then, they retire, sell the farm, and move into a small house in town, and now their NEA is low, the lifestyle has become sedentary, and the adage 'Use it or Lose It' has become a reality. When muscles are flaccid and slow to respond, any movement will begin to cause pain.

Muscles need exercise so that they can do what they are designed for, and that is to keep the body in good working condition. Many people who are seated for long periods of time and don't exercise their abdomen or stomach muscles, won't have developed muscles that can help them with lifting, which then causes the minor muscles of the lower back to engage. As lower-back muscles were designed for support, and not for lifting, the result is lower back pain when lifting heavy objects. The size of your stomach or your desire to have a six-pack don't matter, muscles still need exercising. The larger the stomach, the more exercise your muscles need to balance the weight.

* NEA. Non-exercise activity. This is the activity you do that is not organized sport.

Enjoy your Body

Non-Exercise Activity - NEA
Organized exercise can feel to many of us like a burden. With busy lifestyles and limited time and energy to do something about physical fitness, a gym membership can feel far from achievable, even when starting with the best of intentions. In fact, gyms are counting on people's self-defeating exercise patterns of buying memberships and not using them, because if everyone who bought a membership attended regularly, most gyms would be overcrowded. Gyms and

organized sport make up only a very small percentage of all exercise. But there is an easier solution to keep your body in top condition and obesity far from the doorstep.

Organized exercise is defined as, 'organized bodily exertion for the sake of developing and maintaining physical fitness;' for example, participating in a sport. The vast majority of the world's population does not take part in regular exercise, according to the definition; therefore, their organized exercise activity is zero. Of those that do take part in organized and regular exercise, most will expend only around 100 calories.

There is a much better solution. The *everyday activity* that your body takes on greatly contributes to the health of your body. Not organized sport but exercise such as housework, gardening, mowing the lawn or taking the stairs. This everyday activity is called your Non-Exercise Activity or NEA for short, and it can be more important than having an organized exercise regime. The Mayo Clinic (2007*) has conducted studies that directly compare obesity with a lack of NEA, as your NEA is the counter-response to weight gain. The more you move, the higher your NEA. On average, a lean person tends to have a higher NEA than an obese person. They will move around for two hours longer than a chair-bound person, and can burn an extra 350 calories per day without even consciously increasing any activity.

Non-exercise activity is ongoing and can vary daily, but can be increased by asking yourself these two questions:
- On a scale of 1-10, what amount of activity do I feel I am doing now?
- How can I increase this?

More information on these NEA exercises can be found on our web site: www.6DimensionsofHealing.com

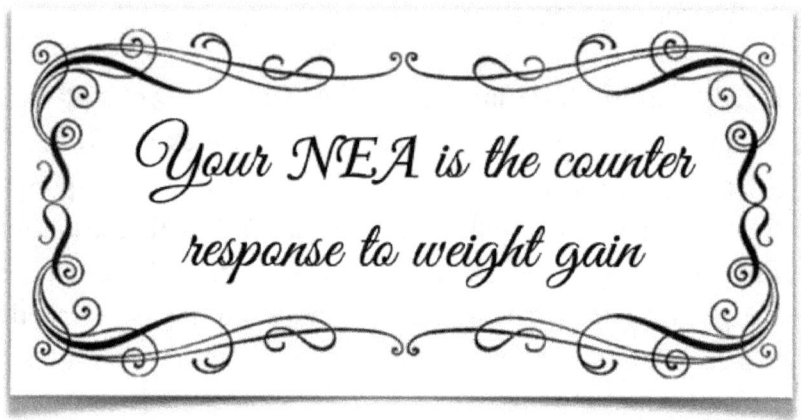

There are two basic types of NEA, Occupational and Leisure.

Depending on their occupation, people can spend anywhere from 300 to 2500 calories per day, differing in their NEA by up to 2000 calories. A waitress is most likely going to have a higher NEA than a desk clerk, so it is more important for the desk-bound person to be aware of how they can increase physical activity during work. For instance, walking whilst talking on the telephone, using stairs instead of elevators, alighting one train station before the station that is closest to work, or choosing a coffee shop a block farther away than usual.

Thirty minutes of sitting in front of the television will burn 30 calories but dancing or moving in front of the television will burn 600. Dormant in the background of your life are hidden gems in the form of ideas to increase your NEA. Gems such as riding instead of taking the car or train, gardening, walking, or dancing while cooking, are opportunities to increase NEA. Then there is housework, especially vacuuming and mopping, mowing the grass, chasing the children or the dog, playing Frisbee in the park, and many other active pursuits. Movement does not need to be difficult; it just needs to be often. Some of your NEA activities maybe commonly outsourced, but by choosing to do them yourself, you will increase the NEA and enhance your physical and emotional body. Why pay someone to get the benefits you can gain for yourself when activity doesn't need to be a burden? It can be fun.

There are endless ways to increase your NEA daily, and they will have the same benefits and cause less wear and tear on your body than organized sport. In fact, if you can find a way of enjoying your NEA, there will be many more benefits than you realize. So, step out, get moving and stop feeling guilty about not exercising regularly.

The benefit of moving is that when you feel good about your body, you tend to move more. Your body is an important part of self-esteem, so you need to enjoy the body you have. This need can be a double-edged sword; if you don't enjoy the body you have, the body you have won't become one you enjoy.

Body Balance

Balance is important, irrespective of age. Everything you do relies heavily on your ability to find balance in your life with respect to health, exercise, and relaxation. Then again, maintaining physical balance is one of the most underrated skills of well-being. As you age, muscle strength, vision and sensory perception begin to decline. These are the main contributors to your ability to balance. The good news is that physical balance is a learned skill that can be maintained and improved by practice. Balance exercises can strengthen perception, which can help the body to better position your muscles. This allows you to sense how you need to move without looking or thinking about it. Practicing balance builds muscle and increases the range of motion in the joints, helping to distribute weight evenly. The benefit is that millions of muscle fibers in the body are kept alert and active. The result is overall stability and confidence in your body.

You are never too old or too young to increase activity. People tend to look for excuses not to exercise rather than look for opportunities to increase their activity, which is much faster and easier to achieve. Our bodies are magnificent organisms that connect to a mind that has endless creativity. Whether walking, running, swimming, dancing, climbing or making love, you were born to move. The more often you move, the better your balance.

In a society driven by diets and body image, people get caught up on what to eat and what not to eat. When you are active and excited about life, you will be naturally drawn to healthier food, as this is a result of mental and physical balance. Moderation is always the key, as your body has the innate ability to assimilate food and drink, and will do so in perfect order unless sabotaging thoughts obstruct the process. There will always be an abundance of available diets as long as there are people not happy with their body weight. These diets don't necessarily help you lose weight, or make you healthy, but according to market research they are part of a $500** billion global industry and are here to stay.

In the long term, the emotional reasons for weight gain are many and varied. It can be beneficial for you to get help to understand your emotional motivators that create excess weight. In this way, you can choose a new plan and decide to either get off or stay on the body image carousel.

* www.mayoclinic.org/documents/mc5810-0307-pdf/doc-20079082 Endocrinology Update Volume 1, 2007 The "NEAT" defect in Human Obesity.

** Global Weight Loss & Gain Markets 2009-2010 www.marketsandmarkets.com

Activity Enjoyment Scale

Variety is the Key

A search for health and fitness books on the Internet will provide over a hundred million results. Exercise, movement and activity, all contribute towards well-being, and this is a subject people are interested in. Well-being encompasses physical, mental, emotional and spiritual dimensions. To achieve well-being, movement is imperative and 'You use it or you lose it'. As humans we are built to move, so why not make it fun and creative? Variety in movement, duration, intensity and combination of exercise, all contribute to the longevity of a routine, which works a range of muscle groups and energy systems.

Whatever exercises you choose as routine, whether NEA or sport, there'll be times when you're expending more energy than others. It's helpful to have a personal scale on which you can value the exercise regime. This scale is about increasing intensity to improve the value of your current activity. In this way, it is easy to increase the energy expenditure by changing very little.

For instance, if walking is your chosen exercise, during the task ask yourself, "On a scale of 1-10, what's my experience on this walk?" The answer may be that you're walking without much exertion and it feels like a 3. If that is how it feels to you, the next question would be, "How can I make it a 5?" Thoughts will arise to increase the pace, and swing your arms. That could take it to a 5. This is a personal scale remember. Introducing a hill, or adding 50 paces of jogging now and again could take it to a 7. You may be happy with a 7 and that's fine. There is no pressure to move beyond what's comfortable for you. How is the enjoyment level? Is the mind running away on its own, or is there an appreciation of the surroundings or the weather? This could take the experience to a higher level. Walking is not just a walk in the park.

The Activity Enjoyment Scale is about awareness of the activity happening in the present, then being able to increase the benefits gained from the same exercise for little increased effort in the same amount of time. It's all about amplifying the experience for body, mind and soul. It's not all about the physical exertion. When you can appreciate the walk and your surroundings, you will have created a beneficial start to your day. More opportunities to appreciate will arise. If you're going to walk, then make it a 7, and you'll gain more benefits in the same amount of time. Don't just say you walk every day. Know that you are walking to set your day up in the best way for what's to come — this will help in clarity and physical stamina. You will start your day with optimism and clarity, a great way to begin.

The same scale can be applied to all activities including housework, gardening or cooking, playing with the children, your relationship or work. When your mind is kept active, looking for ways to increase energy expenditure, the activity becomes fun, and contributes greatly to your well-being.

Movement and exercises can include:

Swimming - To move it up the scale:

- Incorporate different strokes
- Add equipment such as flippers, pull buoy, kick boards, paddles
- Change the routine, by doing long slow easy laps intermittently with spurts of short sprints
- Time your lengths
- Breathe less frequently or do more kicking
- Swim at the lake, or beach instead of the pool

Gym or Fitness Center

There are so many options. The key is to stay interested. To move it up the scale:

- Take on creative combination clusters of exercise and movement
- Change the intensity or duration of the activity
- Set up personal training sessions
- Start group sessions
- Get outdoors, into the park, for example

Walking - To change the intensity scale:

- Quicken the pace
- Swing your arms
- Run sections
- Incorporate hills into your routine
- Take larger steps
- Do some step ups along the way

The benefits of regular exercise are:

1. Feeling great - endorphin levels are elevated, so you're creating happy cells.
2. Healthy longevity - as you live longer your body stays healthy and you gain a prolonged quality of life.
3. Increased blood flow and oxygen delivery - creates more energy and a feeling of lightness.
4. Increased metabolism - which means the body burns fuel in the form of calories.
5. Stronger muscles - your body is 40% muscle. Taut muscles keep you upright and strong. Muscles also keep your heart pumping.
6. Fewer injuries - with regular exercise, you become more stable and bone density increases.
7. Freer movement - getting out of bed or a chair is easier, as exercise keeps the joints lubricated.
8. Alertness - the mind-and-body connection creates an active alertness.
9. Better Sleep - there is nothing like being physically tired to help you sleep.

Change Your Reality and You Change Your Life

Food Consciousness
A new way of looking at the food you eat.

If you are fanatical about food and enjoy indulging in your stomach's favorite pleasures, the general rule of thumb is to be mindful of the HI. That's the Handling Index. The HI indicates how much a fruit or vegetable is handled in becoming the product that is eaten. A low HI would be assigned to fresh fruit and vegetables out of the garden. The more a food is handled (such as fast food), the higher the Handling Index.

The less a food is handled, the more of its original nutrients it contains, as it is closer to its source. The lower the HI, the more vibrant it is likely to be. For example, compare an apple to a deep-fried, fast food apple pie. There really is no resemblance to the apple left in the fast food apple pie, even though it started out as an apple on a tree at one time. The apple has been processed so much, even before it is deep-fried, that there are few nutrients left in it; the HI is too high. The word 'apple' in this context is misleading. If you were to make an apple pie yourself though, the HI would be much lower. The use of fresh apples, peeled and chopped, then cooked in your own pastry case is a sublime way to enjoy an apple. Look for fresh foods that are as close to their source as possible for the highest nutritional and energetic value.

Craving something sweet? Reach for a snack that is loaded with water. Most fruits and vegetables have a high-water content, which will help you stay hydrated and indicate to your brain that your stomach is full. Often when you're dehydrated, your body craves food as a way to hydrate itself, so quite often the cravings dissipate with sufficient water in the body.

When going out for dinner, set your intentions to gravitate towards the simpler food. These will have a lower HI. Stay clear of the foods smothered in sauces and gravies, as the additives used in these have no HI at all. They are chemicals that are not even known as food. American sliced cheese has become so processed that it has little resemblance to cheese, and it has many additives as well; therefore, it cannot legally be called cheese. The health benefits can be very deceptive when a product that is labeled as cheese is actually 'processed cheese', or when yoghurt is labeled 'diet yoghurt' or bread is sold with the claim that it lasts two weeks. Read your labels and if there are ingredients that are chemicals rather than foods, look for another product. For instance the ingredients in butter are just cream, water and salt.

There are thousands of diets on the market designed to create the illusion of health, and there will always be new diets surfacing, as long as there are people wanting to find a shortcut to health. But the easiest path to health is by keeping a low HI.

Conscious Eating

When you are emotionally present and consciously eating a food you enjoy, it will do more good for you than harm. The awareness of how you feel whilst eating anything is the key to having a naturally healthy body. Emotions play a major part in the food that is eaten, not just through emotional cravings which most people are familiar with, but also through the moods with which all food is consumed.

When people are gathered around a table in celebration, food is usually enjoyed, as it is associated with fun and laughter. When this is the experience from a young age, it encourages a pattern of food equaling happiness. Whilst there is balance in life, all is well. As soon as a person is using food to find happiness and needing it to emulate emotional balance, the message to your cells will be that food equals masking pain. When food evokes an emotion of guilty pleasure, it creates mood fluctuations that have both physical and emotional repercussions.

Our inner being is joy, and we will never cease in our exploration for this seemingly elusive emotion. Especially when there are so many situations in life, that seem to create the opposite. But there is only a stream of well-being, so when your emotions are not in alignment with well-being, it makes sense to go looking for relief elsewhere. Some seek it through food, some with alcohol, others use drugs; but whatever is ingested in the pursuit of happiness is short lived, as the connection you seek is always with Source Energy and that connection comes from within.

Be emotionally present and enjoy your every mouthful of your food, no matter what eating regime you choose.

The Quick Fix

Water is critically underestimated in this day and age of supplements and nutrition. From flushing your kidneys to helping maintain optimum weight, water is the elixir of life. It is vitally important for your body to hydrate and the cravings for water can easily be overlooked. Because all food holds water within, thirst can sometimes be disguised as hunger, as your body cries out for hydration. One way to know if you are hungry is to ask yourself if you would like an apple, or similar fruit. If you don't want an apple, you may not be hungry, so drink water.

Your body has an inbuilt detox system that is more effective than any available for purchase. This filter system, called the kidneys, needs fresh water to flush out excess minerals, chemicals, and poisons; otherwise, it is like washing your dishes in dirty water. Allowing clean water to flow through your filtration system enables the body's detoxification to flow freely and easily.

Did you know?
Six Effects of Dehydration are:

1. Headaches
The brain sits inside a sack of fluid that cushions it against the skull. If that fluid sack is depleted because of dehydration, the brain can push up against the skull, causing headaches.

2. Bad Breath
Saliva has inbuilt antibacterial properties, but if your body is not creating enough saliva due to dehydration, bad breath can result.

3. Dizziness & Dry skin
In both winter and summer, you can become very dizzy when standing up from a seating position, or exercising if there isn't enough water in your body. You can also reduce your blood volume, so you could suffer from very dry skin.

4. Muscle cramps
If your muscles are working hard, they can seize up from the heat generated in your body. Changes in the electrolytes and sodium and potassium levels in your body can lead to muscle cramping. Keeping hydrated is as important as adding water to the radiator of your car.

5. Fever and chills
If your body is severely dehydrated, you may experience symptoms like fever or even shivering chills.

6. Food cravings, especially for sweets
When you're dehydrated, it can be difficult for some nutrients and organs to release glycogens and necessary components of your energy stores; so, you can get cravings for sweet food.

How to Check for Dehydration

Try this skin test
Use two fingers to grab a roll of skin on the back of your wrist. Pull the skin up about ½ an inch high and then let go. The skin should spring back to its normal position momentarily. If the skin returns to

the previous shape slowly, you might be dehydrated. Enjoy the cool, refreshing taste of water instead of sugar laden drinks or chemically enhanced sugar-free drinks.

The Anti-Aging Team

Regular exercise can slow down the aging of the brain, and improve your learning capacity for new projects. Ongoing studies begun in 1966* suggest that endurance, resistance, flexibility, and balance training make a significant impact on reversing the aging process. Exercise is also used to optimize mental health** by normalizing insulin resistance and increasing 'good feeling' hormones such as endorphins, serotonin, and dopamine. Through exercise your body can release the stress chemicals that bring about depression.

No matter your age it's never too late for a balanced eating program and a new exercise movement routine with plenty of variety. From five to ten thousand steps per day or thirty minutes of swift walking will help to give your future wellness the platform it needs for mental, physical and spiritual health. The key to success with any activity routine is continuity. It's about being genuinely committed to feeling the best you can. This is for you. For today, tomorrow and a very long time.

There have been many theories released on how to increase your metabolism. The food you eat, when you eat it, the type of exercise, even age can be determining factors on your individual rate of metabolism. The most consistent and efficient way to increase your metabolism is by getting excited about life. When you have a project that you're enthusiastic about, or plan a holiday that you are excited to go on, the cells in your body create endorphins or happy cells.

Looking forward with excitement balances your body so that cravings become less dominant. Together, exercise and excitement are an amazing team for keeping your body trim and healthy. The side effects are also invaluable.

When you get excited, everything becomes faster. Your mind thinks faster. Opportunities arrive faster. You move faster. You don't need to use food as an emotional crutch. Your world revolves around you. When your mind is in alignment with what you want, and your body is traveling in a direction that is good for you, your cells are performing in an optimum manner. This peak performance is natural and can increase metabolism.

There are many methods of increasing your exercise endurance, resistance, flexibility and balance; and there are two methods to purposefully increase your zest for life – by using 'self-talk' and by using your imagination. When you mentally create something for your future in which you become excited (whether real or imagined), your mood and your self-esteem both elevate. As the cells of your body eavesdrop on both of these, you are creating cells that also become excited. Excitement is vital for health as it creates life energy and without life energy flowing through us, we cease to exist.

If you could do, be or have anything, what would it look like? How would it feel?

Imagine it. Write it. Be appreciative of how it feels and really get excited. This is your life and it's up to you to start imagining the most fulfilling life you can.

*http://www.health.harvard.edu/newsweek/Exercise_and_aging_Can_you_walk_away_from_Father_Time.htm
**http://www.mayoclinic.org/diseases-conditions/depression/in-depth/depression-and-exercise/art-2004six495

Dynamic Posture

The average head weighs about the same as a bowling ball. Considering there are some pretty heavy bowling balls, you can understand why it would be of advantage to your body to balance the head perfectly on its axis (neck). The axis is where your head weighs the lightest and the least number of muscles are engaged to maintain balance. When the head is tilted forward on your neck, it increases the tension in the neck and upper back as your bowling-ball head becomes less balanced, and needs more support. Maintaining strength and posture in the upper body is the easiest way to give yourself the lightest head to carry.

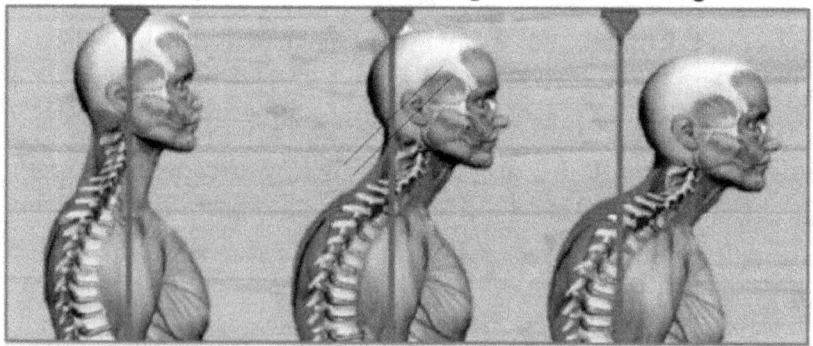

There are two major muscle groups that support the lower back, one being your thighs, and the other being your abdominals. When your belly is large it is important to have strong core muscles and thigh muscles to support your lower back. The bigger your belly, the stronger those stomach muscles need to be to support any lifting. Otherwise it is the lower back that is compromised, as the minor muscle groups may not be able to supply the lifting strength needed.

There are many exercises that promote a good posture and below are a few of our favorites.

Wall Pushups
Stand 2-3 feet from a wall with your arms outstretched and touching the wall in front. Keeping your body taught, lean towards the wall, and push yourself back and forth using your own body as resistance. The further your feet are from the wall, the more difficult the push up.

Horizontal chin-ups
Horizontal chin-ups are easily adapted to any environment. Lie on the floor and with your palms on a broomstick placed between two chairs above you, shoulder width apart, pull yourself up toward the broomstick, keeping your body taught and your legs straight.

The Half Bridge
Lie on your back with your knees bent and your feet flat on the floor. Raise your hips off the floor and pelvis upward, so that your body forms a straight line from your shoulders to your knees. Hold this pose for five breaths, and then slowly lower your body back to the floor. Repeat ten times.

The Plank

The plank is an isometric exercise whereby many of your core muscles are engaged. To hold yourself in a pushup position for thirty-second intervals builds strength in your stomach and core, your shoulders, chest, triceps, and your neck. It is a good all round exercise and can be done anywhere. Start with two thirty-second intervals and build up the repetitions.

Wall Snow Angel

The snow angel is a stretch that retrains the muscles in the upper back and can be executed standing against a wall or lying on a flat surface. Your arms are at right angles with the elbows starting at shoulder height. Slide your bent arms upward to straighten and back into a bent position. Keep as much of your back and head against the surface you are leaning or lying on as possible. Practice seven times, morning, and evening. This helps with your posture.

Mirror Exercise

When being aware of your posture, stand in front of a mirror and imagine a string coming out the top of your head. Imagine pulling that string like those of a marionette and elongating your whole spine. Notice your head is forward and up and your shoulders are relaxed and back. Find a comfortable stance, rather than a severe one, as everyone has their natural posture.

When walking along the street, be aware of your posture. Are you upright and comfortable, or is your head down looking for the dollar bill you lost yesterday? When your head falls forward, your shoulders follow which turns off the muscles of your stomach, similar to when driving a car. Be mindful of your posture so that you engage the muscles, keeping you fit and healthy for much longer.

Create Your Piece of Paradise

Feeling an inner connection with all you have become is the pivotal experience of joy. It provides clarity, and there is safety and knowing in this moment. Unless you have created an inner connection, it is sometimes difficult to process life in a way that is beneficial to you and those around you. Forming this space can be a conscious creation. In times of stress or when you want to feel a deeper connection with Source, there is somewhere to visit that is free and wonderful.

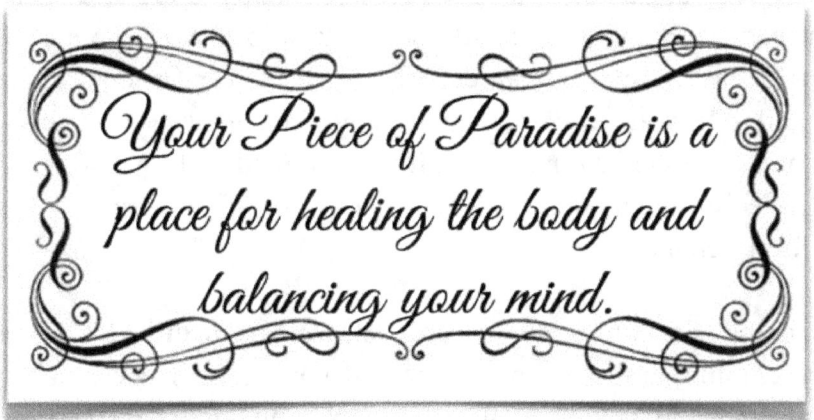

The place of inner connection is what we refer to as your Piece of Paradise. It is a focus you create for healing the physical body and balancing the mind. It can help you find clarity, and gain the information needed to make decisions. This is a place in your mind where you can feel safe, as only those who are invited can enter. This place is comfortable, light, and alive. There's a huge interactive screen, which can project your past, present or future if desired. There's knowledge in all the reference material you could ever need, access to all the information you could ever want and even an elevator with a rainbow, cleansing shower.

You can visit to instigate change in your life or for relaxation, to feel refreshed and revitalized when you leave. It's an innovative place where you can make plans, ask questions, meet your guides and anyone else you would like. This space is uniquely yours and there is not another like it in the whole Universe. It belongs to you and can't be sold or stolen. It's yours to be treasured forever and is completely free.

So how do you create your 'Piece of Paradise'?

This 'Piece of Paradise' is much clearer when you are relaxed so the first part of this journey is all about relaxation. When your Piece of Paradise is set up, you can quickly move there in a few minutes or instantly. If you need to relax at any time in the future, use this method from the beginning. So, if you are ready let's get started. You will need to find a quiet place for at least forty-five minutes to set this up for the first time.

Sit somewhere comfortable where you won't be disturbed. Loosen any tight clothing and put a pillow behind your neck if necessary to get comfortable. It is fine to lie down; the only drawback is that you might fall asleep, but this is a benefit in itself, though not for the purpose of setting up your Piece of Paradise.

Focus gently on your breathing. Feel the ease and flow of each breath in and out, as the life-giving air moves down your throat and into your chest. Feel the breath as it flows in and around your body. Breathe in and out, slowly, and gently. As you breathe out, release all the tension in your body, and allow your body to relax. Take a few slow, gentle breaths and each time you breathe out, breathe out all the tension from your body and allow yourself to relax.

As you gently breathe in and out, use your imagination to see in your mind's eye a gate at the top of a forest path. Open the gate, and in front of you are some mossy, stone steps. Holding the rail, slowly walk down the steps, counting them from ten to one. Each step you take helps your body feel more and more relaxed. Each step allows your mind to let go and feel peaceful. By the time you get to one, you're going to feel very relaxed in your body and peaceful in your mind.

Take the first step now.
Ten: notice the lush forest all around you,
Nine: the steps are easy and there's a handrail if needed.
Eight: going gently down, feeling very relaxed
Seven, six, five: it's easy to see where you're going and very relaxing, it feels just like walking through a veil of relaxation.
Four: your body starts to feel heavy, as though the muscles can't hold it anymore,
Three: you are feeling more and more relaxed,
Two: you are nearly there, and at the count of one, your mind will feel more peaceful than ever before.
Wait for it,
ONE: Your whole body feels relaxed; your mind is peaceful and you're about to embark upon a journey you're really going to enjoy.

NEXT STEP

- You find yourself standing on the earthen edge of a gently flowing stream.
- There's a small jetty nearby, so you walk on over.
- As you get closer, you can see a small boat tied up to this jetty.

- It looks inviting and feels right, so you board the boat, and sit back on the pillows inside it for comfort.
- The weather is just perfect; there's a gentle breeze; and the sun is peeking through the treed canopy and sparkling like diamonds, as it dances on the water.
- The boat becomes free of the jetty, and gently floats down the stream.
- As the gentle current takes it downstream, you lean over the edge of the boat and trail your fingers in the sparkling, crystal-clear water.
- It looks so inviting that you slip over the edge of the boat and into the crystal-clear water.
- It feels cool and refreshing, and you can swim effortlessly.
- You follow the fish and swim down under the water through rainbows of color, swimming down through
- red,
- orange,
- yellow, deeper and deeper through
- green,
- blue and
- purple.
- Just as the color becomes violet, you find yourself on a sunny bank of the stream.
- Following the tree-lined path, you notice your clothes have changed to ones that are dry, flowing, light and comfortable.
- The path opens out into a lush green glade.
- Flowering plants and trees surround it.
- The only piece of furniture is a garden bench, placed purposely to view the vast array of flowers.
- As you sit and watch the splendor, you're amazed that the colors are so effervescent as they have such depth. The light breeze is a

Change Your Reality and You Change Your Life

perfect temperature, there are no bugs and you feel very comfortable.
- You're mesmerized by the plants, as they seem to sway in rhythmic unison.
- The bees are dancing on the flowers, and the whole garden seems to be alive.
- It's a different type of alive than what you've been used to. It's as if the senses are piqued and you're witnessing the clarity of nature, as if for the first time.
- On the far side of the glade, you notice a path meandering through the garden and past the trees.
- It seems to be beckoning.
- You follow the path through the trees to a clearing, where there stands a large house.
- This house seems comfortable and familiar, so you move closer.
- As you reach the front door, it opens and you're greeted by a friendly familiar figure.
- Casually walking through the door, you seem to know exactly where to go.
- Down the long hallway and through a door.
- This door is the entrance to what you will fondly refer to as your workshop.
- As you enter the workshop, you start to imagine things, and where they should be placed.
- To your amazement, as soon as you imagine something, it appears. It's as if you have a direct connection to creation.
- On one wall, you imagine a large television screen that covers the whole wall and it appears. In front of it you position a comfortable lounge, settee, or sofa.
- The wall opposite, houses storage containers but you have no idea yet of what they hold.

- A computer is on a desk next to them.

- Exploring the room, you are drawn to an exquisite solid-crystal bed taking pride of place in the center of the room. Feeling the cool smoothness, the lights of the crystals activate and glow with your touch. You recognize it as a healing bed, and you're excited because you know you can place anybody you like on this crystal bed, and they will gain wonderful benefits, both physically and emotionally.

- There's also a wooden chest next to the crystal bed with a note in your handwriting saying, 'To Fix Things' and curiously you open it to find hardware tools. There's a hammer, a chisel, an electric drill, and a few other tools you haven't used before. With no idea of what needs fixing, you continue to look around knowing that it will be clear when the time comes to use them.

- In the far corner, there's a door. It doesn't open manually but there are buttons on the side. You press a button, the door opens, and a rainbow of colors reaches out to greet you. The most colorful elevator you've ever seen materializes and you realize it's a rainbow shower, which cleanses whoever enters.

- This is the only way another person may visit your sacred workshop. They must be invited and they're greeted by a healing rainbow in the elevator. A note on the table beside the elevator indicates that this is a quicker way for you to arrive at this workshop. Just by counting from 10-1, you can arrive in the elevator with the healing rainbow shower. Moving closer to the rainbow shower, the effects are already being felt by your body as it responds to the deep relaxation. You breathe in the deep relaxation.

- Walking back to the lounge, you sit and ponder, as there is so much to absorb. This place has a wonderful feel about it. You feel a real sense of belonging without knowing why. The huge screen in front of you is looming, but there seems to be no remote controls, only buttons on the armrest. Even as you think of turning it on, the screen springs to life. This is a screen of the mind and it portrays the past, present and the future. The buttons are there in case you want to turn it off or change channels. This is a very safe environment, and if you aren't ready to see or recall something, you have the power to turn it off; it's that easy. This is a place that is comforting and nurturing, so there is nothing to fear.

- You sense a wonderful feeling of privacy without feeling alone, and you realize through its personalized layout that this is a place you have been many times previously. The notes even bear your handwriting.

- Each of the drawers on the wall is vividly labeled. One is labeled 'The Right Words' and when you open the drawer, it is empty but for a piece of paper that is written 'Welcome Back'. You realize that all these drawers are empty until you need them, and this is a tool for communication with your Higher Self.

- As you leave this mesmerizing place through the rainbow shower, you turn for one last look at this wonderful Piece of Paradise to etch the wonderful feeling of belonging into your memory. There's an excitement as you realize that anytime you choose to return, either by the forest path or the elevator, you can feel connected.

Six Dimensions of Healing

Anyone you choose to invite (either physical or non-physical) can only arrive through the elevator, and you will always feel safe and uplifted. You hold yourself proudly, as you walk into this special elevator and press the only button.

- As it travels through ten, nine, eight, seven, six, five, four, three, two and one, the door opens, and you find yourself back where you started at the gate near the forest path. The world looks clear and fresh, and as you begin to doubt that your journey was real, you notice you're holding a piece of paper. In rich text are written the words 'Welcome Back'.

 # Mental Dimension

Six Dimensions of Healing

You Create Your Own Reality

Thinking is a part of being human. Your thoughts define you, as they are different from everyone else's, even though you sometimes share opinions with others. You are the only person who can choose the thoughts you think, and because of this, there has always been persuasion from others to influence the direction of your thoughts. Whether by the media, politicians, parents, or friends, it has long been understood that if one can persuade a person to think in a certain direction, their actions can be anticipated. But the results are unreliable. What is much more significant is how those thoughts create emotions, which then translate to behavior that is predictable.

What you think and how you feel creates your reality, and since your thoughts rarely cease, consciously choosing how you perceive life is invaluable. You need to control your thinking, or your thoughts will direct your life in ways that are unwanted. Just one thought that is focused on for as little as a minute will become a thought-form, which gathers momentum and soon you are automatically looking for more thoughts that are similar. Your thought form is rapidly becoming matter. It makes no difference whether the thoughts you think are about things wanted or unwanted, as they are all included.

When thoughts in your head have gathered momentum, and spiraled out of control, the turmoil is reflected in your life by the situations around you. This feeling of being out of control will result in blame, either of self or others. As all situations in our lives are reflected back to us like a movie, with the people closest to us playing pivotal roles, it is easy to think that someone else is to blame for the chaos now experienced. But blaming others will only keep momentum increasing in the same unwanted direction, it is never the path to a solution.

Rather than looking at disagreeable situations as someone else's fault, ask yourself what you would like to happen and how would you prefer to feel? This will help you choose the path that feels like relief, as this is the path of least resistance, which leads in the direction of clarity and Source Energy.

Your Mood Map always leads you toward your Higher Self, and your thoughts are the communication that indicates the direction in which you are traveling. You are always moving either toward your Source Energy or away from it. Blame is never the path that takes you towards what you want, as it is pushing hard against something you don't want, and when you do this you include more of what you don't want into your reality, as it becomes the focus of your thoughts. Ultimately you want to *consciously choose* the direction of your thoughts, and not let them run in the old path of past patterns of thinking.

The following steps will be valuable whenever you are in a situation where your thoughts are moving in an unwanted direction. Use them as a tool to refine where you are going, or to discover what you want.

Firstly, choose not to react. Reactions have consequences that gather momentum and many times you don't know what your reactions are until the momentum is strong. Reactions are common and often a first response, like the fight or flight of a survival response. But most situations are not about survival, they just initially feel as though they are, so reactions are often regretted. If you do react to a person or situation, which spirals out of control, you will just have to ride the wave, and let the scenario take its course. The momentum will dwindle eventually.

Next, redirect the inner voice of complaint. By consciously choosing thoughts that are abstract, you can move the self-talk in a direction that gives you relief. This is important, as it will diffuse the momentum that can create any more unwanted situations. (It is much easier to stop an avalanche at the beginning while it is still a snowflake, than to do so at the bottom of the hill.)

Loraine had a successful hairdressing salon, and introduced two extra partners that offered a variety of skills to compliment her own. After a few months, the two new partners decided that they would like to push Lorraine out of the business and own it themselves. Loraine knew there was something wrong, and her self-talk was filled with fear and resentment. She reacted to the situation by going to a solicitor. The other two women also got their own solicitor, and it was an uncomfortable situation, so the clientele started to dwindle. The talk at the salon was all about what was happening, the reality at hand. It ended with the two women opening a salon elsewhere and Loraine wanting to sell, as she no longer enjoyed being in a place that had caused her so much anxiety.

It's important to understand there is no right or wrong in this situation, as both parties could show evidence as to why their story should be the truth. When you have a situation where all parties react, it doesn't create a favorable outcome for anyone. It is the self-talk that spirals out of control by choosing more of the same toxic thoughts as you have been thinking. If you recognize this type of reaction in your own life, you might want to introduce some changes. To interrupt this pattern of thought, look for something abstract to focus on. This may be a flower, the lush green grass, the scent of a rose, a sunny day. Anything that gives you relief from recent thoughts is effective, as you are creating a space amongst the chaotic thoughts. When you have interrupted the pattern with abstract thoughts, you can then choose the path in which your thoughts travel by choosing thoughts that feel better and better.

You are the creator of your own reality, as your thinking creates an emotion, and a focused emotion creates your vibration. Everyone and everything has vibration, which becomes your focused point of attraction in the Universe. Thoughts and people are attracted to you by vibration. You are free to choose your own vibration (and therefore what is attracted to you) by choosing your thoughts. Being conscious of creating good-feeling thoughts translates to a vibration, which attracts good feeling situations and people in your life. This is an empowering place to stand, as although it means you can no longer blame anyone else for your situation, you have the opportunity to change your future by simply changing the pattern of your thoughts.

You can't change how another person thinks, nor are you responsible for how they feel, no matter how much they try to convince you otherwise. Some people would have you believe that you are responsible for their anger or unhappiness, but that is never the case. Just like you, only they can choose how to think and feel.

Find something to focus on that is working in your life. There only needs to be one thing that's working, and as you focus on that one thing, it expands. As you practice looking at situations in a perspective that feels good, the feeling grows and in just a short while, you have changed your mood. That sort of practice creates a pattern that creates a positive outlook as your default perspective. Your focused thoughts create your vibration and your vibration creates your reality.

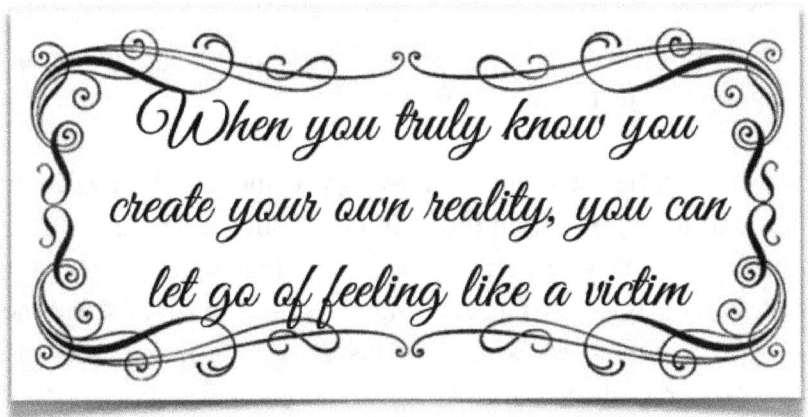

When you truly know you create your own reality, you can let go of feeling like a victim

When you *truly* know that you create your own reality, you can move from feeling like a victim to standing in your own Universal power. This transition changes your focus from the problem to a solution. There is no right or wrong way of looking at anything, but whatever you focus on you create more of that same emotional vibration.

Be comfortable in the knowledge that your thoughts won't always be joyous, and you won't always stay in a good mood. With practice, however, you will feel good more often and the lows will become less frequent. When you practice moving your thoughts and emotions towards subjects that feel good, you will find you bounce from low to high much more quickly. When you experience joy frequently, you really won't settle for anything less.

Fairness Vs. Worthiness

A friend of mine was relating a story of someone she knew who had won the lotto. She said he was the type of person who would go every week to drink with friends and eat their food, and when challenged as to why he didn't contribute to the bounty, he never returned to the group. She mentioned that she didn't understand how someone who was seemingly there only to take, could now be receiving so much by winning lotto. It just didn't seem fair to her.

She was under the illusion that fairness was judged by how deserving one seemed to be, based on the opinion of others. These are illusions of your reality, as you don't know their bigger picture. A sense of fairness is focusing on what *isn't* wanted, and a sense of worthiness is focusing on what *is* wanted. Observing fairness and making judgments is based on your own perceptions and beliefs, as there is the thinking it will be noticed and acted upon by others and ultimately a higher power. But your judgments have no bearing on how others feel about themselves. You have no influence on the Universe as regards another person; in other words, you can't wish ill on them, to influence an outcome in their lives. The only person a sense of unfairness affects is the person feeling the disharmony. Fairness is an opinion you express, based upon your perception of a situation. Fairness is the opinion of another's deeds.

Worthiness is an emotion you feel for yourself, as nobody else can make you feel worthy. It is everyone's birthright to feel worthy in one respect or another, but we have so much free will that we can actually choose whether we want to feel worthy or not.

Feeling worthy will align you with all the joy in the Universe; it is the emotion that allows dreams to come true. Nobody else can take your worthiness away, and nobody else's opinion of your worth matters. You were born worthy, you are worthy and your feeling of worthiness will move you beyond the dreams of ordinary men.

Universal Truth

There are many truths in the Universe, as it isn't a set equation like mathematics. The Universe is filled with people who have questions and there are as many truthful answers as there are opinions, understandings and human beings to think them. In fact, your own truth will change many times over a lifetime.

Focusing on a subject will bring more subjects with the same emotion into your reality. If you were looking for evidence that the subject was true, you would always find some. If you thought the government was spying on you, there would be evidence to support this theory, and if you thought they were protecting you would find evidence of that as well. That is the paradox of Universal Truth. Whatever truth you want to prove, whether it be an abundance of something, or the absence thereof, you will always find evidence of that which you believe. The evidence of your belief will physically manifest in your life, and when it does, you will call it the truth, as it is your reality.

Reality and truth are not the same, as reality is a manifestation of your vibration. It may or may not have any bearing on your truth. When you have focused your attention on a subject that you have observed, and created a reality of unfairness with the world, this sense of unfairness will show up in your reality constantly. The Universe will give you evidence of your practiced vibration of unfairness. However, this is usually a short-term mood as you will observe something different and your vibration will change. You don't necessarily hold the truth that the world is unfair, just because it became your reality for a short time.

There is always evidence of what you are seeking, either for the affirmative or the negative. You can find evidence that God exists, and you can find evidence that a God does not. You can find evidence that an afterlife exists, and you can find evidence that it doesn't, that the world is unfair or that it provides what you need. That is the paradox. The more you try to prove the existence of something, the more contrary evidence that can be found by those who are searching for evidence. This is the reason people disagree, as one knows from their experience a definite truth and the other is convinced of the opposite. They are both right. There is not one truth but the truth that is right for you.

The key to finding your own truth is in letting go of having to prove your truth is right to anyone. When you measure truth by the alignment of your elevated mood, you will know which is right for you and will march to the beat of your own drum. Your eyes and your ears are not the best guides on the journey of truth as they give you evidence of where you are, but have no concept of where you are going. Even standing in a place of illness and fear is no evidence of what is to come. *Sickness is not your truth, it is a temporary reality.* Just as a university degree does not guarantee success, neither does your current reality necessarily have a bearing on your future. You can only see what has already been created, and what manifests itself is determined by the truths you believe.

You do have eyes that can guide you along your path of truth. These are inner eyes. There is no need to be psychic, though; you just need to use the imagination.

The eyes of your soul await your direction by using imagination to create what you want, to direct you as to which path you want to take.

The path of truth is made up of all your perceptions and beliefs, and has been woven out of the fabric of life, but truth is unlike mathematics. It is not solid and unrelenting, but organic and changes with your new perceptions and beliefs. Your truth grows with you, and as you imagine the truth of who you are, you will come to understand that nobody has the same truth as you.

Metaphors Illuminate Truth

Life is filled with metaphors. My youngest son was solving a Rubik's cube and made the first move out of sequence, so that the cube didn't work out the way he expected. He then noticed it wasn't working and said, "Well that didn't work; I'll just have to do it this way". He solved the cube puzzle in no time. He reminded me of the time when I missed a turn leaving Sydney airport for the unfamiliar journey home. I thought I knew the way, but missing the very first right turn took me in a completely different direction. When I realized this, I had to use a map to eventually get myself on to a familiar path home. (This took three hours, and was a daunting experience.) Sometimes you know you are on the wrong track and need to acknowledge it, so you can make some adjustments and feel confident you are back on course in your desired direction.

Examples of how the Universe works are everywhere, because Universal Truth is made up of the sum of all its parts. Just as cells divide in your body to create new cells every day, every hour, and every minute, the new cell has the same properties as the parent cell. It is not a part of the cell; it is a cell like the parent, complete with its own DNA. As everything that exists is created from the Universe, so too is even the smallest creation whole and complete. There is a misconception that we as human beings were put on this earth to learn and that we are somehow inferior to that which we came from, and so need to improve. But the expansion of human beings is not about learning or improvement, it is about choosing and creating. The forest with all its bio-diversity doesn't need to improve, and the ocean in all its majestic vastness does not need to improve. They are complete without any help from us.

An example of the Universe can be illustrated through the ocean. When you take a glass of water from the ocean, you have part of the ocean. Or do you? You actually have much more than that. You have a glass of water from the ocean, but it is not *a part*. The ocean doesn't divide itself so that some is sacrificed to the glass. The ocean within the glass is *whole and complete*. There is a small ocean with all its properties and components intact inside that glass. It has the DNA, the minerals, and the cells of the ocean. It is not a part but *an extension* of the water it stands for.

To understand a little more of the Universe, you only need look closer to home. As a human being, you are like the glass of water from the ocean. You came from Source Energy and you remain Source Energy, so you are not a part, but an extension of that which you came from. This Earth you chose wasn't random or by chance; it was because of the opportunities it presented for you. Amongst these were freedom of thought, and the opportunity to choose any situation that would create circumstances from which you could expand and grow. This growth is very personal, yet is influenced by many. It represents the forefront of reality in which you gain knowledge and momentum from a myriad of experiences, which influence further change and growth. The purpose is to create in a path forward that is joyous and fulfilling. Your reality is what makes you unique, as it is created from the choices that are different from those of every other person in the Universe; nobody has the same experiences and perceptions as you do. You are truly unique.

When your belief is that you are here to learn, the power to consciously create is diminished, as that sort of learning sets you up for a life experience as a student. But, life learning is natural and is more accurately described as expansion. All thoughts, situations and experiences contribute to your expansion and because of this, there is no wrong path. Your truth creates your reality, because your reality is created by the thoughts you think, guided by your perception, so that your Higher Self expands, and the Universe becomes so much more than it was before you came into this world. This is a noble path you have set forth upon; to participate with those around you, so that each and every person contributes to a broader, expanded Universe. You were born a leader of your own path, not a follower of others, and you can always create new truths that determine any reality you can conceive.

I had a conversation with a man from South Africa who came to live in North Queensland, Australia, quite a few years ago, as he thought the world was going to become chaotic and disastrous. It seems that, after Armageddon, only one hundred and forty-four thousand people were to be left in the whole of the world, and our way of life would decline because of the lack of a particular chemical. He felt that it didn't matter how positive you were, this would still happen. His truth was that the world would rapidly deteriorate. I couldn't help but offer the contrary truth that I had come to realize, namely that opportunity would still be sought, and creativity would flourish even in the absence of plenty. There would be those who created more abundance out of what they had, and those who complained about the lack. When we spoke about what he believed, I realized that we are all living that way now. There would always be some who believed in devastation and imminent disaster and others who chose a truth that made them flourish. Just as there are always people who create wealth in a financial crisis and those who remain optimistic in a state of emergency. Each person lives their own truth; it's just a matter of what they have perceived their truth to be.

Does the truth become your reality, or does your reality become the truth?

Benefits of Self-talk

Self-talk is the voice inside your head that chatters away, day and night, whether you are aware of it or not. Self-talk can be your friend or worst nightmare, as this inward voice is fueled by what you see, think, and the opinions you currently hold. There is no other person controlling that inward voice or telling you what to say; it is merely responding to the stimulation you are providing. Self-talk is self-programming, for better or for worse. When you feel good, the inner voice endorses your experiences and makes them even better. You are endorsing an understanding that life is great. When you don't feel good, the inner voice will chatter away with thoughts that make you feel worse. You are accumulating evidence that life doesn't feel good.

Self-talk is not independent of you; it's always a reflection of how you are feeling. These thoughts belong to you, so it is helpful to be aware of them. When you don't control your thoughts, self-talk seems to have a mind of its own as it follows an established path. It's sometimes referred to as the ego talking, but remember that *all* your thoughts are self-established.

Change Your Reality and You Change Your Life

You're not crazy if you have a conversation with yourself. In fact, some of the most amazing discoveries have come about because people have taken the time to talk things out in their own heads. When you are pondering a decision, imagining, and talking it out in your mind, this will assist you in deciding if you have selected the right choice for you. It is self-talk at its best; with you in control and determining the track it flows on. When your thought process spirals in a direction that seems self-destructive, this isn't because your self-talk has a mind of its own, but because it just hasn't been given a new track to run along.

Sometimes it may be difficult to believe you are the controller of your own self-talk, but thinking is personal, so nobody else can control it. Nobody really ever knows what you're thinking. Most don't care. Others can share their observations or opinions, but there is still a choice as to what you allow yourself to think about. Opinions or observations that don't serve you are the reason many thoughts spiral out of control. And when the thoughts running through your mind are realized, there is a risk of letting these dominate how you feel. This is creating a reality you don't want, and is like letting a two-year-old decide what's for dinner every night. Eventually your body will crave more nourishment than chicken nuggets and cotton candy can provide. The best opportunity to achieve harmonious self-talk and balance for your body, is by feeling your way. Your mood is the guide and your Mood Map can be the best ally you have, as it offers a new thinking track for self-talk to travel.

Some signs that unwanted self-talk is making an impact on your life can be:
Lack of Concentration
Sleeplessness

Obsessive Compulsive Disorder
Post-Traumatic Stress Disorder
Chronic Fatigue Syndrome
Inability to hold relationships
Incessant busyness
Fatigue
Anxiety
Depression
Not being able to keep up with life
Fear and Paranoia

All habit patterns are created when thoughts repeatedly travel in the same direction. As thoughts become the path of behaviors, these patterns can be wanted or unwanted. It's up to you to decide what thoughts you want to think and in which direction you would like your life to unfold. How you feel at anytime, will reflect your patterns of self-talk. Nobody asks outright for depression, schizophrenia, paranoia, anxiety, or a myriad of other disorders. You don't say, "Depression, come to me," but by allowing your mind to wind into default negative patterns that have been created over many years, your natural flow of well-being is obstructed.

It can be difficult to change spiraling thought patterns, even when you are aware that they're not taking you where what you want to go. The most powerful insight about these patterns is that you can't think your way out of the abyss; you can only *feel* your way. Instead of recognizing what you are thinking, connect with how you're *feeling*, then look for a feeling that is more neutral, and then one that is a little better.

As you become the guardian of your own thoughts by consciously sifting through the observations and choosing what to think, you gain an awareness of your own self-talk. This gives you the opportunity to catch thoughts early, so momentum doesn't take hold of thoughts moving in an unwanted direction. With practice at noticing your thoughts, you can become sensitive enough to recognize uncomfortable patterns as soon as they begin to occur. This is the pivotal point of changing your reality. When you decide to change self-talk patterns, giving less attention to what isn't wanted and more attention to what is wanted is the secret to setting up an empowering reality.

Being aware of your self-talk is the key to change. If you wish to cease the self-talk you can interrupt the pattern with a mantra such as: "I let you go, I let you go. You too, you too." Be gentle with yourself, as you are a worthy and loving being. Understand that your thoughts and feelings go together, so when unwanted thoughts have gathered momentum, and you can't change them, sleep and meditation can be a valuable interception. On waking, you can choose the thoughts you want to think, such as ease and flow. Remember, habit patterns of thought have been developed like the groove on a record, and now a new groove is being etched. It takes twenty-one days for a new pattern to be created. Take notice of your thoughts, and the ways in which they influence your mood and etch a new groove on your record.

For twenty-one days, practice turning your thoughts around, and you will begin to notice a significant difference in your life.

Remember:
- Be aware and let go of the thoughts that don't serve you.
- Meditate or sleep to interrupt the pattern.
- Consciously choose thoughts that feel better.
- Feel your way, as thinking will get you in a tangle.

Each of your habit patterns are a process and every person processes differently. What you think of someone and their circumstances may not be the same as the way *they* feel about their own experience. You are looking at their situation through your own perspective. You don't really know what anyone else thinks and feels. It's not your job to change the world for others, just as it's not your job to fix anything you think is wrong with others. There is nothing in this world that is broken, so when you align yourself with the starving and poor in the world, your self-talk follows your observations and you feel powerless. As you focus on what is lacking in society, your self-talk follows the path of lack. When you understand that focusing on the best in people, even if they can't see it, brings out the best in people, you will understand the influence you can have on the world in a very positive way.

As I'm a busy person, I know I can handle several different jobs at one time, and I find it exciting and exhilarating. My parents were well organized, and I adopted their patterns. It's never been my life's journey to sit on a mountaintop and meditate; I'd rather be involved in my community and live life. Automatically checking my self-talk to make sure I stay balanced is one of the patterns I have developed. Balance is important to me, as it makes me feel good.

When I was working for a couple of charitable organizations at one time, a couple of people said to me, "You've taken on too much. Don't you feel stressed?"

I didn't. However, I started to buy into their story and found my self-talk following those thoughts, and then I started to doubt myself. Maybe I *was* taking on too much. As the self-talk eroded the confidence I had felt, the pendulum of self-talk started to swing in the direction of feeling overwhelmed. Within a day, I felt tired and thought that others must have been correct in their assumption; but when this happened a second time, I understood what was happening.

You see, my perspective of life was different from those who had made the comments about my taking on too much. Through their eyes, they could imagine how overwhelmed they would feel in the same position. But not everybody is the same, and some people thrive on handling many projects at once, and that was me. I was the only person who could gauge how I felt and I felt great. I knew it wasn't a lifestyle, so I would immerse myself in events for a while, and then spend time on my own. That was my balance. You never know what someone else is thinking or what is right for them, so it's a good idea to mind your own self-talk.

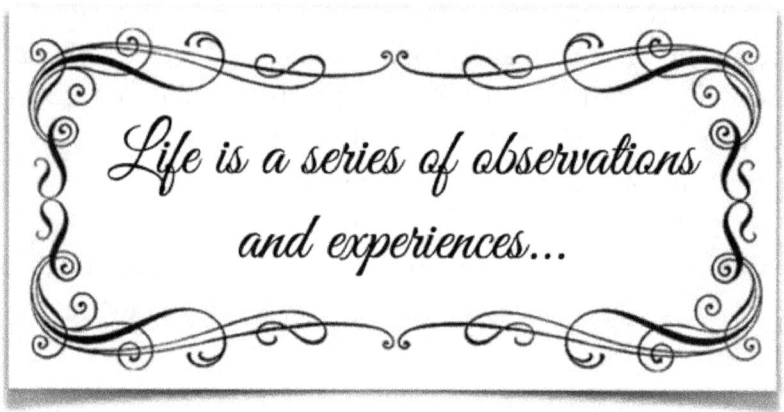

Life is a series of observations and experiences...

Life is a series of observations and experiences that cause expansion. The expansion that is born within you creates a new platform from which to dream and create. It is the self-talk that will move you forward along your own path of expansion, or keep you a prisoner in your own head. It's good practice to monitor the thoughts that run through your head, because when you feel good you're moving in the direction of your own expansion, and when you feel discomfort you aren't. Self-talk can be the tool to help you close the gap. As you consciously choose thoughts that make you feel better, you are creating a new reality – one that encompasses the new expanded version of you.

Overriding the Cells of your Body

As we have seen earlier in Section 1, each cell in the body has intelligence. It knows exactly how to work for optimum health. The body is an amazing creation. When it needs nutrition, it can create the nutrition needed from the food provided. When it needs Vitamin B, the body can create it from the food you eat. Your body is amazingly efficient, as each cell is whole and complete, and knows the joy of the Universe; the cells ring in a chorus of health and well-being.

So how does the body become misaligned, so that the natural balance is affected? The cells are efficient and effective at what they do, but you guide them, and they follow your directions. You don't give instructions with your conversation, as nobody would consciously direct their body to illness, but instructions to the body don't come in the form of words; they come in the form of thoughts and feelings. So, when you are feeling great, you have happy cells, and when you are depressed your cells are depleted.

The thoughts you think can either enhance or override the messages automatically sent to the trillions of cells throughout your body. Your body doesn't have a mind of its own, of course; it uses yours. Your cells eavesdrop on the conversations you take part in; either with yourself or with others, and your self-talk is just as coercive as outward conversations. Just as you were influenced by your parent's emotions as you grew up, so are your cells influenced by your self-talk. It doesn't matter what another person thinks or says about you or your body, it only matters how you feel about what they've said. If the messages your cells are receiving via your own self-talk are unloving, they will listen and act per the instructions your feelings are emitting, so that your body feels the same way as you do. Your thoughts give directions to the body, whether you mean them to or not. This is how you override the cells' intelligence. Every cell in your body knows exactly where it is supposed to be, and how it is supposed to be performing, but if you think thoughts that are unloving on a regular basis, these become instructions which override the cells' ability for well-being. Constantly thinking negative or deprecating thoughts will have dire consequences on your health. If you don't notice what you're thinking and how you're feeling on a regular basis, don't worry, as the evidence will eventually become clear in your body.

Your body doesn't have a mind of its own; it uses yours, so every thought you think is a direct communication with the body's healing system. Every thought you think makes a difference to your well-being.

If you can imagine your body as the hardware, then your thoughts are the software. Your thoughts are the programming for your body. Whatever the mind conceives, the body will achieve, especially when the software is played repeatedly. Whatever you are thinking places an order to your body for what you want, whether you are aware of it or not, and the body will respond accordingly. When your mood is one of constant anger, you are placing an order for pain. When your mood is chronically one of abundance and joy, you are placing an order to feel great. You don't ask with words, but with your *mood*.

Enhancing your thoughts is free; it doesn't interfere with any medication, and will give immediate benefits. I know of surgeons who refuse to operate on cancer patients if the patient's thinking is detrimental to their health. The medics have noticed that results change dramatically when the patient is optimistic and feels loved. Uplifting thoughts can enhance your life at once, and the body will follow your thoughts.

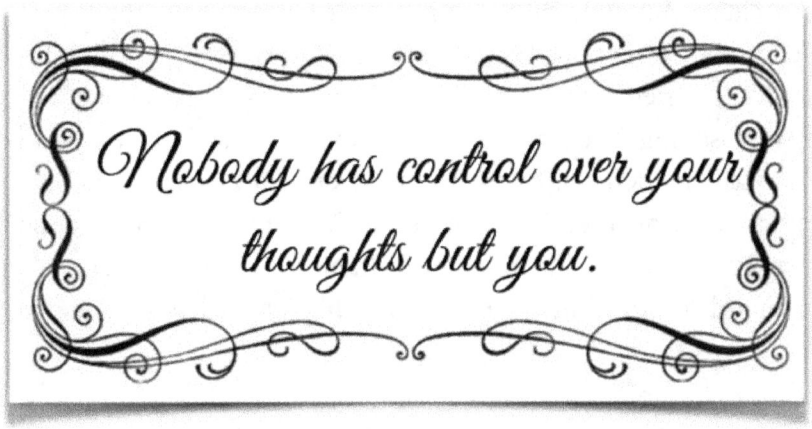

It may not seem obvious at times but nobody has control over your thoughts. People can influence you by what they say, only if you invite their thoughts to be yours. You are the only person who can choose whether to be influenced by others. A doctor may inform a patient they have six weeks to live, and if the patient believes the doctor, they then *do* have six weeks to live. Yet, there are many who have chosen to ignore their doctor's prediction, and have lived a much longer and fulfilled life.

Balance Vs. Imbalance

When someone is blaming you for how they feel, it can be easy for you to think it's your fault. Especially if you feel guilty from when you were a child. Allowing others to influence your thinking by their story, if their story isn't empowering, creates imbalance in your life, as you have chosen their story as your own. For example, when you were spontaneous and youthful, you were probably told to 'stop it' or 'grow up', or to modify your behavior in some restrictive way. It wasn't because you were doing something wrong, or even harmful; it was because someone else thought it would be better for *them* if you acted in a different manner. Only you know what is right for you. When you started being mindful of the way you were acting and what you were saying in case you upset someone, that is when you set up the patterns of being influenced by others, and living someone else's story rather than creating your own. You became more concerned with how *someone else* felt, rather than how *you* felt. You changed your mood to suit that of others and that created imbalance in your life.

People are naturally coercive and can persuade others that they are right, even if the evidence is absent. Politicians are experts at this game. They are counting on the parents of every society to create a sheep-like behavior in their offspring, as it helps them, the politicians, greatly. It is much easier to convince someone to adopt an idea, if they can show how much it will hurt another if you don't. Advertising companies make billions from this practice. They know that, if they can convince you that buying an item will make someone else happy, you will very likely buy it. Advantage is being taken of the conditioning that was created when you were young – and that is the belief that making someone else happy is more important than your own happiness.

With this belief, your happiness becomes dependent on others around you being happy. You become unsure of how you feel yourself, and wonder why your experience is of a deep dissatisfaction with life, when logically you should be happy. The winners in this imbalance are therapists and pharmaceutical companies. You can lose yourself in someone else's story, as your cells eavesdrop on the emotions that affect health, weight, confidence, relationships, and joy.

Create your own story. Just because your mother was dependent on pleasing people, or your father pretended he was happy yet drank a lot, doesn't have to be your story. Your past need not have any bearing on your future, as your cells eavesdrop in the present. It is the *patterns* of thought that you need to be conscious of. Change the cycle and choose your own story to allow a healthy, happy body.

Create Your Own Story

"As a single footstep will not make a path on the earth, so a single thought will not make a pathway in the mind. To make a deep physical path, we walk again and again. To make a deep mental path, we must think over and over the kind of thoughts we wish to dominate our lives."
Henry David Thoreau: *Walden*

A cheerful friend of mine was opening a wonderful, whimsical café. It was turning out to be a fun-filled, entertaining and joyful place. However, the proprietors of café down the road that she had owned a few years previously said they were going to sue Amy if she opened another one in their vicinity. Another rival cafe owner from a few streets over abused her for setting up, and the townspeople were talking boycott. Amy's early excitement quickly vanished; as she thought about the consequences other people's actions could have upon her life. Amy had many supporters, but had bought into the rivals' story of fear. Following the recent, unexpected death of her brother, Amy knew she was fragile, and so she also bought easily into the story of her unworthiness.

It can be tempting to get caught up in someone else's reality, as others often make a point of convincing you that their situation is your fault, but another person's mood is never your fault and you can't do anything to change it for them. We all seem to live in the same world, but all of us are actually walking around in our own worlds, seeing evidence of the reality we have created. There are billions of people walking our planet, all with a different reality, as none of us is the same. It's easy to believe that other people affect your life, but it's you who chooses to be a part of the other's story or not.

When Amy spoke to me about the situation, she was very concerned about it, and ready to withdraw from her dream. I helped her to understand that she was buying into other people's stories. They didn't have to become her reality.

When you become the object of attention from fearful people, there's always a chance you'll get caught up in their momentum. With all the threats and the animosity, it was enough to send Amy back to the recent low place she had been in when her brother died. She certainly didn't have the fair mood she wanted to be in, to create the fun place of her dreams.

There were only two choices for Amy. She could create her own story, or live in someone else's reality. Only one of those choices would make her happy. For Amy to find a solution that suited her, she needed to find a way of letting the problem go. Things have a way of working themselves out when you don't focus on them. There really is a reason you don't add fuel to a fire. You can't challenge someone else and win, when you're playing a role in their story.

There were many things that were working in Amy's life so when she focused on the excitement she felt with this new venture, the choice of colors and decor, the kitchen design, the layout of the tables and chairs, and many more challenging decisions that were available to her, she started to create her own story. That was her salvation. If you don't like the way you are feeling, change your mood, and tell a different story. As Amy was creating an Alice in Wonderland themed café, she chose to focus on a well-timed quote received under the door.

"Imagination is the only weapon in the war against reality."
Lewis Carroll: Alice in Wonderland.
This was just what she needed and it brightened her spirits immensely.

Nobody has influence over your business. Not the government or the economy, as they don't control you, and they aren't responsible for what happens in your life. How you feel either attracts people to your business or repels them. When you are angry or worried about someone opening up down the road, you are certainly not attracting. So, when your business takes a dive, it's not because of the business down the road opening, but the way you have chosen to feel about it, as this is the story you are telling. You have the option of telling any story, so change your mood and change your life.

Thoughts are tangible. They exist along with every plant, animal and object as matter and energy. We too are made of matter and energy. Thoughts are real, and as such, are influential in our own lives. Thoughts have emotion, and when focused upon, create vibration as they gather momentum in the Universe, like a snowball that rolls downhill. As we focus upon a thought, it creates momentum and gathers more thoughts that are of a similar emotion.

Thoughts have the biggest impact on the thinker. You can't think someone into having an accident, or maiming themselves in some way, and your thoughts can't be forced on others. The only way thoughts can be given to another is by sharing them. Some of the best orators in the world were people who shared their thoughts in a convincing way. When you persuade people that your thoughts are valid, those suggestions gain new thinkers, who then gather together. One famous analogy was *The War of the Worlds*, written by HG Wells. The text was adapted for radio by Orson Welles in 1938, and was broadcast over the airwaves in and near New York as a series of bulletins announcing the arrival of alien space ships landing and taking over the world. This created panic amongst listeners to the point where many actually believed the story, and took steps to flee the city. The listeners thus shared Welles' thoughts, and created a reality for themselves that was based on someone else's story.

Shared thoughts or suggestions can lead to groups, towns, religions, and countries all sharing some of the same thoughts. Propaganda is exaggerated stories that are fed to groups of people to cause chaos. These stories work because they feed fearful thoughts to fearful people, which perpetuate chaos. Nobody was born to be a follower; but another's thoughts and suggestions can define and limit people. Women are second-class citizens in many countries, and that works so long as everyone believes the same story. In some cases, another's story can free people, such as when children are brought up to believe in themselves. The story is one you want to hold on to as it is empowering. A thought you think over and over becomes a belief – not because it is true, but because it derives from a persistent pattern of thought.

If you wanted to inspire children to believe in themselves, you wouldn't consciously tell them they were useless. You may uplift them with stories of people who had overcome obstacles to win, anecdotes of people who came from less than suitable backgrounds to become the people others admired. You wouldn't build a picture of those who kept failing, and eventually gave up to settle for mediocrity. It would seem obvious not to tell them a derogatory story if you were wanting them to believe in themselves, so it would make sense not to tell those self-defeating stories to yourself either. Life paths aren't set in concrete; they change constantly. When the evidence presented in your life, shows you what you don't want, it's time to change your mood and tell a new story.

Everything you think becomes your personal story. This is the story of where you are right now, with all your hopes and dreams of the future and active memories of the past. A single thought may not make a pathway in the mind, but if you've ever spoken to an adult who was abused as a child, you will know that just one thought about that experience sows the seed for more similar thoughts to appear, and in the absence of anything else, this becomes their truth. Their old story becomes the current story and this creates their reality. Abuse may be an extreme example, but as an adult, you now need to choose which stories from your past you would like to believe and which stories not to perpetuate. You are the creator of your own reality, so any story you tell over and over becomes a self-fulfilling prophecy. Just as you can pick up any book you'd like to read, so too can you choose any story you'd like to create. The story doesn't have to be based in reality. In fact, unless your reality is something that is happy and joyful, you would be better off immersing your imagination in a new story. The importance of having a story you love is to guide your life in the direction of a joyful reality.

To keep focus on her own story, Amy took the opportunity to do the things she loved most. There was a crater lake near her home, so early every morning she would kayak, walk or swim in the lake. This connection with nature centered her for the day ahead. Amy was developing roots to form a solid foundation for the growth of her business. She would eventually attract the people into her business she wanted, those that were fun and happy. There aren't many business owners who can say that.

When sitting down to create a new story, allow your imagination to wander. Ask yourself what you want and why? What are the reasons for wanting what you want? There is no right or wrong answer, but understanding the emotional reasons for wanting what you do helps you immerse yourself in the dream. It's changeable, and you will refine your desires often. Then, just as Amy did, you can expect your will to be done, and you can go and have fun. Forget about the bad things. Enjoy each moment, and when you don't enjoy it any more, change your mood to something better, repeatedly.

The Lost World of Imagination

"You can't depend on your eyes when your imagination is out of focus." Mark Twain

Did you know your mind doesn't know the difference between a thought you think and something you imagine? That's why a dream can seem so real. Your body will go through the same emotions as if you were living the scenario. So how can you use this to your advantage? Your imagination is the most influential tool you have in your repertoire for creating a reality you love. When you were at school, you may have gotten into trouble (as most of us did) because you were daydreaming, but the reason you were imagining had more to do with choosing to be somewhere more pleasant than the classroom, rather than listening to dreary arithmetic drills.

Most young children were discouraged from daydreaming with a slap on the wrist, or a blackboard duster thrown across the classroom with practiced accuracy to wake them up. Some children stopped daydreaming and others didn't. It was seen as a childish pursuit that would amount to nothing, and just as with anything, either you use your imagination or you lose it. So, some people now daydream often as adults and others don't, but the importance of childhood daydreaming is that it was practice in using the imagination.

Nothing in this world exists that wasn't first imagined? This is a very powerful statement, isn't it? Just think, there are so many wonderful things in this world, and they were all imagined before any words or drawings took place. In a classroom, just like the one you were in, someone imagined, then refined and put down on paper the workings of something you use today, and they ducked the blackboard duster more than a few times.

Imagining what you want ignites the passion that becomes your story. The story you live in your mind becomes your reality, so if your current reality is not the one you want repeated, then focus instead on the one you've imagined.

If you've lost the ability to imagine a more fulfilling life, then using visualization techniques can help you feel comfortable in the pursuit of imagining. Whether you call it Imagination or Visualization, the key is that you ignite the emotions and it feels real. As you become immersed in the image, you are creating a new story. Writing this story down on paper as you imagine the scene, is endorsing the imagination and you become immersed in the story for longer, as it takes time to write the words.

When using your imagination for joyous creating becomes a regular part of life, you'll find that changes occur quickly. It's not the picture you want to create but the *emotion*. What if you could imagine yourself as fit and healthy, feeling the strength of your body in every step taken, spending endless energy playing with your children in the park, running, laughing and feeling the breeze on your face, with the smells of fresh pine forest around you. This is an image you can feel, see, taste, touch, and smell. That's the daydream, and this new scenario of freedom, ease and fun, becomes your story.

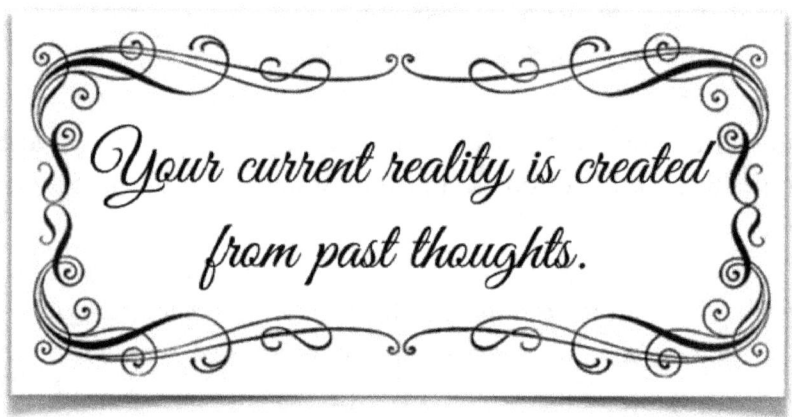

You have the power to change the focus of your life. You may describe a movie to someone to say that you didn't like it and give it a bad review but you wouldn't keep focusing on the movie, so why do this with your life? It is a popular human pastime to focus on what isn't working. It could be lack of money, being overweight, the wars in the world, on drugs, or even a disgruntled neighbor. Your focus becomes your vibration, and your vibration brings you more experiences that are similar to your thoughts. This means you can't focus on being overweight if you want to become thin, and you can't focus on war to create peace. You can only focus on health to become healthy, abundance to become abundant, peace to create peace in your life, and so on. The formula is simple; when you don't like certain aspects of your life, don't focus on them. Use your imagination and create something better.

Your imagination was a gift designed to mold a better life, to create a reality that would inspire and excite you. Daydreaming can occur anywhere, anytime, and it can make short shrift of waiting in long lines. There is no need to worry about 'not facing reality' or getting lost in the abyss. There is none of that, and so much to gain.

Some places are truly inspirational. They often occur in nature, such as waterfalls, lush mountains tops, the ocean, an isolated beach. I have a beautiful physical space as I write. I'm in the mountains, with a lake view framed by my window, and nobody around during the day but the birds and the little dog beside me. Not everyone has this environment, yet we are all drawn to somewhere in nature we would love to be. This is where your imagination can help as you may not be able to physically move to your favorite place but you can always go there in your mind. (See *'Your Piece of Paradise'* at the end of the *Mental* Dimension for instructions, or visit the website http://6DimensionsofHealing.com.) Remember, your mind does not know the difference between imagination and reality, so visiting a healing place in your mind can have the same rejuvenating effect as being there. Indeed, it can be better, as there are no bugs and no traffic noise; you can even control all aspects of the weather!

Give yourself permission now to start using your imagination as much as possible – from now on and forever more.

The Possibles and the Probables
"Follow your bliss and the Universe will open doors where there were only walls." Joseph Campbell

Your perspective on life is important, as how you perceive is how you receive. Everything is possible, but not everything feels probable. Winning lotto is possible, but it's not probable. Finding peace within is possible, but in times of chaos it doesn't always seem probable. Healing an illness is possible, but it's not necessarily probable. The things that are possible and probable for you depend on your personal perspective, and, in turn, depend on the beliefs you currently hold, and how you are feeling. If something is possible, it tends to carry a tinge of doubt, as it feels a bit distant. If it seems probable, then you believe it is imminent or even likely.

Nobody was born with limiting beliefs. These were adopted at an early age from the environment which you saw as you grew up. These were the parameters that shaped your life and became your beliefs. If you saw success as financial wealth, it was possible for you, while to others it may only have been probable. Everything about your life is changeable, including thought patterns and beliefs. A belief is only a thought you reinforce over and over again. The beliefs you hold are shared by some, but not by all, as there are no right and wrong beliefs. If a pattern of thought is serving you by creating the joy and happiness you want, you are on the track to freedom. If they're creating pain and tension, you might want to consider adopting some new beliefs.

When a record of accomplishment of circumstances going well has been established, it's easy to buy into the momentum that probability affords. A football team that has won the last few games is much more likely to win the next, because they are starting their game with a feeling of positive expectation. They feel winning is probable. When a team hasn't won all season, their chances of winning feel only possible. Try as they may to get excited, their ability is tinged with doubt. They can change their mood if they can draw on winning in the past, and use their imagination to keep that alive. The team with the higher vibration will always win the game. An interesting experience in any game is that the vibration of the team is not usually stable throughout the game. Because of events that occur during the game, team members change moods and emotions. If the team that started on the higher vibration can keep that mood and use it as a platform to fly even higher, they will not only win, they will annihilate the opposition. Therefore, 99% of turning a possible into a probable happens long before the game begins.

Can a team that isn't on a winning streak come out on top? Of course they can. The team who are the probables can change their mood to one of frustration, for instance, at a referee's decision; the other team can take the opportunity of the referee's calls going their way and change their mood to one of hope. If they score in this mood, it gives them momentum and they also become more capable of winning. The most valuable players on any team would be the ones who can quickly realign their mood to one of positive expectation, and inspire the rest of their team to do the same.

Changing a possible into a probable is a process. The process is closing the distance between your thinking you want something and believing it can be achieved. For instance, it's always possible for you to make a million dollars this year, but how likely is it to happen, in your opinion? Closing the gap between thinking you might and knowing you will, is the work that needs to be done. It is just as easy to manifest a castle as a button; it just depends on whether you think a castle is as probable as a button.

Using emotional leverage is the best way to consciously move from a possible to a probable. When you have created income through your own devices, you then know how it feels to be empowered through abundance. This is leverage for the next income and the next. It fuels desire, whets the appetite, and creates excitement. If you know what it feels like to be a millionaire, and have gone broke, you are more likely to become a millionaire again, and much more quickly than the first time, as you have emotional leverage. There is an understanding of how it feels to be prosperous.

When your dream is to move to another country, it is more likely to happen if you have visited or lived for some time in that other country, as you already know what it feels like. You have moved it from the 'possible', into the 'probables' basket. Of course, you can move without visiting the country, but it is likely to take longer as it is still on the 'possibles' list. Find a way of getting your desire into the 'probables' basket. This doesn't mean you focus upon the desire all day. In fact, if you can forget about it, a 'possible' will move its way to the 'probables' automatically when you feel great. Since most people can't think about a desire without activating the absence, which keeps the desire away, imagine your desire only when you are feeling great. Your job is to find a way of feeling great by generating patterns of self-talk that will influence a mood of fun, and then the things you want will start to seem more probable.

The more often you can change your mind from the direction of disappointment to one of hopefulness, the more momentum is created that transforms 'possibles' into 'probables'. When you feel great, even the most incredible dreams seem probable, and it all seems so easy. Moving 'possibles' to 'probables' is automatic whilst you feel great. So, change your mood and change your life.

Cleaning up Stress

Stress bridges many gaps and crosses all boundaries, as worrying thoughts are interlocked with emotions that wreak messages of havoc throughout your physical body. Stress can be caused by a situation, but, if prolonged, it leads to anxiety, which is a way of processing that feels out of control, where thoughts and emotions. When you understand that the only thing you ever have control over is how you feel right now, then you can reduce stress dramatically. Your focus becomes the present and you can choose your mood. Picking a shell up off the beach is much safer when there is a ripple than when there's a tidal wave, just as changing your thoughts early is much simpler than when you are having to deal with a tidal wave of emotional energy. When you practice changing your self-talk as you become aware of the early signs of anxiety presenting itself in your body, in other words at the mere hint of distress, you will decrease the momentum of stress.

Stress is a form of worrying, and the way you process thoughts can affect the amount of stress you feel. Nobody was born worrying; it's a learned behavior, a pattern that has usually been adopted from a parent, who also learnt it from a parent, and so on through the generations. If your mother tended to worry or stress, those thoughts and behaviors of hers have been communicated to you since the day you were born. It's the patterns of processing that are the hereditary part, and not the illness or the worrying. There are many patterns you may have adopted that don't serve you, but they are all changeable.

Worrying is allowing your emotions to take over in the pattern to which they are accustomed. This practiced pattern of thought and emotion becomes a default behavior, and if left unattended, loss of control is experienced, as the mind wanders into directions of what could happen. When the mind has traveled down a spiraling path, that feeling of dread is felt as a knot in the pit of your stomach, which combines with your imagination in overdrive. The bodily sensations of fear have become your reality, and this serves as evidence to you that your thoughts are correct. But your mind does not know the difference between what is real, and what is imagined, so the body responds as though each event is real. This is the effect of anxiety.

When you are chronically stressed or worried, the health of your body is at risk, as the stress interferes with the performance of your cells, and overrides their system of well-being. Chronic worrying can lead to anxiety, which affects your life so much that it changes your appetite, lifestyle habits, relationships, sleep, and job performance. People who worry excessively are so anxiety-ridden that they often seek relief in harmful lifestyle habits such as overeating, cigarette smoking, or using alcohol and drugs, just to operate on a daily basis.

Worry is a pattern that can be changed by focusing on what you want, rather than on what you don't. Catching your signs early, and self-talk are the keys to moving your emotions in the direction of relief, as that helps you to develop new habit patterns. One of these new patterns will be the habit of meditation. Another is affirmation. Both are dealt with below.

1. *Meditation is relaxation for the mind,* and it relieves tension just as a cool drink relieves thirst on a hot day; it is a soothing lozenge for a sore throat, and a tropical island for a city dweller in winter. It is the relief your mind needs, so that tension does not lead to stress, worry, and anxiety, by allowing your mind to relax and find freedom. There is no right or wrong way to meditate. It's as simple as focusing on the breath, listening to the sounds of nature, or listening to a guided-meditation talk. It may be difficult, at first, as your patterns of thought may object, but persist with it. Twenty-one days creates a habit and meditation helps to get the mind out of the way.

It is important for the mind to relax because, as you now know, every cell in your body has intelligence, which eavesdrops on the chatter in your head. All that chatter serves as directions to your cells, which then match their performance with how you feel. That works wonderfully if you are conscious of feeding your cells healthy thoughts, but when you feed them patterns of stressful thoughts, your body can react in the form of heart palpitations, rapid heartbeat, dry mouth, and even diarrhea*. The eavesdropping of the cells can be effective for healing, but in the case of worrying, controlling your thoughts and emotions rebalances your body.

When you feel sick there is a tendency to sleep, and when you can't sleep, you doze. This is a natural healing mechanism for the body, as it stops your mind from interfering. That's when the trillions of cells in your body move into the only pattern they know, the pattern of balance and well-being. There is a saying: "If you don't make time for your body, you'll have to make time to be sick". This saying has proven itself many times for our clients over the years. Don't wait until you are sick to make changes in your life; notice the early indicators of ill health and take preventive measures. Take control of your thoughts, rather than allowing your thoughts to be in control of you. Relaxing the mind allows your thoughts go on holiday. The calmness felt through meditation is reflected in the whole Six Dimensions of your Being.

2. *Feed your body nourishing thoughts* by looking for things that feel good. Create some affirmations that feel aligned. Affirmations are statements that affirm your well-being and connection, but the key to an affirmation's power is in its ability to move you closer to Source, so it must resonate. There is no point to an affirmation if your mind opposes it, so write an affirmative statement that you are synchronized with. For instance, to affirm you are healthy when you are in pain is counter-productive, as every time you say you are healthy your mind at once objects, "No, you're not. You've got this terrible pain." This means you aren't at one with the affirmation, and so it won't be of benefit. To write instead:

"It would be nice if I could find a way of handling this pain. It would be lovely if my body could find some relief," is to create an affirmative statement to which your mind can accede, an affirmation, in other words. These affirmations shouldn't oppose your mind in relation to how your body is feeling, and eventually you can move your statements on to become even more positive.

Look for things to feel good about. Worrying is created by allowing yourself to move into a pattern of looking for things that aren't working, so be conscious of how you feel and create a new pattern by looking for things in your life that are working. There could be many things that aren't going well, and only one that is, so that one thing becomes your focus, which will expand. Whatever subject you focus on will expand.

Patterns of belief are not just thoughts; they can be rigid and all encompassing, and this is what creates your reality. But you get to choose what you want, and with practice you can start to change your thoughts and create a new reality.

*   https://www.healthstatus.com/health_blog/depression-stress-anxiety/how-is-anxiety-different-from-stress/

Methods of Relaxation

"Your sacred space is where you can find yourself again and again."
Joseph Campbell

As we have seen, meditation is a term used for relaxing the body and releasing the mind from active thought. Fifteen minutes of meditation or mental relaxation a day can change your life. This is enough time to interrupt any patterns of behavior that are disrupting your lifestyle. At the end of fifteen minutes you can choose a new direction for thoughts. The pause for meditation allows you to change your thinking to a new mood, a new program, and a new groove on the record, as it's a new choice.

Methods of meditation can be as simple as sitting and focusing on your breath, taking a walk-in nature, listening to relaxation music, dancing as if there is no tomorrow, or petting your dog, and so on There are many methods of relaxation that offer you peace and tranquility, and that is their purpose. If you have difficulty sitting and relaxing for fifteen minutes, then remember it is a new pattern you are developing, so let go of expectations and make a commitment to yourself to persist gently for twenty-one days. This will help you develop a new pattern, which will become easier and easier to adhere to. As this method becomes your default pattern, stress levels will fall dramatically.

Here are six meditations, and practicing one of these daily can change your life.

When you find fifteen minutes out of your twenty-four hours is not available, or the mind is too active, then the first method offered takes just two minutes and when you have practiced the Two-Minute Method, it can be done anywhere, even in a traffic jam or waiting in line at the bank. Read through the whole set of processes before starting so you will be aware of the choices you could make.

1. Two-Minute Method of Relaxation

Sit comfortably in a quiet place as you breathe in and out. Look out the window at nature or focus on a picture on your desk; sing in the car, or just close your eyes on the train (not when driving) and focus on your breathing. If you can't find a quiet place, use some earbuds, and listen to gentle background music for just two minutes. Do this three times per day. Simply focus on your gentle breathing, and allow your thoughts to float past.

Use this simple Two-Minute Method a few times throughout the day. You may start off three times a day and increase to ten times a day. This is something you will enjoy, and no doubt the two minutes will become longer until, eventually you can string all your two-minute breaks together. It is a handy method to practice as you are commuting, taking a lunch-break, or waiting in line at a bank, all the while performing these gentle breathing exercises. It may be helpful at first (but it is not necessary) to close your eyes, so no one will ever know what you are doing, but it will change how you feel and allow your body to move into its natural healing place. This balances your body from the inside out.

It can take a while to find the peaceful space you are looking for, but practicing relaxation exercises regularly will create a new habit pattern, as this is a lifestyle and not a fad.

2. Breathing (Twenty minutes)

Focus on your breath, gently breathing in and out. Notice how your breath winds through your entire body. As you breathe out, expel all the air in your lungs, then gently breathe in the beautiful life-giving energy again throughout your body. This is a gentle and easy exercise that brings focus to your body, and lets go of all the clutter of your mind. In Hindu philosophy, the breath is known as kundalini or energy and it ignites the chakras as you breathe and focus.

You breathe because you are alive, so enjoy this amazing process that happens without you even thinking about it. You don't need to work out how to pump the air through your body; it happens automatically. Your heart beats by itself without your help, and your breath oxygenates your blood cells automatically. Not once do you have to think about how this process works; it is an amazing system, a marvel of creation.

Sit comfortably upright, close your eyes, and bring your awareness inward. Follow your breath in and out. As you breathe out, breathe out all the tension in your body. Breathe in relaxation. Occasionally, gently say to yourself, " With every breath I take I feel more relaxed, and more peaceful." Then focus on your breathing once more.

Repeat this process for fifteen minutes. If unwanted thoughts appear, just watch them float by and focus on your breathing again.

3. Body-Breathing

A slightly different method of following your breath is the body-breathing method of relaxation. It helps to release tension from the body, and occupies your mind as it requires you to talk to yourself when relaxing one area, and then another. This gets easier with practice, but the words aren't as important as the relaxation so you are welcome to ad-lib.

Lie down in some place where you won't be disturbed for fifteen minutes. Just lie comfortably on the bed or a floor, or whatever other surface you choose. You can record the following instructions in a slow, gentle voice and play them back, or you can make up your own.
- Close your eyes and gently focus on your breathing in and out. In your mind's eye watch the easy breaths moving in and out of your body.
- With each breath, your body feels more relaxed, and more and more peaceful.
- Each time you breathe out, allow the tension to leave your body and relax.

- Focus attention down at your feet.
- As you breathe in, tense your feet, and hold the tension for a few seconds, then relax and breathe out. Breathe in and out. In and out.
- Next, your calves. Tense them for a few seconds as you breathe and relax.
- Breathe out the tension in the calves.
- Tense your buttocks for a few seconds breathing in and out, and relax. Breathe in and out. In and out.
- Tense your stomach for a few seconds breathing in and out, and relax. Breathe in and out. In and out.
- Tense your back for a few seconds breathing in and out, and relax. Breathe in and out. In and out. In and out.
- Tense your chest for a few seconds breathing in and out, and relax. Breathe in and out. In and out.
- Tense your shoulders for a few seconds breathing in and out, and relax. Breathe in and out. In and out.
- Tense your arms for a few seconds breathing out the tension from your body, and relax. Breathe in and out. In and out.
- Tense your hands and fingers for a few seconds, still breathing and letting go of any tension, and relax. Breathe in and out.
- Tense your neck and hold for a few seconds, then breathe out all the tension, and relax. Breathe in and out. In and out.
- Tense your head and hold for a few seconds breathing out any tension, and relax. Breathe in and out. In and out.
- Tense your face and jaw for a few seconds, then breathe out the tension, and relax. Breathe in and out. In and out.
- Tense your whole body, every part and hold for a few seconds. Breathe out any tension, so that your whole body is more relaxed than it has ever been before.
- Gently breathe in and out. Notice the tingling in your body, as the tension is released, and a balance is achieved.

- Breathe in and out. In and out.

This is a great method to use in bed at night, if you can't sleep. It helps both your body and your mind to relax.

4. Healing Light Visualization

- Use the Body-Breathing method. When you are relaxed and gently breathing at the end of the Body-Breathing exercise, imagine a light, a healing light of a color you choose coming in through the top of your head.
- Imagine the light coming in through the top of your head, and spreading its way through your body. Everywhere it touches it heals and rejuvenates.
- Imagine this beautiful healing light spreading through your head, and around your face and jaw. It's now dancing around your head, and flowing around inside your neck, rejuvenating every cell it touches, as it winds its way gently through your shoulders and down your arms to your fingertips.
- The beautiful healing light flows across your chest, and into your heart.
- It expands your heart, and dances down your spine, flicking color in every direction so that all the cells encounter this beautiful healing light, as it dances its way through your body.
- It expands down to your stomach and your thighs, through your knees and down around your ankles and feet, moving into every toe. It dances in and through every part of your body, healing and rejuvenating and energizing.
- Your whole body feels alive, it feels alive and fresh and new.
- This beautiful, vibrant, healing light expands to fill your whole body and bursts outward from your body so that it is flowing in, through and around your body with effervescent rays of light.

- It feels wonderful and rejuvenating as you breathe healing light; it is one with you, and feels gentle and loving. You feel as though you could stay in this light forever, as this is the best you've ever felt.

5. Expanding Light Visualization

You can use the healing light method, or just breathe and imagine yourself filled with light, any color healing light you are attracted to.
- Breathe the light, so that it fills your body, and expands so much that it is bursting out of your body, and flowing all around you. Breathe the light so that you can feel the effervescence of this beautiful healing color.
- As the light dances around you, it becomes one with the room, and expands its way through the room to incorporate the trees in your yard. You watch it flow from tree to tree, and it moves farther afield flowing into the trees of the whole town and city as it expands through the ground and the trees and everyone who walks on the ground or touches the trees, absorbs this beautiful light.
- Everyone who absorbs the light walks around with this healing effervescence, which flows into all that they meet.
- It spreads through the ground, incorporates the water and the lakes, flowing across the sea and whilst it spreads its way across your city, state and continent, this beautiful healing light also travels through the sea to other continents and cities, and spreads through the trees and the ground there also. This glowing effervescence affects each and every thing it touches, until the whole world is a pulsating, vibrating glowing light.
- Everyone who meets this light is filled with the effervescent glow of love.
- The light keeps expanding out into the sky and the universe, as it reaches its arms out to embrace the moon, the stars and the planets.

The whole universe pulsates with this beautiful glowing effervescent light.
° Breathe in the energy of this beautiful light, as you are experience being at the center of the Universe, — the center of this beautiful loving, all-encompassing light.

6. Flower Focus (fifteen minutes)

This was the first meditation we were ever taught. It was at a Sri Chinmoy meditation weekend in Melbourne Australia many years ago. I have used it successfully over the years in Healing Conferences and workshops for people who haven't been able to relax their mind. It offers something tangible to focus upon, rather than relying on your imagination.

° *Sit comfortably* with a flower propped up in front of you, a red rose, or another flower.
° *Focus* on your breathing and relax; notice how your breath flows gently in and out.
° *Be present with the flower.* Notice all the colors and the shades. See how it starts with one color and blends into another. Spend some time looking at the colors blended together, see how they change from the base to the tip and take note of the colors of the petals inside.
° *Gently look at the folds of the flower*, and note how they move into the other petals. Notice the shape of the petals, and how uniquely different they are, and how each is perfect in its own way.
° *As you breathe,* start to appreciate how the flower is formed, the texture of the flower, the fragrance.
° *Notice* how the flower connects to the stem, and how robust the stem is that supports the leaves and the thorns etc.

- *Focus on your own breathing now*, and notice how your breath encompasses the flower. You have become one with the gentle peacefulness of the flower.
- *There are so many more aspects* to focus upon, so form your own observations as you go. You want to absorb yourself in this exercise for ten to fifteen minutes, or longer if you prefer. You are slowly moving from one aspect of the flower to the next. It really depends on the type of flower you have as to what questions you ask. When you are first using this process, it can be helpful to record the questions, giving yourself time to form an appreciation of what you're observing.

Make sure to keep the flower in water when you've finished the meditation. We have noticed flowers last much longer when you have focused loving attention in their direction. A prominent biologist from the 1950s, Luther Burbank, conducted extensive studies into the benefit of giving plants appreciation and love. He found the ones that had been cared for with loving attention lasted significantly longer than those that hadn't. We are like the plants, as we flourish under loving attention, especially if that loving attention comes from within.

The Path of Dreams

Take a few minutes to imagine a path from where you are now to where you want to go. It's an evenly paved path, easy to see and fun to walk along. Sunshine and clear skies make it well lit, and the path of your future winds through valleys and over gentle hills. You are pleased with the foliage-lined path and it feels interesting and easy to move along. But then obstacles arise in the once-clear path; your thoughts become cluttered with opinions, fear, resentment, or resistance. As you become more worried, the path seems more overgrown, much darker and more difficult to traverse. It's easy to give up moving along it. Eventually, the path disappears, lost in the wilderness. Just as we lose sight of the path, so too do we lose sight of our dreams.

When you can no longer keep moving forward, sleep or meditation will help you start afresh. We all put obstacles in our paths from time to time. When you remember how the path used to look and how the dream felt, the emotion returns, the excitement becomes stronger, and the path is cleared of any self-imposed obstacles.

Most people don't keep the practice of meditation or relaxation alive, as there is an expectation that thought will cease completely. This is not necessarily the case, but when you see the thoughts as if watching a movie, you can allow them to gently float by. If you find your mind wandering down a pathway you would prefer it didn't traverse, gently bring it back in line with your path. Congratulate yourself on a job well done, rather than become frustrated, as there is no right and wrong in this practice. As most humans prefer negative thought to no thought at all, it will be easiest to use a visualization technique so that the mind is suitably occupied. If you fall asleep, you have achieved the same results as meditation. Of course, sleep is not always appropriate; relaxation may be preferable at work.

Using visualization techniques helps you to know the benefits of being in control of your own mind rather than your mind controlling the thoughts. Meditation will become easier in very little time.

Your Life is a Reflection of You

"A man who carries a cat by the tail learns something he can learn in no other way." Mark Twain

Have you ever wondered why on some days, happy people are in your life, and on other days, the people there are rude and offensive? Everyone showing up in your life is there to help in your growth, by reflecting what you've been thinking about. The way you feel about your thoughts is most often directly reflected back to you by what is happening in your life right now. If the people and situations that come into your life are pleasing to you, then keep thinking the thoughts you are thinking. If they aren't, it's an indicator to change your line of thinking to something that feels better.

You never stray far off track, so thoughts can be finely tuned to move you in the direction you want to go. Sometimes it feels you are a whole ocean off course but just shifting one train of thought can move you from a path of distress to a path of hope. It makes sense then, that if you want different results, you need to do something differently, and the difference is changing your thoughts. When you change the direction in which your mind travels, ideas recommence their flow, thoughts get faster and gather momentum, people come into your life with friendships and opportunities that are far beyond what you imagined. It seems as though the better it gets, the better it gets, and life is really good.

Hard Luck Janie

We had a client that was very down on herself. Janie was a woman in her sixties who could have passed for late seventies easily. Her appearance was withered, she felt pain in many regions of her body, and she used a walking stick. There was no end to her tales of woe: the elderly man next door spied on her, and played his music too loudly; the city council wouldn't do anything about renovating the apartment she lived in; she didn't like living in the village she had come to call home; and she couldn't afford to move. She shuffled along, bent over and no matter what you said, it was a bad day, and there were a lot of people that were to blame for this.

One thing she did look forward to was her only son visiting from overseas. Janie was the most excited I had seen her for months when he was due to arrive, and I didn't know what would happen when he left again. She shopped and made food in advance and spoke about her plans of how he was going to change her life. They would build a house together, somewhere nice away from the Council estate.

As you might have guessed, things didn't quite go to plan. When her son was visiting, he didn't want to spend all his time with his mother. So, he spent some time with his friends. She became angry at him, and by the time he left, he said that she was a grumpy, bitter old woman, and he didn't want anything to do with her.

Janie was devastated, but not upset enough to bring about change. She recommenced her bitter attacks, and nobody was excluded from the firing line. Most people avoided her, as nobody wants to be party to bitterness. Janie was not going to change until she became uncomfortable enough to do so and there is no time frame on change.

Sympathy and Compassion

Sympathy can keep you stuck. When someone sympathizes with you they are saying, "I'm glad it's you and not me." You have become a victim of the story you tell. Sympathy is jumping in the mud hole with someone, and trying to push them out, when they're not willing to go. After all, the victim never indicated they wanted to feel better. Repeating their story justified their powerlessness, so people felt sorry for them. Many people are addicted to sympathy, and their pay-off is attention that otherwise wouldn't be received.

Compassion is different. When somebody is compassionate, they have aligned with your Higher Self. If they happen to cross your path at all, they listen and offer clarity, so that you can find your own way to move forward. They don't try to fix things, and they don't get into blaming. They understand how you are feeling but they don't play a part in the relationship triangle. Instead they stand where you want to be, and they shine a light for you. This is much more empowering than sympathy. Compassionate people stand out of the puddle on solid ground, and extend a hand when you are ready. If you aren't ready, that's OK by them. They have no personal stake in your movement forward, as they will love you, irrespective of the choices you make. Respecting the path you have chosen, compassionate people understand you have your own guidance, and know that you will find it when you are ready.

Reflections of Your Life

There is a common misconception that the way others see you is a reflection of you. The opposite is true; how others see you is a reflection of *them*. How *you* see them is a reflection of *you*. Or more accurately, how you *feel* about them is a reflection of your dominant emotions. Everyone's life is mirrored to offer insight into what you are manifesting, so you can be pleased with the reflection or change the vibrational offering to create something different. Either way there is no right or wrong, as the perspective you hold of everything around you is a reflection of your thoughts and feelings. Janie's perspective was a reflection of her life, and her son gravitated towards people that were a reflection of his life. Your mood defines your perspective, and creates your reality, so when your mood is anger, the light your Higher Self shines to show the way will seem like anger. When your mood is disappointment, so too will the calling of your Higher Self sound like disappointment.

People often mistake their reflection of life, for somebody to blame.

Instead of wanting or needing others to be happy for you to feel good, the key is to find what makes you feel great, and stay there for as long as you can, no matter what. When you find yourself gravitating towards feeling negative, you can change how you think before momentum gathers and similar people are gathered to you. The reflections in your life can serve as early warning signs, as they are instigators for changing direction. You don't have to heed the warning signs, and you don't have to change, but the reflections become more pronounced and your mood less healthy.

The little boy next door had a broken arm when he came to play, and a short while later I watched him go home crying. It was not because he had hurt his arm again, but because his toe hurt. There were five boys playing, but this one had been stung on the toe by the only bee around. Of all the boys in the backyard, how come he was the one who found the bee rather than one of the others? Fact is, he already had momentum with dominant thoughts of feeling a victim, so he was a match to the bee sting. It may not seem fair, but fairness has nothing to do with how we perceive our lives at any age. How we feel about ourselves makes a difference to the reflection of our lives.

Role Model or Anti-Role Model

As we grow and look for patterns to adopt and form the quilt we become, Role Models take on a distinct importance in our lives. They shape the direction of our path. Nobody I know chooses to be a Role Model, but we all do become Role Models to someone at one time or another, whether we want to or not. Default Role Models are the people we grew up with, as the habit patterns of their routines were already set up and they become the patterns we gravitated towards. Many people have said they would never want to become parents like the ones they had, and yet they follow in the same footsteps, or rather move into the same mindset, worsening the traits they once deplored.

When you consciously choose what you want rather than what you don't want, a whole new world of opportunities arises. When I had my first baby, I decided I wanted a new Role Model for parenting skills. A person I chose for this role was a friend whom I admired for how she handled the parenting of her young daughter. It was the type of parenting I wanted to adopt, so I said, "yes, that's for me". I didn't want to emulate the parenting skills of my parents, so I chose another.

It wasn't until many years later I realized I had changed the direction of my life by choosing the path of parenting I preferred.

You can choose a Role Model for every aspect of your life. In business, in health, in relationships of many kinds, there is no need to choose the whole person; you can choose just the aspect of their life that you admire. In doing this, you are adding their skill set to your own, and becoming the person you admire most. It's important to note that when you choose a Role Model you don't necessarily choose everything about that person but you choose the skill set you are interested in adopting. A Role Model is offering a change of focus, which is very powerful in creating your new reality. I know people who have chosen Arnold Schwarzenegger as their physical Role Model, and moved in the direction of a strong, lean physique. The Role Model does not need to know they are an inspiration for your life, as this is *your* journey and not *theirs*. Many Role Models will influence your life and shape the direction of your journey. The more consciously you choose a Role Model, the more consciously you choose your reality.

Just as Role Models are important, whether chosen or by default, so are Anti-Role Models. An Anti-Role Model is a person who is involved in your life that you don't ever want to be like. I have had several of these and they have helped me in refining my life immeasurably.

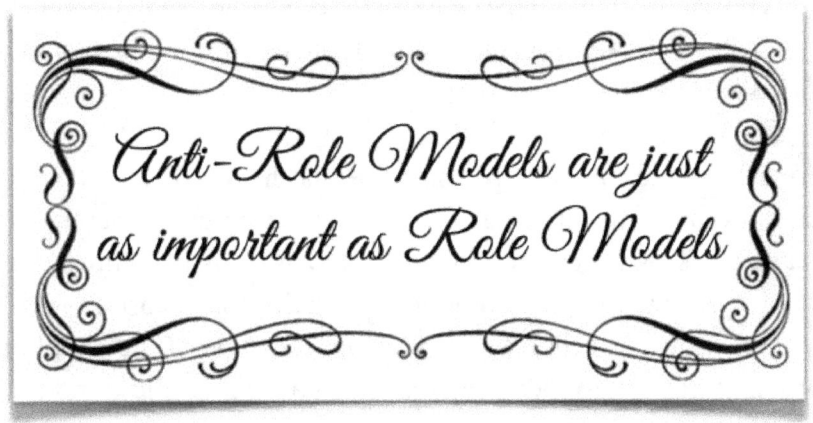

Anti-Role Models are just as important as Role Models

One of these influential people happened to be John, my boss when I was an impressionable twenty-three-year-old. He wasn't really the boss; he was the husband of my boss, but he thought he was in charge. His confidence translated to cockiness, as it was well known he'd come into the business to rescue the financials, and the business had in fact turned around. It was a happy time in my life, and John wanted a part of that, so he was eager to be a Role Model for me. The more time at work I spent in his company the more I felt sad for him. He had announced his dream was to be in front of an audience as a personal trainer and inspirational leader. That was my dream as well, so it piqued my attention. As I looked at him, the only thought that ran through my mind was that there was no way he could achieve this dream; he may have had the knowledge, but was so arrogant that nobody would have cared what he had to say. John was the last person you would have been inspired by. It was a slap in the face for me, as I knew I had some of those traits, so I made a conscious decision without delay that I would never be like him. I could see aspects of myself in John that I didn't like, and that scared me. I recognized that if I followed the path I was on, my dream would never be realized, so I changed my direction. My mantra for years became "Nobody cares how much you know, until they know how much you care". This experience was truly a shining beacon in my life and I'm forever appreciative to John for becoming that pivotal Anti-Role Model.

There are people in every person's life that have caused them to say, "I don't want to be like that". They can be parents, friends or just acquaintances, but they are realizations of what is becoming, and are of immense value. People come into your life for a reason – even the scoundrels you don't like. When you ponder some of the people from your past with a new perspective, you may notice the opportunities they were offering. This could be by the impact they had in causing you to change direction, or by sticking with the path you had chosen already, with renewed fervor. When an Anti-Role Model enters your life, it's like a sharp jab in the ribs, as the realization dawns on you: 'That could be me in the future'. How do you know if these people are Anti-Role Models or just objectionable? When a person comes into your life, and presses your buttons, there is always the opportunity to change paths. The offer is to stay on the same path, or choose another. One will offer you the same mood and the other, an improved mood. Choices to change paths are as prolific as the people we see. Some may need a mere tweak and others a sharp turn in the road, but don't get caught up in feeling as though opportunities are missed. There is no end to the opportunities available to create a new reality.

Anti-Role Models are just as important as Role Models because whilst the positive Role Model offers you a glimpse into the future of what you *do* want, the Anti-Role Model allows you to see a future of what you *don't* want, and this makes your choices easier. The Anti-Role Model's actions are a shining beacon of what's to come if you take the same path. The advantage of this insight is that you get to choose a path consciously, before it becomes your reality. That's a huge benefit, as this insight is not for learning but for choosing a path that is wanted or rejecting one that is not wanted. There are no wrong decisions, but some are more harmonious than others.

A misconception arises when you see the Anti-Role Model as a bad person, or one who is on the scene to give you a hard time. It's better to recognize an Anti-Role Model as an opportunity for change. When your attention is focused on what you don't like about the Anti-Role Model, instead of using the opportunity to change direction, you invite what you don't like into your vibration. The way you feel becomes your vibrational request to the Universe. There is no wrong decision, of course, and sometimes it is easier to gain the clarity of an Anti-Role Model in hindsight.

There's no need to move along the path of any pattern of thinking that doesn't serve your best interests, as everything is changeable. Anti-Role Models are here to help you refine these choices. If what you're doing now, or how you are behaving in the present moment doesn't work for you, then change it. When you do, you'll get a different result, and a brand-new reality. Now that's self-empowerment!

Opportunities for Growth
"There is no end to the opportunities that present themselves."
Fraser Watts & Mark Williams (1988)

Opportunities for growth constantly present themselves to every one of us. Whether it is your child complaining, or someone telling you it's your fault for their pain, every situation holds a seed for growth. It's not the situation that is important, but your reaction that serves the purpose. Every situation is personal, and every person involved in the same situation will experience it differently.

Being retrenched from a job you have been working for the past twenty years may not feel like an opportunity for growth as it seems out of your control, but how you respond to this situation determines the path of your growth. If you quickly come to the understanding that this new freedom gives you the opportunity to travel you have always wanted, your growth will move in the direction of things working out for you, but if you get stuck in fear of the unknown and blame of others, life will become more difficult. You may not have control over the situation but you do have control over what you think and feel and that determines the direction of your future.

The opportunity that presents itself is the ability to choose a perspective different from that of previous habit patterns. A new outlook may seem trivial but it is pivotal for changing the direction of your life. Opportunities constantly present themselves to you through your experiences. Some are harmonious and others are chaotic, but all will serve your higher purpose.

My uncle was ninety-six when he died. It should have been peaceful as he wasn't in physical pain but the truth was, he was in emotional turmoil. I spoke to him a few years before he passed on, and as he perused his life, he felt remorse for things he had done when younger and much regret about things he hadn't done. Many people think the elderly are peaceful because of their years, and yet most are not. They too, receive opportunities for growth up until they die. These could be in the form of acceptance, receiving from others, patience or unconditional love. Many times, the opportunities are presented from people they don't like or are annoyed with. This isn't to get back at them; it is a reflection of how they feel. These can be the same subjects they were dealing with when young, but the subjects become more pronounced as we age so that the opportunities can be noticed above all the noise of the mind. When the opportunity has been accepted, there is a serene peace that fills people, whether old or young. They expand into this understanding and there is no longer an opportunity for growth needed on that subject. It is good advice to take the opportunities that present themselves in the form of chaos in your life, as when you do, the chaos dissipates.

Opportunities are constant and infinite.

The Determining Factor

Without obvious warning, a seemingly thoughtless individual has changed your wonderful-feeling day, and what you think next determines the direction of your future; it helps create your reality. As the situation is churning over in your mind, familiar feelings of fear and uncertainty may raise their heads. Gone is the morning's mood of enjoying the day, as movement into the familiar patterns of uncertainty seems inevitable.

Now is a good time to notice what is really going on. Not the situation, but the thoughts that turn your attention to old patterns of thinking; that someone else has control over your life and you don't create your own reality. These are patterns that ceased their momentum long ago, but still exist when re-ignited. Just as a waterfall becomes a trickle when there is a drought, it is still a dormant waterfall awaiting the next storm when it will be a raging torrent once again. The power is in the present moment, as the immediate opportunity is the choice of allowing a dormant pattern to gain momentum, or to consciously choose your own focus. Either decision will reinforce a pattern, so the question is, "What do you want more of?"

Allowing the mind to wander will increase momentum on the path it wanders along and the old path is well trodden. Just as the water meanders its way through the grooves it has carved in the earth over time to a cascading waterfall, so too do thoughts return to repeat along their etched patterns. Over time, the most familiar patterns will be your default or dominant patterns.

However, this time you may have decided you want something different. You want to go beyond feeling afraid and not being in control, but no matter how much you want something new, there can be a niggle in the back of your mind that says you can't do it alone, that it's too big. But that is why it is an opportunity! Take heart in knowing that doubt is common in the embryonic part of a new pattern that has just begun its journey.

At this early stage, momentum on the new pattern of thought has begun, but as it's still relatively easy to move back into a more dominant thought pattern from the past, awareness is the key. Mind your own thoughts, as this is an influential stage of growth, one where you get to choose which direction your life takes. If you don't consciously choose what you want, your most dominant thoughts will direct you. To understand what your dominant thoughts are, you only need look at how your life has unfolded thus far. When thoughts are consciously chosen, your life path moves in the direction of your new thoughts.

If you talk to a lot of people about the situation and try to gain their support it will perpetuate the current situation, and make it much larger than it was, because whatever you focus upon, you expand. Your new patterns are vulnerable, so practice independently if able.

This is the time for finding out how well your platform of joy is going to perform. How stable is it? How well established are your patterns of feeling great? All the insecurities that are still present in your life will announce themselves presently, and if you don't consciously choose what to focus on, they will take over. You will be sent spiraling fast into the arms of fear. This is high contrast, and contrasts are vital to growth, but remember, you've done this all before. You know how it ends, so you can change how far you fall this time. The determining factor is being aware of how you are feeling and choosing a new story.

Building a Platform

Each opportunity that presents itself allows you to build a more stable platform, a more solid foundation so that when a problem arises, the choice of moving into a more powerful position also arises. As problems occur from time to time (and they will), your practiced platform will be solid, so you won't topple into an emotional abyss. Because of your foundation, it won't be long before alignment with a solution presents itself. Blame will keep you from moving forward, so take great pains to avoid it.

When you have talked yourself into a great feeling-place where you can practice the feeling of joy, fun and love, you are building a platform of strength from which you can choose your own reality.

Never underestimate the opportunity to change patterns of thought, as thoughts create your emotions, and emotions mold your life-experiences. Without changing your mind and your mood, you will find that your life stays the same as it was yesterday, is today and will be tomorrow.

The chapter on 'Emotions & Spirituality' will help you understand how interconnected your thoughts are. Suffice it to say here that thoughts create emotion, and your emotions are the connection to your soul.

How do I attract bad stuff when I'm feeling so good?

"You're only a thought away from changing your life. "
Dr Wayne Dyer (2006)

There are times when it seems that a good mood is too much for those around you. A simple smile can spread the light of joy, yet it will annoy the heck out of others. The people who object to your smiles aren't happy, and the fact that you're feeling great tends to shine a spotlight on what's not going well in their lives. It would be futile and damaging to your self-esteem to try and change these people, or their opinions. You won't convince them of why you are feeling great, or succeed in encouraging them to do so too. In any case, it doesn't matter, as you don't need anyone else to feel good for you to be happy in yourself. When the others are ready, another person will help, though it may not be in your lifetime. Accept people just as they are, as their mood will never be any threat to you or to your well-being.

Detractors are really doing you a favor, as they are helping you find out how well you are plugged into your energy system. If your light is plugged into another's mood you will always be looking for ways to please that other person, so that your light may shine through them. When they aren't happy, neither will you be. Eventually, you will realize they aren't your energy source. Nobody outside of you is responsible for your happiness. When your light is plugged into Source, your energy is always abundant, and the light shines brightly in every circumstance.

Occasionally our son would call and vent about his employers. The café where he worked had changed hands, so it was being run differently. He didn't have a lot of respect for one of the owners, and the changes weren't working for the business. Ben was frustrated as he could see the owner was driving customers away. As the café business wasn't Ben's first love, he wondered why he was even still there. I gently pointed out that he was doing what most of the population in the world did. He was focusing on what he didn't want – in this case, the negative changes made by one owner. When you focus on something, it becomes accentuated in your reality. He thought he was there because he needed to feel good amongst the chaos. I told him not to try to change the environment just so he could feel better. He could change his focus and accentuate something preferred in his reality. In this way, he could find his own source of energy, and not expect circumstances to be made right just for him to feel good. This is a common mistake that leads to frustration and blame for many.

To change how he felt about the situation, we suggested three things.
1. *Set his intentions to feel good, no matter what.* He could set up his day before entering the workplace. The environment does not have to change for a person to feel good. Ben started playing little games at work, and became more interested in the customers, showing them he cared, and getting a smile out of each.
2. *See his new boss the way his boss would like to be seen*, not the way he was. Noticing someone's attitude only perpetuates a situation nobody wants to be in. When you imagine somebody as they would like to see themselves, you align yourself with the best of them, shining the way.
3. *Find a new focus.* Something he loved which didn't need to be work related. It could be anything.

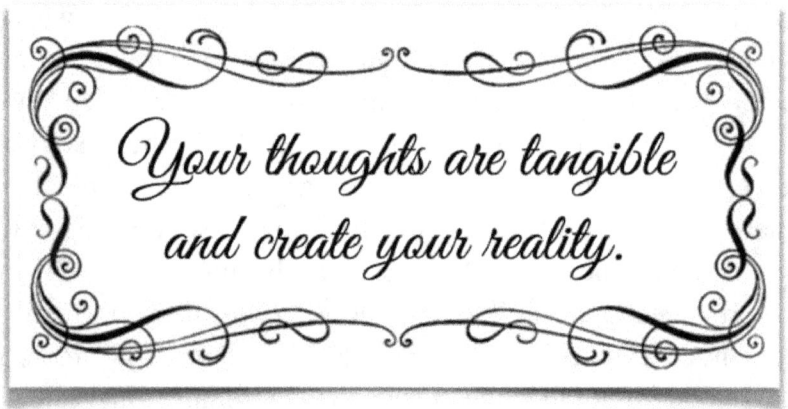

Thoughts have Momentum

You know that what someone thinks of you is none of your business, so the more steadfast you become at practicing feeling good, the more momentum you have in the *mood* of feeling good. You are building a platform of joy as deactivation of old subjects occurs by activating new ones. When you are no longer giving your attention to a subject that creates a negative mood, it becomes less activated in your vibration. This means the momentum of any unwanted subject is no longer easily triggered.

Thoughts are tangible and create your reality; they influence your mood and outline your life. So, what you think and how you feel is always a match with what's happening in your life. What occurs in your life is called your reality. When you have been angry for a while and turn it around so that you start to feel good, the momentum of that angry feeling is still active for a while longer in your vibration, so remnants can show up elsewhere in your life. It's like a roller coaster. All those ups and downs and loops make you feel like the world is spinning. Even when you are standing on flat ground, you still have momentum and seem to be moving. You feel like you are still on the rollercoaster even when you have moved on to something else. That's the feeling of momentum. You don't say, "I feel dizzy for no reason" as you're aware it was the recent rollercoaster ride.

So, it is with your thoughts. If you have been on the rollercoaster of 'someone did me wrong' for an hour, you have some strong momentum starting in the direction of feeling victimized. Ride the rollercoaster of victimization for days or weeks or months, and then you are vibrating in a place that attracts more of the same into your life. Occasionally you move into a place of thinking thoughts of relief, but you can still feel the momentum of that, 'someone did me wrong' rollercoaster. When you find some thoughts of relief and gather momentum in that direction, you may be off the rollercoaster, but the dizziness is still around. So, you will keep attracting the balance of the momentum you created by feeling victimized. You could be feeling quite hopeful and still be attracting situations that offer you the opportunity to feel victimized. It's easy to think the good-feeling thoughts have not worked but it's just that you have both subjects flowing at the moment. A train does not come to a sudden stop; it slows gradually, and so does momentum. Keep your focus on where you are going and let the past go by. Focus on a better future.

All dominant thoughts create momentum in your future so to direct your future you need to be conscious of your thoughts. The indicator of what you are creating is your mood, and not the situations currently occurring around you, as they could be from an old momentum. How you respond to what you are seeing is pivotal, as this creates your future reality.

It is good practice to look for things to feel good about each day and each moment. Write down the things you have appreciated during the day in a journal before going to bed each night. During the day, take a moment to sit, tune in and notice what you are thinking. If your mind wanders to subjects in which you don't want to create momentum, just change it within sixty-eight seconds. That's how long it takes before it is activated in your vibration, and starts to gather momentum.

Change Your Reality and You Change Your Life

Emotional Dimension

Six Dimensions of Healing

Connection and Contrast

As you now know, your emotions are your connection with the Universe and with your Higher Self. Your mood is the center of your Universe as it creates the experiences that unfold as your life. So, your reality is designed by your emotions. Emotions become your guiding light down the path of life. They help you understand why things happen the way they do, and they show you the direction in which you are traveling.

Many people have learned to block their emotions early in life. There are many reasons that lead to the suppression of emotions, and all of them are associated with pain. It is a natural part of life to feel your way in own life and interpret what is going on around you into emotions. In this way, you can feel fear and it can warn you of danger, and you can feel love and it will guide your path in the direction of joy. Getting through life without noticing your emotions is common, as many have felt 'burnt' by wearing their heart on their sleeve, so they prefer their mind to be the life guide. The mind is fickle and influenced by what it can see. It is influenced by reality. But emotions can't be blocked completely, only dulled. When you start being aware of how you are feeling and use these emotions as your guide, they become stronger. It is possible to attune yourself to being guided by emotions in such a way that even a subtle change can be noticed and lead quickly to a change in your mood. The only thing in life you have any control over is your own mood. You are the sole owner of your emotions and you are the person who controls your moods.

This world moved into the Age of Aquarius in the year 2000, and according to the ancient science of Numerology, the Age of Aquarius is the age of emotions, of feeling and of co-creating with the people around us. Each person is born with a unique set of numbers that are the result of adding their birth date and names together. There are nine single numbers and many combinations that are influenced by the mental, emotional and physical planes. During the last century, the 1900s, every person born had at least one number on the mental plane, signified by the number nine, and this gave many people a mental learning capacity. During not only the next century, but the next millennium, only a few children will be born with numbers on the mental plane but all will have numbers on the emotional plane which is where the number two is situated. As the millennium progresses, it will become obvious in schools, that teaching children via their mental capacities will not be as effective as teaching them through their emotions. As every child born in this millennium has numbers on the emotional plane, it indicates they connect to others through emotions. These are the adults of the future. They are the business people, the inventors and entrepreneurs; they are the sales people, the sportsmen and the soldiers. They are the parents of the future, and they will find much value in connecting with their own emotions, as communication through emotions is the path of understanding and compassion.

Moods are an indicator of the emotion you are projecting for the world to see. A sad mood is but a glimmer of hope and a light of sadness, and a happy mood is a beacon that shines brightly in the darkness.

A Mood Map shows how you are traveling along your emotional path. I was sitting at a railroad station a few years back. This was a country station with no guard or ticket-box attendant. A teenage boy was also seated waiting for the train. I asked him where he was going, and he told me. Then I asked him if he knew how to read the railway schedule but he didn't, so he wasn't sure which train to catch. The schedule was behind him, so we used the time we were waiting for our train to familiarize him with the map. I remembered being his age once, lost in a big city with a map I didn't know how to read. Nobody I asked knew either. It was a harrowing experience, and made me realize you can have a map but it's useless, unless you know how to read it.

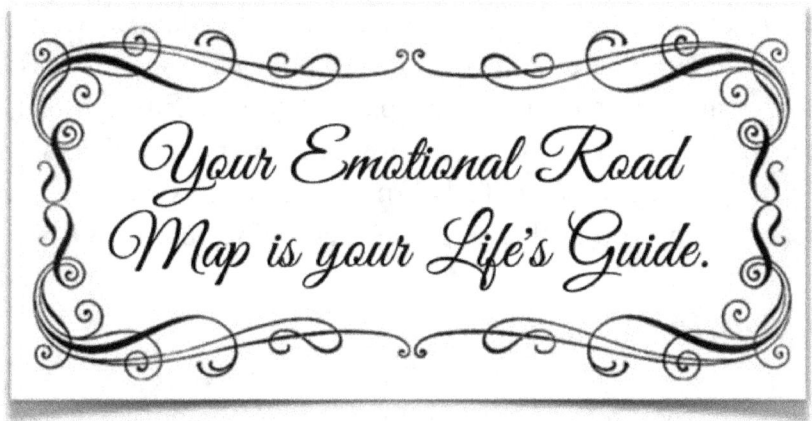

Your Emotional Road Map is your Life's Guide.

It would be to your advantage if you were to learn how to read your Emotional Mood Map. So, here goes. When your mood is happy, you are in the company of your Higher Self. When it's not so chirpy, you have strayed a little further away. Taking an emotional detour to somewhere other than the place that is desired is OK. Surprisingly, being somewhere other than where you thought you wanted to be isn't wrong at all, and nowhere is so far away that you can't go back and find your desired track again. When your Mood Map is familiar, you have the advantage of always knowing where you are traveling. Then, if you find yourself off track somewhere, the error is easily corrected.

Knowing your path can be the difference between being afraid and being confident about where you are going.

Any pain felt by being off-track is only ever the distance between what you are feeling and what your Higher Self is feeling. If what you are feeling is a long way from what your Higher Self feels, then there is intense emotional discomfort. When you experience discomfort, you get a clearer idea of what you want. If the emotion is a mild discomfort, the request for fulfillment is a whisper, but when you feel abject poverty the request for abundance becomes louder within you. But remember! There is never a distance so far away from Source Energy that you can't rejoin the path of your desires. Moods are merely indicators of the direction in which you are traveling, so when the path you walk down feels frustrating, this is your emotional indicator telling you to change paths by changing your mood.

Contrasting Emotions

Technically speaking, as it is used in this book, contrast is a focus on something unwanted, whether consciously or subconsciously, and it is a vital ingredient along the path to finding a life of fun and happiness. There are many ups and downs in life, with both joyous and unhappy moods. The more practiced the feeling of happiness becomes through focus, the easier it is to find your way back when contrast knocks you down. The knocks will come and, through contrast, new desires are born.

It is a misconception to think that, once you feel great, you should be able to stay in that happy space forever, as nothing could be further from the truth. Feeling joy is the most wonderful experience, but it would not be so wonderful if you had never known depression or oppression. Clarity is a magnificent tool, and it gives you a window into the universal mind, but it would not come into being if you hadn't known confusion or disempowerment. You wouldn't know peace, if you had never felt anger. The reason for the clarity is the contrast. The reason for the joy is the contrast. The reason for the peace is the contrast. Without contrast there is no desire, and without desire there is no focus, and without focus we cease to exist.

Contrast is the opposing emotion, which travels together with every joyous emotion. Focus is what gives life to either the wanted or unwanted emotions experienced. (Unwanted emotions can be experienced through situations, observations and imagination.) Contrast gives wings to the opposite, which is born within you when the emotion of pain exists. When you feel anger, automatically the Higher Self moves to the opposite emotion, waiting for you to join the expansion that has just taken place. The mood of anger is the contrast. If you were to move your mood quickly to the same emotion as your Higher Self, there would be no gap in emotions and the anger would be in the past. If you choose to keep the contrasting anger, tension becomes the emotional distance between your opinion on the subject and that of your Higher Self. As humans, we reach beyond where thought has gone before with our ideas and imagination. Contrasting moods have instigated some of the most magnificent creations in the world. We call it 'evolution', but there were many who were frustrated before they could find an invention to solve an inadequacy. When you look back two thousand years, you can see how far we as creative beings have come. I truly love flicking a switch for electricity, I couldn't do without the Internet, and I really enjoy driving my new car.

When experiencing contrast as everyone does, you can either get stuck on the adverse emotion or turn your attention in a new direction. Because it is easier to stay in a particular mood than it is to change it, focusing on any contrast is creating your new reality with the stamp of the past. Contrast is an important ingredient of creation, as it helps define and refine desires.

A desire to win the American Civil War inspired the designing and redefining of the submarine, steamboat, telegraph, and the newspaper, as there was an urgency and a focus for machines to become more streamlined, and for information to be made more readily available to the public. Devastation after earthquakes and cyclones led to the innovation of seismic grade steel and cyclone bolts, while a painfully slow Internet created the need for better cabling and faster broadband speeds. A busier world brought about many automated machines and devices. Many items we take for granted today are the result of people experiencing contrast through which was born desire, then focus, and, finally, inspiration.

Contrast serves as an indicator for what you don't want, and opens the gate of opportunity pointing the way to a solution. The most important step after experiencing contrast is to identify the desire, and turn your focus towards what is wanted. Instead of going down the common path of focusing on the contrast and becoming stuck, use it to inspire the turning point towards a new creation.

Contrast is vital for growth, but how long you experience any contrast is determined by your focus.

Your Mood Map

"If you have faith in your future you will have power in your present."
John Maxwell

Just as your Mood Barometer translates emotions, you were also born with a Mood Map. This is the guide for creating the life you want through consciously choosing your emotions. The Mood Barometer shows you what you are feeling, and the Mood Map shows you the direction in which you are traveling. This Mood Map has been a guiding path all your life. When you are moving in a direction that is *in alignment with your Higher Self* who holds the light for you, your emotions are fun, joy, love, enthusiasm, and appreciation. If you make choices that move you in a direction that is *not* in alignment with your Higher Self you feel emotions of fear, anger, depression, disappointment, or blame. If you experienced these emotions at any time in your life, you were witnessing your Mood Map in motion. Unlike the GPS in your car, it does not have to be plugged in or given directions, as it's always working to guide you towards your Source Energy. You can recognize some of the guideposts easily, as, 'fear' or 'love.' Most you probably don't recognize these as such, but understanding your Mood Map is an opportunity to consciously choose your emotions and choose a new reality.

Your Mood Map

Joy/Knowing/Empowerment/Freedom/Love/Appreciation
Passion
Enthusiasm/Eagerness/Happiness
Positive Expectations/Belief
Optimism
Hopefulness
Contentment
Boredom
Pessimism
Frustration/Impatience/Irritation
Overwhelment
Disappointment
Doubt
Worry
Blame
Discouragement
Anger
Revenge
Hatred/Rage
Jealousy
Insecurity/Guilt/Unworthiness
Fear/Grief/Depression/Despair/Powerlessness

When you experienced a negative emotion in response to something you were observing, you may have blamed someone else for how you felt, instead of understanding the emotion as the guidance of your Mood Barometer. The person who was the object of your blame may have participated in the experience, but no one is to blame for how you *felt* about it. Your emotion was an indicator of how you were traveling on your Mood Map in relation to where you were going. When you feel the tension and the emotion repeatedly, you have built some momentum on the subject and it will manifest in your life. Whether you want this subject or not, your focus on that emotion will manifest in either your surroundings or your body.

The purpose of your Mood Map is to coax you toward that which you really want. Source Energy knows what you want, as you have asked through contrast and vibration. All that has been requested by you awaits the moment when you will be ready for it to manifest itself, and, because Source knows what you want, it calls you toward what you have asked for, guiding you by your emotions. You are always being guided towards that which is best for you, and that is the reason that tension is felt when you have moved further away on the Mood Map from Source. Your mood always matches how you feel. When you get excited about something, opportunities arise, there is flow and life seems easy. There is freedom and no tension. When something feels scary or uncertain, and you need to try really hard to make things happen, life feels tough and alone, and there is a great deal of tension. Innately, you know to move toward that which feels good. The only reason you ever want anything is that you think that in having it, you will feel good. Your moods guide you by letting you know if you feel good or not and therefore if you are on track to your desires.

Every Subject is Really Two Subjects

Every subject you could think about has two ends, just like a sword. It has a handle and it has a blade. One is comfortable, empowering, and useful, the other is sharp and is filled with tension. Say, for instance, that you want more money, and you think about all the money you can imagine, forming a scenario in your mind that feels as if money is easy to find and abundant. If you're thinking that, you're grabbing the sword by the handle. It feels easy and powerful, and you have found the path to your desires. When you think about money and wonder when or even if it is coming, or why it hasn't arrived in your bank account yet, you're grabbing the subject of money by the blade. Every subject is always potentially two subjects; that which is wanted and that which isn't. Wielding a sword by the blade will hurt, just as focusing on what isn't wanted in any subject, also hurts. The idea is to grab the subject by the handle, the thoughts of the subject that feel good and then you can notice by your mood that you are moving in a direction that is wanted. This is the your Mood Barometer in action. Feel your way on your mood map to less and less tension and more and more freedom. One mood will bring you closer to what you want, and one will keep you distant.

For instance: "Isn't it going to be wonderful when my loving mate shows up in my life? We'll have such fun together. I really look forward to the new places we'll discover. It'll be so great to have someone sharing the laughter. That feels alive and exciting. I can just imagine it now."

You can feel that these statements are grabbing the sword by the handle, as they feel powerful, alive, and exciting. This is the mood you need to be in for your mate to arrive.

The opposite example would be: "I feel utterly abandoned. I really want someone who completes me. Then, I won't feel so alone anymore. It'll be good when they get here. I don't know when that will be, but I hope it's soon." You can feel from this statement that there is the distinct focus upon need for an absent or elusive mate. As the mood is sadness and disappointment, the request to the Universe is for more of the same.

Creating a mood of fun, excitement, freedom, appreciation, and love is alignment with your Higher Self. As your mood shifts to an emotion further away from Source, a feeling of tension begins to arrive, because you are moving further from the innately desired emotions of appreciation, where Source is located. The further you move from Source, the more tension you will feel. Release the tension and you will automatically spring back towards fun, excitement, appreciation, and love. This is naturally where you belong.

It's up to you to choose a mood that is closer to Source as that is where you will always feel your best. More enlightened, intuitive, happy and fulfilled.

Opposing Subjects

When you've identified a desire, the image of it is larger than life in your imagination. The thoughts you think, the self-talk, the conversations you have, are all pointed toward what you want and how good it will be when the object of your desire shows up. As this idea comes more into focus, so does its opposite. Remember, 'for every action, there is an equal and opposite reaction.'

This is Newton's Third Law of Motion, and just as it helps us in Physics, so too can it help you to understand life. As your desire becomes large and alive, a bridge to its opposite also becomes large and alive. It takes *focus* to keep your thoughts on your desires, and not on the lack of them. When you are excited, there is a bridge across the unknown to fear. Both your desire and its opposite are vivid and real. As both wanted and unwanted are present in your vibration, your focus becomes valuable. Knowing you want great love in your life creates a bridge to loneliness, which also comes into focus as the fear of that great love being absent. Desire for a healthy and fit body comes with the fear of illness and frailty. Grabbing hold of the blade, which is the loneliness or the frailty, is what keeps you distant from your desires, and it creates the highs and lows in life. Practice at focusing on your desires is required to keep you on the path of your dreams, and to be vigilant in observing your moods, so that it is easy to correct an adverse one before tension builds and momentum takes you in an unwanted direction.

Recognizing the lows as an effective means of clarification can be very empowering. When you know pain and sorrow, it causes you to ask for joy. Ill health provides a bouncing-off point for health, and destitution provides a strong desire for abundance. There are many billionaires and famous people who have rags-to-riches stories, as these situations are pivotal in creating a new reality. The contrast is very strong, and that strength amplifies what is desired. The key is not staying in the mood of the unwanted, even if it is your current reality. The contrast has caused a strong desire for its opposite, but you can't get to the desire when you are focused on the contrast. There has to be movement. This is where the Mood Map can be your best friend.

This Mood Map is the communication between how you feel and how your Higher Self feels. Before you began this physical journey, you decided a Map would be a good idea to guide your way, so that if you ever strayed from the direction of your desires, this map would act as an indicator to guide you back on track. The Mood Map and instructions on how to use it were familiar when you were young. Innately, you knew that if something made you happy it was good for you, and if it made you upset, it wasn't. There was a simple and effective set of instructions. When you laughed, and smiled, you were happy, and this was moving you automatically in the direction of what you wanted, which was to feel great. When a person hurt you, you moved away from them, and gravitated towards what made you feel good. The instructions for the Mood Map seemed clear.

There were adult Role Models in most children's lives that were influential in their growth. Unfortunately, many of these adults had already lost their way. They didn't know the instructions for their own Mood Map, and just moved along bumping into one situation after another. In most cases, as a child, you started getting mixed messages about what feeling good meant. When you did something to please your parents, they were happy, and you decided their happiness translated into your happiness. Then there were those who convinced you that it was selfish to think of how you felt, and that pleasing them was far more important, so your Mood Map started to feel confusing. When people close to you responded in a way that didn't match yours, you changed your interpretation of the Mood Map to suit them, concluding that when others were happy you could be as well. So began your quest to please others.

You listened to what others told you, rather than to the emotional guidance of your Mood Map, and soon the inner voice was but a whisper. Lost amongst the cascading debris of selflessness, you learnt it was wrong to be angry, so you became depressed. When it was wrong to blame others, you blamed yourself. These Role Models convinced you that you weren't the center of the Universe, and you needed to fit in somewhere. The truth that you create your own reality became lost and unreal, as you didn't know what made you feel free and happy anymore.

These are merely examples of how the translation for your Mood Map got lost. When emotional pain was felt, it should've been an indicator to move to a better feeling mood. Instead, most of us were taught to play the 'blame game.'

The Mood Map was designed as a tool for you to consciously create your own reality. It is simple and consistent. When you feel that you are in your flow of Source Energy, which feels natural and alive, you feel great. As you experience emotions that are further away from this, you feel tension, until it is stretched tightly and you feel pain. But the Universe really does mold itself around your desires. When you feel good, more situations are created to help you maintain a good feeling. When disappointment is dominant, more situations are created that help you remain disappointed. The Map can't disappear or get lost. Try as you might, it can't even be ignored. This Mood Map has been working for you the whole of your life, and it's only the communication that has gone a little off track. You have felt the tension when the emotions stray further from Source, and you have experienced the elation when having fun. Imagine if you had been taught as a child that it was your job to feel good, and that nobody else could ever create that feeling for you. What sensitivity you would develop without the side effects of guilt or blame! The relationships you would attract would be balanced, and powerful. The platform from which you would create, would be more of the very best of life. People would call you lucky.

This Mood Map is guidance. At one end is Source Energy, Higher Self which equates to Joy, Love and Excitement. The further down the mood of emotions you travel, the further from Source and the more uncomfortable you will feel. Choosing another mood is the freedom of your Mood Map and the guiding light to a wonderful future.

Understanding Your Mood Barometer

Monitoring your life at any point in time can be valuable for understanding which direction to take next. A barometer for the soul isn't necessary, as the emotions you experience are a direct connection with Source. The barometer required for a fulfilled life is built-in, as your Mood Barometer registers the way you feel about someone or something. This doesn't arrive on your doorstep as an optional accessories pack; it came pre-installed. The Mood Barometer is always working, as it's illuminating your path via the emotions at any point in time. Sometimes it can be difficult to understand your emotions, as they can become clouded by outside opinions, but your Mood Barometer will work at all times. When you meet, talk to, or even observe people, your Mood Barometer interprets how you feel about them.

Everybody who comes into your life reflects your mood, and how you feel about them is your interpretation of it and them. You get to decide how you feel about anything by observing yourself through the people you're coming into contact with. These are the reflections of your mood. It's not how they feel about you that count, but how you feel about them. Do you remember the saying, "What someone thinks of you is none of your business"? Never a truer word was spoken, because what someone thinks or feels about you is a reflection of themselves, as experienced through their Mood Barometer. As you observe how you feel about others, the people in your life will give you many opportunities to create a wonderful reality just by being there.

We all think we want to be truthful with ourselves, and sometimes we are, but the truth is that none of us really wants others to know how we're feeling, so we pretend. It might be that we try to pass ourselves off as happy by putting on a smile, whilst inside feeling a mood of anxiety. When people respond to this anxiety, as they invariably do, we get upset. We always wear our hearts on our sleeves, as our Mood Barometer cannot be fooled. It will bring us evidence of how we're feeling through the observation of those around us. This is not felt in words but in emotions. Often people are labeled as rude or insensitive, but how we feel about someone is a reflection of us, not them.

The Mood Barometer amplifies how we feel so we can choose which mood we would prefer. As we cannot see or experience outside of our own beliefs, it gives us an opportunity to feel our way towards the life of joy that is innately ours. This is much deeper than a smiling façade, as it is the connection to Source Energy. If we're ever confused about whether what we see or how we feel is the correction perception, we should always go with how we feel. Some label this 'intuition', but it is much more than that. When we notice how we are feeling, we have the opportunity to change the direction of our thoughts and change our mood. Our Mood Barometer is always presenting us with opportunities to choose which direction to move in. It's not there to guide others or judge them; it's a method of steering us on course again and again and again. Through the practice of noticing our moods, we will begin to trust our Mood Barometer and be aware of the subtle changes that offer us a different direction. In this way, we will be aware of when another's moods and opinions are influencing us.

When my youngest son was three, he attended a community kindergarten. On occasion, I would speak with his teacher, and when she talked about herself, I would usually come away feeling confused. One day I stopped and thought about what was happening, and concluded that when the teacher was trying to convince me of a truth she held, I could feel it was the opposite. That created confusion within me, as my well-tuned Barometer was indicating one emotion, and she was telling me it was another. There was a lot of mistrust at that kindergarten. There was an incident where a child had climbed the fence to get out and was found by a local cafe owner, who called up the kindergarten to report him lost. The first person the teacher called was the Kindergarten President for legal advice. Not the parents.

No matter how hard you try to hide behind a happy face, your mood will present itself in your reality loudly and clearly for others to observe and react to. Instead of reading her own Barometer and changing how she felt, the teacher stayed with the pretense, and a resulting mood of mistrust wound its way like a spell throughout the kindergarten community. Not everything is to be taken at face value. Your mood barometer will guide you as to what is the truth and what isn't.

You don't always need to feel good, but your Mood Barometer is the guide to moving you in the direction of your higher purpose. However you feel and whatever the mood, you can't hide it, but you can change it. Ten minutes is all it takes to sit and focus on something that makes you feel better. We are born vibrational beings and we are exceptional at reading vibration, so good, in fact, that we aren't even aware it is done naturally,

Having an awareness of how the Mood Barometer works will assist you in understanding if you're in a feeling-good mood of your own, or whether others are influencing you. It gives an immediate mood reading, as there is no time delay. Of course, the only situation in which you want to be influenced by another's mood is when it is an uplifting one.

The Mood Barometer is one of the most valuable tools you have, as it helps to determine how you're feeling at any given time. The job of the Mood Barometer is to guide you towards feeling great. This is where you rendezvous with your Higher Self. The importance of feeling great is that everything you have ever wanted is created from that space of joy.

The Game of Triangles

We all create relationships with many people throughout a lifetime. Relationships with lovers or family members are few compared to those of the acquaintances we make. A relationship is defined as the way in which two or more people regard or behave towards each other. When a connection is made with a person, there is an exchange of energy. This creates an emotion and an opinion. This opinion can change your perspective and therefore create a new reality. The unions we have with people other than family can be immensely influential in our reality, whether they are with a bus conductor, a neighbor or a schoolteacher.

Not every relationship is harmonious; you won't get along with everyone, ever. Making an effort to constantly please people or affect another's behavior is tiring, as people can be fickle. They often want different things. The more you try to please another, the more often you're expected to do so and you can't bend yourself in enough ways to please someone all the time.

Now, think about this. If the people you are pleasing are your children, then stop it now. You're not going to be there for the rest of their lives to please them, so they will need to find someone else to fill that role. This is creating needy or toxic relationships. Don't prop them up; just give them a soft place to land when they fall. This way they can decide what works and change what doesn't. This is their grounding for the real world. You will have helped them create a platform to emerge into the world and feel safe.

The relationship triangle (see below) is used in our workshops to demonstrate patterns of behavior. It's a handy tool to help you understand the type of relationship you gravitate towards. There are basically three types of role-relationships in this potentially toxic triangle and each one of us gravitates towards playing the Victim, the Rescuer/Caretaker or the Perpetrator. We use the Caretaker and the Rescuer roles interchangeably, and this is not to be confused with a Caregiver. A Caretaker is one that enables the behavior of another for their own emotional benefit, and a Caregiver is one that takes care of another's physical needs. Caretaker is the description of an emotional state, and not the physical help that's required of a Caregiver. When you have been emotionally hurt, you seek a Caretaker or Rescuer.

To understand which of these three areas you gravitate towards is quite simple, as you'll attract the others in the triangle to form a relationship. This works rather like the rules of a game. Whatever role you play, the game is toxic to all relationships eventually.

You enter the triangle by playing a Victim role. A Rescuer/Caretaker is sought to help you feel a little better as they feel sorry for the Victim.

When you are at a low point and looking for validation, you can be a Rescuer and will attract Victims to bolster your mood. When you are feeling resentful, you will act as a Perpetrator and a Victim will seek you out.

The game of triangles can be played in one's head as well as in physical reality. All roles are interchangeable in the same person, but you are taught early, within the family unit, which role you are to play, as children want to fit in and we all want to feel loved. This triangle gives the illusion of both connection and love. Eventually the conditions for the love are not worth the emotional trauma.

As you can see, Victims are pretty popular, but don't worry about that. Even though people gravitate towards one role on the triangle, we are a versatile collection of humans. We change roles to suit our needs. There is no right or wrong role here. A Victim will work just as hard to reel in a Perpetrator as a Caretaker wills a Victim. It's a game, and therefore follows rules.

The rules are:
1. You need to fill the role I'm looking for; and,
2. If you don't play the game, I'll find someone who will.

When you choose not to play the game, the players pick up their bat and ball, so to speak, and take their game elsewhere. In other words, when you choose not to play this game anymore, you may need to find new friends, as those who are currently playing the game with you are not necessarily willing to change.

It only takes two people to play these roles, which can change, as the situation requires. You don't need a person to be aware of the rules to play the game, either, as like attracts like, and compatible players will find each other from all over the world. Most people are taught these roles from the day they are born, and will seek others to complete the game. The players can be complete strangers. A friend of mine has played these games in a self-help forum online, so you don't even need to be face to face.

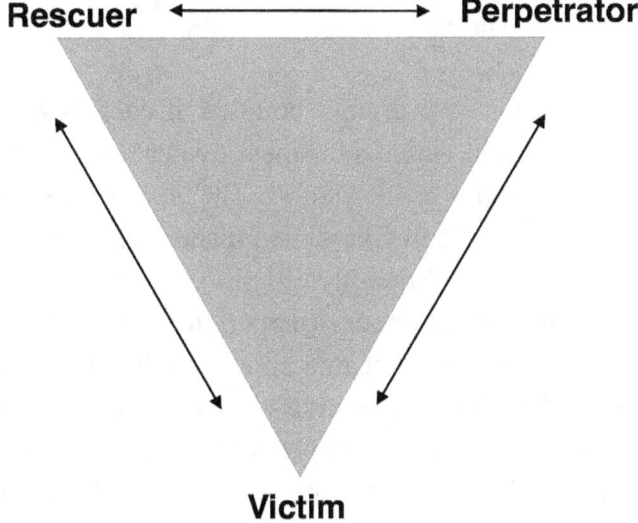

This game is one you learned growing up. You may have experienced that when your father hurt your mother for instance. You needed to feel sorry for her, so you became the rescuer. When you were being picked on at school, your mother felt sorry for you. She taught you how to become a victim, and have other people feel sorry for you. The problem with this logic is that it is disempowering, and you become trapped in a time warp of your own creation. There are variations of these scenarios played out throughout your life. It's not because someone *makes* you respond in a particular way, it is that you *learned*

the patterns of how you thought life worked from those you grew up with.

You'll keep using these patterns of behavior at home, work and socially until they no longer work for you. It may take a while for you to realize they're no longer working, as the vibrational pull of someone to fill a need is always met. There is always another need, and another, for as long as you believe the empty void can be filled by others, because it never can.

This drama cycle not only divides couples; it can divide towns. We lived in a small town in which a business owner was afraid of another similar business opening its doors. The fearful owner (victim) gathered her supporters (caretakers) and made it clear that she was the victim in all of this. Consequently, gossip ensued and the supporters (caretakers) became executioners (perpetrators) of a boycott against the new business. The town became divided. What usually happens in this scenario is that the new business becomes so victimized that it shuts its doors. This method of engendering fear is otherwise known as 'bullying tactics.' The new business owner asked me for guidance, and I made sure she moved into her own mood of feeling great, and focusing on what was working. In doing this, she moved outside the drama triangle. I would not enter into any gossip, and I made sure that those who expressed an opinion in my presence were aware of the part they were playing. As with all fear and gossip, if you can rise above it by moving into a better-feeling place, which is outside the drama cycle, the gossip dwindles. People gravitate towards fun, and the new owner's business is now both flourishing and fun.

Your language choice can indicate a tendency towards your drama cycle. A client was discussing her staff, and I noticed she often used the preposition 'luv' in relation to them. This was a stylish business, and I asked her how often she used the terms, 'luv' or 'darlin' with her staff. She reluctantly admitted that it might have been more than she realized, and rather than being their boss, she was acting as their caretaker. She agreed to play a game to find out if this was a problem. If anyone heard her use those terms at work, she would fine herself a quarter. After two times, I raised the amount to $1. It was a slow day, and already she was up to $5. This knowledge came as a shock to her, and she wanted to change her patronizing behavior. You don't want to act as a Rescuer or Caretaker for anyone, let alone your staff, as you will attract staff that will play the victim, and this is not a healthy working relationship. The only way out of a drama triangle is to be conscious of the role you are playing, so you can choose differently.

A disadvantage of playing the Game of Triangles is that you are always looking for someone to fill your drama. There is never the satisfaction or feeling happy with yourself, because you're looking for others to fill the gap in the triangle. People will go to great lengths of creating a drama so they can fulfill their role. It's not just something you play at home; it's a pattern you play everywhere.

Honoring yourself means feeling good about who you are. When that happens, there is no need to play the Game of Triangles. To opt out, you need to be conscious of playing the game and choosing differently. It will be difficult at first, as there is still momentum in your life from the part you used to play. Make sure you have in place a routine that will maintain your vibration or redirect it if necessary; you will find then that the relationships attracted to you become more balanced and empowering. Being aware of how you are feeling and what emotion you are reaching for on your Mood Map is the key to changing your reality. That's a wonderful springboard for any venture, business, or personal endeavor.

We Teach only by Example

Nobody will ever see things the same way you do, but in a relationship, it is advantageous for both partners to have similar intentions. Often one will try and change the other, even though difference was the very thing that attracted them to each other in the first place. Making peace with others who are different is an acceptance born of love. Words don't teach; only your actions teach, and when you look at the people throughout your life that have made the biggest impact, both good and bad, it wasn't because of the words they said, but because of the actions they practiced. Your parents could have yelled at you to be nice all they liked, but if they weren't nice people, they weren't going to influence you to be nice.

My son was in a relationship where his partner didn't like the circumstances at work. Her job was becoming a burden to her; that was the reality she had created. He explained this to her and tried to persuade her to change the way she felt about things by looking at her job as she wanted it to be. In that way, a new reality could be created, but this girl wasn't having a bar of it. For her, there was comfort in playing the familiar role of Victim, and nobody moves until they're uncomfortable. He was now in the position of doing one of two things. Either holding his own good feeling or becoming the Rescuer, which is what she was seeking. Since he knew there was nothing he could do for her if he didn't feel good himself, he opted to keep his own mood uplifted.

If how you felt was important to you, and you knew that nothing could be gained by entering the Game of Triangles, in fact that everything you wanted would be gained by moving in the direction of your Source, wouldn't you do that? Wouldn't you mind your own mood no matter what? The biggest influence you have on another person, and indeed on the world, is to feel good and look at things in a way that makes your heart sing. As you hold the vibration of Source, you gently and automatically guide people toward their Higher Self when they're ready.

Resistance is Your Friend

Resistance is the tension felt by emotionally pushing against a subject that you are giving attention to. In Physics, resistance is that which opposes motion and flow. Imagine you have a stream of well-being that instinctively you allow flow to. All of the dreams and desires that have grown with you and expanded as you have flow in this stream. When you are feeling great, you have no resistance and you are flowing along happily with this stream of well-being. Now imagine that you are in disagreement with a *subject* (a person or an idea) and you are standing in that stream of well-being that is flowing very fast, but instead of allowing it to flow you have turned upstream and are pushing against the current for all your worth. The more disagreement you feel, the stronger the current, and the more difficult it is trying to battle against the stream. Battling against the current is what is known as resistance.

Resistance is the distance between your opinion and the opinion your Higher Self has on that subject. Your Source will always take the higher opinion on any subject, so if you have an opinion that is any less than the one your Higher Self is expressing, you experience resistance. When you are resisting moving your mood towards the opinion of the Higher Self (Who, of course, has your best interests at heart) tension is felt. Seeing the best in every subject is the natural flow of who you really are. When you feel resistance, it's not punishment or a lesson; it's an indicator that you should move your thoughts to a place that is closer to that of your Higher Self. Resistance is gently prodding you toward your highest goal, where you merge with Source.

So, how do you get to a place of being in opposition to your Higher Self? It's a process. Let's explore it.

You have an opinion. Now think about that for a moment. When you are in a great mood, in high spirits, with a great sense of Well-being, you don't have opinions. You just flow, as life is good. There is no need for an opinion about anything, as all is wonderful with the world. Clarity is your companion, and a broader perspective is natural. When you have an opinion, it's usually about someone or some group being right and another person or group being wrong. Your Higher Self will not join you in admonishing anybody – ever – and your opinion creates tension. You give up on your dreams. Having a dream that feels good and not being able to maintain the vision creates resistance; you find yourself thinking you don't deserve the dream. You feel unworthy, because you are allowing the opinion of others to be an important factor in how you feel. You start to believe in the black and white of right and wrong. You feel anger or resentment towards anybody, for any reason at all, whether you feel justified or not. You think you should be doing something you're not. You get irritated by not being 'present' in any moment. You feel victimized, blaming anybody, yourself included, for something they or you did or didn't do. You feel guilty about the past.

Resistance is an early indicator of distance and discomfort. The only way to eliminate it is to change how you feel. Change your mood and make peace with whatever it is.

Have you ever noticed when you get into a conversation that takes a direction you don't want it to, that very soon you are adding more hard luck stories to the pot? As you listen to a conversation, it becomes a part of your vibration as the thoughts inside your head move toward the topic, and soon there are stories coming to mind that match the conversation at hand. You have now included this new cascade of thoughts into your reality, and they are quickly building momentum in a direction that is not wanted. In as little as a minute, more situations will come to mind, and you could be on this tangent for a long time. This could become your vibrational request, namely, to create a new reality in the direction of your unwanted thoughts. More of the same kinds of stories will emerge, and you will have allowed another person or group to influence your reality without even realizing it.

As like attracts like, an emotion attracts more circumstances that will create the same emotion. If the mood experienced is anger, and you have gained momentum by being angry for an hour or so, the request to the Universe is for more situations that will cause you to feel angry. People will cross your path that will contribute to your anger. Nobody can *make* you feel angry but your newfound momentum wants to be fed, and an emotional match is the only sustenance it will recognize. The quicker you notice resistance the better, as momentum has a way of spiraling out of control. The longer resistance stays around, the more momentum is created, until you are surrounded by opportunities to feel more of the same. You have changed your reality. The same works for feeling great. When you have moved your mood to excitement, you will look for more things to be excited about and everybody who comes into your vicinity will feel exciting. To create your own joyous reality, it is beneficial to be a conscious creator.

The Benefits of Resistance

If resistance feels bad why does it exist? The benefit of resistance is to help clarify new desires and perspectives. We are born creators and, without resistance, we would not have new desires and dreams. The emotions we experienced would feel flat, as without the lows the highs would not feel so good. Resistance allows us to reach forth, and expand into the new growth our desires have created. It is a constant reaching, fulfilling, and expanding.

Resistance is an indicator, and not a lifestyle choice so to move beyond resistance, take these steps:

- Notice the indicators of resistance by observing your emotions; this is the indication of your Mood Barometer;
- Recognize what you would prefer; then
- Focus your attention on what you want and why you want it.

When the emotional indicators are ignored and the focus is on uncomfortable emotions, resistance can be felt in the body. All pain is an indicator of a build-up of resistance. The key is to notice how you are feeling, early. When you notice that your mood is a bit 'ordinary', move your mood on the Mood Map towards Source and something that feels like relief. Change your mind, and change your mood. The solution is simple, and with practice it gets easy. The secret is to catch the unwanted emotion before momentum builds.

Any resistance felt is never about another person. The pain you feel is the tension between where you are and where your Source is. It's easy to blame someone else for how you feel, but it is not their job to make you happy, and it isn't in their highest good to do so. From an early age, we have been taught to associate emotional pain with another person, real or imagined, alive or dead, yet this is far from the truth. Emotional pain is brought about by a differing opinion from Source, expressed in response to a person or situation.

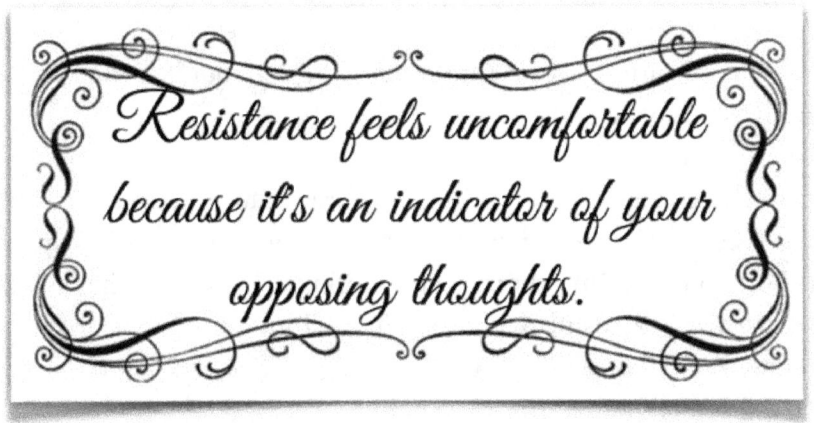

If you don't take notice of the resistance you're creating with your thoughts, you will feel the emotion express itself in your body in some way. It could be as a stubbed toe, a headache, or frustration with heavy traffic on the road. It follows along the path of, the thought, the mood, the feeling, and a stubbed toe. Didn't notice? What about the unhappy thoughts, the mood, the car accident, the gout or the kidney stones? Do you still not notice the resistance you have created? Don't worry; it will grow.

Resistance is a persistent indicator that it would be wise to heed by using the Mood Map you were born with. Moods gently guide the way to the reality you have always wanted, even if you don't know what that is. Becoming sensitive to resistance means you can change your mood before it builds momentum. As your mood improves, flow is felt, and the stream of well-being carries you on the current to manifesting those desires that were brought about by the resistance. Continual resistance is letting you know whether you are on the path to your dreams, or moving away from your desires.

Emotional Baggage

We have all heard the term Emotional Baggage but how do you know if you if you have it?

Emotional Baggage is rarely the description people use about themselves. It is more often the term they give to habitual behaviors that they don't like in others. The emotional heaviness that weighs a person down is a result of the beliefs holding them back from being who they really want to be. A belief is a practiced thought, one that is practiced often enough to form a habit.

The signs of emotional baggage are frequent unwanted behaviors.
For example:
°Prolonged Bad Moods
°Being Quick to Anger
°Depression or Despondency
°Lack of Joy
°Expecting things to go wrong – Murphy's Law
°Blaming people and feeling 'Out of Control'
°Being Judgmental
°Feeling a need to please people

Any frequently occurring behavior that has a detrimental effect on your life is emotional baggage. It is carrying the burden of unwanted emotions, either inwardly or outwardly. We could call it, practiced resistance over a long period of time. Emotional baggage can range from mild irritation to severe debilitation; all will entail the fear of letting go. That is the feeling that if you were to let go of some of the beliefs that seem to support you, you would fall and there would be nothing to catch you. At one time these habit patterns served to create a feeling of relief, and that's why they were established. Just like all thoughts, depending on your mood, they will take you closer to or further from Source on the Mood Map.

All habit patterns are practiced thoughts, and they can become so entrenched that it is easy to mistake the thought patterns as being necessary to your happiness. Patterns are often created to imitate or fit in with a family unit. A niche is then carved in the fabric of reality by adopting patterns of behavior that are acceptable to others. If a behavior was adopted that resulted in you feeling accepted by others, it improved the way you felt. All patterns you adopted gave relief at one time; they made you feel better and that's why you developed them but they aren't necessarily life enhancing anymore. They are now repeated, as there is a familiar way of feeling when the pattern is played out. Logic does not play a role in belief systems, as habit patterns were created for the purpose of feeling better. Noticing how you feel will help in understanding whether the patterns you have adopted are working for you or not. Because of the full embodiment of habit patterns, they're usually not uncovered until a conscious choice has been made to move forward. When moving forward becomes difficult these habits are often referred to as blocks. Everybody thinks they want to remove blocks.

I had a call for help about 9.00 pm one rainy evening. The mother of one of my son's friends wanted a lift to the airport, as her partner had ejected her from home. Her son was away at his grandparents' home at the time. I said I was happy to take her to the airport the next day. (The airport is 90 minutes away and taxis weren't available.) She could stay with us for the night, as we had a spare room. I knew the relationship with her partner was volatile, so when he told her to leave he didn't sugar coat the demand. She thanked me and said she was sorry she'd rung and hung up.

After thirty minutes, I picked up my umbrella and my cell phone and walked down towards her house. I could hear the shouting over the rain as I approached the landing. She was in tears as I sat with her and we talked. I asked her partner to come into the front room and talk with us. After a little while he did this. From my counselor training I had come to understand that there was no right and wrong in these situations. All I could do was to ask questions and place all the answers on the table for both of them to find some clarity. There was no solution. Nobody wanted a solution. They only wanted someone to blame for their misery and circumstances. There was much water under the bridge, and a lot of very warped perspectives. I left knowing I had done all I could do.

In some toxic situations, the blame is even shifted to the counselor (or parent, etc.) and this can serve to bind the relationship temporarily, until the blame is shifted back to the partner again. I knew with some certainty that the blame would be shifted to me, and that was ok. They would be on talking terms with each other, at least for a while.

As I walked away that night, I made a promise to myself not to counsel DV (Domestic Violence) cases, as generally, the partners are not ready to move forward; they only want to blame each other for how they feel. Unless a person is ready to say to their partner, "I don't hold you responsible for my mood, as the way I feel is up to me", then they aren't going to move forward just yet.

It is human nature to want to help people, but if the people don't want any help, there is nothing you can do. When they are ready they will find the next step, as it's always available. Listening is a key component in therapy, and it is also a key component to becoming a friend. Every person needs to feel as though they are being listened to, as it is a basic human need for health and well-being.

Everyone can let go of the emotional baggage they carry by developing new habit patterns. Focusing on the problem or trying to push it away, only serves to make it bigger. The only way it can be alleviated is by slowing the momentum, and we do this by adopting new patterns. One undesired habit pattern can be replaced by a chosen pattern. The empowering factor arises when you choose to create an uplifting pattern, rather than moving to another default pattern of demeaning behavior. That is consciously creating your reality.

People often don't mind their own business, as they don't like what they're looking at in their own lives. When you don't feel comfortable with where your mind wanders, unwanted thoughts are accumulative and create momentum. Then you look to others to find value in yourself, hoping they will make you feel better. Looking for someone to value you when you do not value yourself has become commonplace in our society, but it doesn't work for long, as people are fickle and don't always find value in you consistently. It is also much easier to find fault with someone else's life than to enjoy your own life. This is all baggage as the habit-patterns in such cases were developed long ago. Needing a partner to uplift you or value what you do is to bring baggage to a relationship, and does not have its roots in joy. You are much better off to find your own power, and then you will find somebody who stands in their own power. In this way, there is mutual respect and much joy.

Validation comes from within. Rather than diminishing who you are, expand into who you want to be and allow the light to shine brightly, no matter what anyone else thinks.

Shortcut to Manifestation

The only reason you want anything in life is because you think that when you have it you'll feel better. So, the mind tends to wander in the direction of, when I have a great body I will feel amazing, or when I am healthy I can go on holiday and that will be fun, and when I win lotto I will feel financially free. You know your own list.

When you peruse the list, you will notice that the common denominator is one of feeling great, fun, and free. Rather than thinking you will only feel great when these desires become manifest, you can use your imagination to create that good-feeling mood immediately – by imagining yourself as fit and healthy, and walking to the supermarket, or running that marathon. When you imagine the fit and healthy body and feel the emotion of the sense of achievement, you have manifested the desired emotion. As you connect with this vision and immerse yourself in the imagined scenario, allow it to be fluid, as if you were watching a movie in which you were the star. Refine the shape and size of your body and imagine people looking in admiration as they pass by. Use imagery to define the aspects of this dream to personalize your experience. Notice how wonderful you feel as you've manifested the desire. The physical evidence may not be in your life, but the emotion is present, and when you feel it, you will see it.

Making Decisions

Favorable decisions are made through the path of least resistance, which means that if presented with two choices, the one that feels best is the *favorable* one. Imagine each choice and play it out in your mind to get an understanding of how it feels. If choices are available but there is no clear decision, it's usually because you don't have enough information. This is the time to refine the questions you ask yourself, so that you are clear about what you want. Don't force a decision, as clarity is not about timing but alignment. When you are in the same emotional alignment as your desire, then the decision is easy.

To align yourself with your desire, find a way of moving your mood towards love, joy, appreciation, enthusiasm, or excitement. The choice that feels easiest or most fun, or feels exciting as you think about the unfolding, is the path of least resistance. This is the choice that feels the best once you have imagined the consequences. Whilst there is no right or wrong decision, you'll find the path of least resistance unfolds organically.

Power of a Mantra

Everyone has big ideas we call dreams. These are desires for things that haven't arrived in your life yet, and sometimes they feel a very long way away.

If you feel your dreams are distant, they're probably hanging around the ether looking for an opportunity to ignite. Find what is holding you back from achieving your dreams. It will be an emotion of some type; perhaps it's doubt, fear of the unknown, or of another person or of failure. There is sure to be some emotion that is the resistance that stops you from being the best you can be — physically, monetarily or in your relationships.

When you have found that emotion, name it and write it down. Then create a statement that's the opposite. Keep tweaking this statement until it's something you can relate to. Choose words that can resonate the power within, and let this statement be your mantra.

For instance, I used to doubt that certain things would come into my life, as I couldn't see a logical way for them to turn up. *Doubt* was the emotion that was my resistance. The opposite statement I created was, "I believe in myself and I can create anything". I tweaked that to a more powerful statement, which was "I create my own reality and I can do anything". That became my mantra.

A mantra is a handy tool as it fills the space that could otherwise be used to create negative self-talk.

Dowsing

This is a type of dowsing method using the breath. If you are wondering if a particular food is of value to your body, there are methods you can use to find out. The body has a communication system that sends information to you in the form of vibration.

Put your hand on the food, or its picture in an article from a magazine. Take a nice long breath in through the nose. If the breath goes all the way down to your stomach, the item is of value. When the breath only inflates the chest, the item is of less value. Don't just assume because you were told that broccoli was good for you that it is good for everyone.

A note of warning: Dowsing is not recommended as a reason to give up prescribed medication. Instead use this method as an indicator for a better communication with your body.

Vision Board

A vision board is a shortcut to reminding you of the dreams that first inspired you to action. Also known as Dream Boards, they can be topical and cover a broad range of desires and subjects. On a vision board, there is a collection of pictures and phrases that you either want to accomplish or receive. The idea of a Vision Board is to place the collection of images on a board in any fashion and place the board in a position where you will see it often. It will inspire you every time you catch sight of it, and can serve to readjust your mood often. Make this board big and put it somewhere prominent. Preferably in a location that is private, as you don't want to be explaining and justifying to those who don't believe in your dreams.

The Power of a Waterfall

A waterfall is created by a collection of thoughts that have gathered momentum over time. You have many waterfalls flowing at any one time. These represent the subjects that have gained momentum in your life, both wanted and unwanted. When you have focused thoughts and gained momentum on a subject, the waterfall is flowing freely. When you have momentum flowing on a subject you *don't* like, the only thing you can do is to start a new waterfall on a subject that you *do* like. The new subject will start with a trickle whilst the old one continues gushing, but gradually the momentum will change from one waterfall to the other. It's worth the persistence, as momentum on a subject that is wanted becomes clarity.

Starting a new waterfall on a subject that is exciting sometimes needs a bridge, and that bridge is made from self-talk. Self-talk that is uplifting on any subject will gather momentum quickly, and a new uplifting waterfall begins. You will need to feel your way when building this bridge, as some statements will give momentum to a new direction and some to the old.

The key is to use statements that don't contradict how you are feeling, but coax the water to flow in this new direction. For instance, if you were feeling angry and had gathered some momentum, so that your waterfall was flowing freely, you would have to get to a stage of firstly wanting to move on from this mood, and secondly deciding upon the alternative that you want to replace it. This is where your Mood Map comes to the fore, as it will guide you in finding your way. If you decided you wanted to go beyond anger and feel good, you might make a statement such as: "I feel happy all the time." This statement may represent what you want but the mind is screaming at

you. "No, you don't. That's not true." This is an indicator that you are moving in the opposite direction so a gentler approach may be:
"I've had enough of being angry."
It doesn't make you happy but it doesn't cause resistance either. This statement might make you relax a little. The next one may say:
" I don't need to do this anymore."
"If I can move into different feeling place, I know I'll feel a little better."
You've put a wedge in the anger now, but you can't feel any contradiction, so that's good.
"I can find other things to focus on"
"There are some things that are working for me"
You're making a shift now, and because you're still feeling your way, you can gauge whether there is resistance or not.
"I like the feeling of things working for me."
"It's a real 'ease and flow' feeling"
Moving up the mood scale now. Stay with an improved mood for a while to gain some momentum, and get water flowing over that waterfall.
"I can feel that ease and flow"
"It's a sure feeling."
"It feels like knowing."
"It feels like this is how it should be."
"It feels sure."
"It feels knowing."
"It feels real."
"I feel optimistic that I can move in a direction that makes my heart sing."

You are now in a completely different mood from the one you were in when you first started this waterfall. After a couple of minutes more,

more thoughts that are like these will come, as momentum has already started. The only thing to be done now is to be aware of looking for things that feel good, and not going back to the old waterfall that is still flowing.

It's important to note that the old waterfall may become a trickle but it will never cease to exist. Giving attention to that subject will always cause the momentum to recommence. That's why it can seem easier to manifest a bad mood than a good one. The waterfalls are already established. So are the ones for disappointment, abandonment, blame, victimization and many more.

We all create our own reality, but consciously creating your reality is about setting up new desired waterfalls and allowing them to flow and when the unwanted ones start to gain momentum, being quick to change to a preferred waterfall.

5 Easy Steps to Change your Life

From the time you were born, there has been guidance and knowledge available from within. Not for one moment have you been alone, or without the advantage of a higher perspective. You came into this life knowing there was no risk, as nothing was ever too big to handle. You were also aware that getting what you wanted involved focusing your attention in the direction of joy.

 That knowledge is still active within you, and it is empowering to know you have built-in guidance. You only need to be guided by your moods, which show how you are feeling, and how you are feeling is indicative of what you are creating in your reality. These five steps will help you stay on track.

1. Recognize your mood.
2. Change to a better feeling mood.
3. Imagine what you want and how it would feel.
4. Use your Mood Barometer and the people around you as a guide for how you're going and
5. Constantly look for things to feel good about.

These steps can be used to realign each area of your life, whether they be health, relationships, money, or any other.

If you can imagine a new desire and you can feel the power of it and get excited, it has become a part of your pool of creation. You don't need to keep focusing on the desire; you only need to stop focusing on the lack of it, no matter what the desire consists of, whether a new life, a new car, a puppy, or a baby. There is no difference between manifesting a large or a small desire, but many people find it much easier to imagine a small desire than a large one.

It is no easier to imagine healing a sore finger than a cancer but many people just know the sore finger will heal and have a lot of resistance around the cancer. When creating, ask yourself what it is that you want and does it feel easy? Or are you fighting with yourself over the thing that you want for any reason? Are you grabbing the handle or the blade of the sword on this subject?

The Universe does not judge or decide who is worthy and who is not. Judgment is purely a man-made creation, and many have chosen to believe that some are worthy and others aren't. The Universe delivers in response to your request, no matter who you are. There is no judgment, and it is *you* who feels worthy or the opposite. When you feel worthy then you match the desires you have requested, and the

Universe delivers accordingly. You are at one with the Universe and life flows beautifully.

Your Feelings Guide Your Reality

As you look at something or someone, your eyes record what you are seeing. As they record what you see, you process the vision according to your current emotional state.

A friend of mine was writing a book and was very excited about it. She was so sure that this book was going to change her life and create that which had always been a cherished dream. The mere thought of the opportunities this book was going to create inspired feelings of excitement and anticipation. She felt empowered, and knowing. This was the opportunity she had been waiting for all her life, and it was now. There was no thought of the book *not* creating what she wanted.

She was right. The book not only became successful, but also opened doors to many paths of fulfillment, including areas she had never thought about. This was not a chance event, but something that had been consciously created; she had believed it, felt the joy and nurtured this dream well before her success became a self-fulfilling prophecy. When you want something so much that you know it will come about, and are so excited for the plan to be fulfilled that you know beyond any doubt that it will be so, it can't ever be otherwise. When you are focused in a particular direction that becomes your reality.

Her dream of success would not have come about if she had not become excited and felt that it had already happened. That was the key to her dreams unfolding. If you have a dream but not the knowing and the excitement, you haven't ignited the dream enough for it to show up in your reality yet. If you can imagine the dream as if it is a sure thing, and are excited that it is coming, so excited that you see it in your mind in your waking hours, then you are becoming a match to your dream. Your mind doesn't know the difference between what is real, and what is imagined. Your reality responds to your emotions.

Dreams are neither dormant nor fleeting; they are alive and real. It's your ability to ignite visions with the flame of emotion that allows them to take shape and come forth. When you feel your way to the edge of reality, the only thing that can happen is that reality expands to accommodate the 'more' you are imagining. Creation is never-ending expanding moments of joy and excitement, strung together to create something new and extraordinary. It begins with you.

Giving Up is Good

The term 'giving up' has a meaning that is diversified and varied but for many it is classified as meaning 'failure'. One of the most difficult decisions in life is deciding when is the right time to give up on something?
Is it when you fall constantly?
Is it when you become financially destitute and can't keep going?
Is it when your health is at risk?
Is it when you are broken?
Or maybe it is never?

In this world of striving for success as a means of comparing your life to another's, there is a popular belief that giving up is for the weak. The adage that you keep doing what you are doing, and eventually it will work, reigns supreme. However, if you are hitting your head against a brick wall, it's more likely your head will give way first. If you're slicing a golf ball, or you're constantly tired, then you're doing something that's not working, and you have probably been doing it for a long time. In these cases, it seems obvious that something must change.

I remember being in a Multi-Level Marketing company once, and I had to knock on doors to get sales. It was a numbers game, and the more doors you knocked on, the more chance you would have of success, right? In theory that was correct, but in reality, it was quite different. When you had been rejected many times, and expected to get rejected again, your confidence was so low that you were better off to give up, as the persistence was causing more harm than good. If you were a sprinter who was practicing a technique that didn't improve your time, you would want to give up on that one and use another. A national swimmer I know wanted the best coach in the nation, but the two were of a similar personality, and they battled each other constantly. It just wasn't a winning combination. Not all methods work for everyone. It seems obvious that one should change techniques under such circumstances, but that is all giving up is about. It's never about giving up on life; it's about letting go of the pushing against something that isn't working, so that another solution can present itself.

Change Your Reality and You Change Your Life

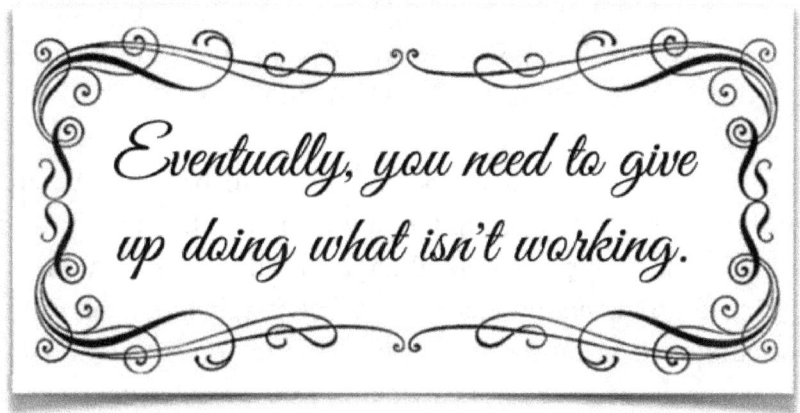

Eventually, you need to give up doing what isn't working.

When you get to a stage that it's emotionally uncomfortable doing something, that's when you should give up. You give up doing it this way and let it go. You don't give up on your dreams and desires, though; you hold on to the dream and remind yourself why you want it. But the quicker you let go of what isn't working, the quicker the Universe can deliver a method that will work.

The path to any success is not in doing something wrongly enough times that it changes. The path to success is letting go of what doesn't work so that what does work can emerge. The problem and the solution are never in the same emotional space. Desperation will never emerge victorious, but if you can give up on the feeling of desperation long enough to find a mood of hope, then opportunity emerges in the most unlikely of places. Pushing against something so hard that it hurts is a difficult way of living life as the desired results only come when you let go of the pushing against. Hard work needs to be fun for it to be worthwhile, and the Universe is your partner in successful decisions.

How do you find a coach who can help you refine a method that works for you? There is no need to look outside yourself; you have a coach within. Your emotions guide your path, and the Mood Map shows you which direction you are moving in. Understanding this Mood Map is the coach that will lead you to victory.

Giving up the pain and fear does not serve to banish your dreams. Quite the opposite; they are ignited by excitement. It is only struggle that leads to suffering. Emotional anguish will not take you to where you want to go, as no amount of physical or mental action can make up for emotional misalignment. Use your emotions to guide you, and give up early, when pain is evident. Life wasn't supposed to be difficult or a struggle, so be careful which patterns you practice. Give up the ones that don't serve you, and create new ones that do.

Change Your Reality and You Change Your Life

Attitude Dimension

Six Dimensions of Healing

What is Attitude Anyway?

"You cannot tailor-make the situations in life but you can tailor-make the attitudes to fit those situations before they arise." Zig Ziglar

It's not how you present yourself to the world that defines you, but your reaction to what you notice. Attitude is your demeanor in life. It is how you process what life has presented you with. This is a learned behavior that has been cultivated over many lifetimes. Attitude does not commence as an outward expression but an inward observation and observing your thoughts is the key to understanding your own attitude towards life. There are as many different attitudes as there are opinions but they can easily be categorized into two main sections, which are a *positive* or a *negative* attitude. Nobody is born with a negative attitude but has developed a negative response to some situations. Even people with a predominantly positive attitude will feel negative sometimes, as it is common to waiver from one to the other. Consciously moving towards a positive attitude is pivotal to a healthy and happy life. When people tell you they have a positive attitude yet their life is in chaos, you know their understanding is deceptive, as your life will always reflect your attitude.

When I was a teenager, it was regularly endorsed by 'those in authority' that I had a bad attitude. Teachers, parents and non-significant others would exasperatedly conclude I had a bad attitude. Throughout my life, I had come to believe I had been born and was consequently stuck with an unfavorable attitude. What these supposedly well-meaning people never explained was that the affliction was changeable. (To be fair maybe they never knew it was a pattern and could be changed.) Having no idea it was a learned behavior that had been adopted, resentment became my frequent mood. Remembering the great relief in my early 20's with a daughter and a divorce, that I could change this behavior, opened the world to me and I never looked back.

Whatever you don't like about yourself is changeable and change doesn't cost a cent. It's completely free! You may spend money on a book or become inspired at a seminar but all the best information in the world is useless unless you consciously choose to change. Just as attitude is an inward observation, change is an inner choice. Death and change are the only two certainties in life. Most people fear both, yet change can be fluid and as simple as making a choice.

Change is feared because of the perceived discomfort in the unknown as if controlling the future somehow makes it easier. When you're aware things aren't working out as you want there is much more discomfort in noticing more of the same, so change should be a blessing. Getting fired from a job you don't like isn't necessarily a conscious decision because the consequences of not having an income are not desirable but if you can move with the change rather than get stuck in fear, doors will open in a more welcome direction. Nothing needs to be done outwardly but much to be decided upon inwardly.

As a new path is chosen and habits of thought that are encouraging dominate, doors open to opportunities that until recently were hidden.

If your reality could benefit from a positive attitude, then conscious change is the next step. There is a wonderful <u>method of change</u> that is completely painless and anonymous. No one ever need know. You will need at least 30 minutes on your own in a quiet place. Find a pen or pencil and a piece of paper.

- Draw a line down the center of the landscape page. On the left side, place a heading at the top, 'How I see myself'. On the right side, place a heading 'How I would like to see myself'.

- On the left-hand side under the heading, 'How I see Myself', write a list of every word and phrase that comes to mind. You will need to be honest here. It is a private conversation and is for your eyes only. Write down how you think others feel about you. Write the words and phrases of the things you don't like as well. This is a description of how you really see yourself. How you look, think and feel. When you have exhausted the adjectives, give yourself a couple of minutes to digest this before moving on to the next part.

- On the half under the heading 'How I would like to see Myself' imagine yourself as the person you have always wanted to be and write a list of descriptions and emotions about how you want to see yourself. How do you want to look, think and feel? How would you like to be described by others? If you are having trouble with this, just imagine yourself at your funeral listening to your eulogy. At the end of your life, how would you like people to describe you? What would you like people to say about you? Take some time to ponder and imagine this as reality. Place your signature at the bottom of this list only.

- The next step is to tear the page down the centerline. Throw the 'How I see Myself' half away or burn it if you want. Keep the half with the signature and put it away. There is no need to look at it again or to say it aloud as reinforcement is not necessary to change the path of your life.

This is your order to the Universe for a new path, a different direction for your journey. Take this piece of paper out in a couple of years and see how many of the descriptions on the list can be checked off. You will be pleasantly surprised.

The only reason a person would display a bad attitude is if they feel the Universe does not yield to them. Feeling a victim of circumstance can create resentment and give a jaded perspective. When someone doesn't have knowledge, or understanding of how they attract what is in their life and feel they aren't in control of their own reality, then there is often fear that others have control over their life. This is never the case and as you create a new perspective, so too does your attitude begin to change. You are the one who has the ability to change your self-talk from negative to positive and when you do, changes are imminent. The Universe is always consistent so when you ask for what you want with your vibration and not your words, excitement is created within that changes your attitude to one of knowing things are working out. Relax your mind and gently enjoy life with a zest and enthusiasm that maintains a positive attitude.

You were born to make manifest the joys of life.

Right and Wrong Decisions

Making a decision can be difficult when emotion is invested in the outcome. The path is lined with reasons to make a choice and not to make a choice. We all want to be sure that the choice we've made is right, as making a right decision is perceived to create positive consequences. But how do you know whether a decision is right or wrong? Do you measure it upon the outcome, does it elevate you in society's eyes, and does it make you a lot of money or maybe please others? The first question to ask yourself is "What makes my decision right?"

There are times when people seem frozen in their ability to make a decision that seems important. Fear of making the wrong decision is a common reason for procrastinating but sometimes there's not enough information to gain clarity and so the decision-making process isn't automatic. When enough information has been gathered that supports a favorable outcome the decision isn't difficult at all as it's the next logical step to take.

There are times in everyone's life that seem stagnant. Movement here or there seems elusive, as there is a lack of direction where decisions don't come into focus. Dr Seuss describes this stagnant time as the 'Waiting Place' in his inspiring rendition of life, *Oh the Places We'll Go*. This is the time that a life changing decision is not the next step. Instead it would be preferable to align yourself with Source Energy so that clarity is gained and no decision needs to be made. Meditation, sleep, writing lists of aspects about your life that you love, playing with the kids or the dog, walking along the beach and enjoying nature. These are some activities that will bring you into the mode of aligned decision making which is the space where opportunities are actively waiting. This is a place of focus where all the decisions you make are inspired.

Contrary to popular belief there are no right or wrong choices. When you feel good about an opportunity and move into the path of that choice it is called an inspired decision. You back yourself and that makes the decision right. All decisions have the seeds of greatness but you need to believe in them as worry will undermine the best of decisions. Making a choice then regretting the decision is decision remorse where you commence to back yourself and later become overwhelmed with doubt. Even a seemingly wrong decision can be made right by believing in it.

When uncomfortable decisions were made in the family that affected their emotional well-being, such as job loss or divorce, many children learned that decision making was painful. This creates the seeds of fear about making a right decision rather than learning the joy of making choices. Unless children are brought up to value the decisions that form their lives, they don't gain balance from noticing the myriad of choices that work smoothly. There are so many decisions that make up a day that most people aren't even aware they are constantly making decisions, let alone thinking about teaching their children the benefits.

Making a Decision

As there is no handbook on recognizing a right decision you can be waiting a long time to notice. One of our clients was having difficulty in recognizing the next step for her and her family. Taking any step available, even a small one, and making a decision to get to the next opportunity, then the next, and so on, gathers momentum along the way. Decision-making is rather like a hilly landscape. You want to make a decision that moves you all the way to the horizon, but as you can't see the horizon from where you're standing you just need to make the decision that gets you to the next hill. From there you have a new vantage point from which to make the next choice and the next.

Life is a series of decisions and nobody can really judge what is a right choice and what is wrong for you. We expect to move in a straight line from where we are to where we want to go, because we're under the illusion that there is a destination to reach, but there isn't any destination; that's why it's called a journey. The twists and turns are supposed to be enjoyed, as that's where the fun is, and fun is a purpose not a destination. When there is no expectation attached to a decision, it is unlikely ever to be considered wrong. Most major decisions you make will not turn out as you expect but it doesn't mean they're wrong. The tendency is to look for the lesson behind a decision gone wrong, but the wrongness is only in comparison to the expectation and not the experience. Life is a journey and sometimes decisions are a scouting trip, getting us ready for the main event, of which there may be several. When you trust the process of life and understand all your decisions are right, a broader understanding of life will be gained, from which you will enjoy your decisions.

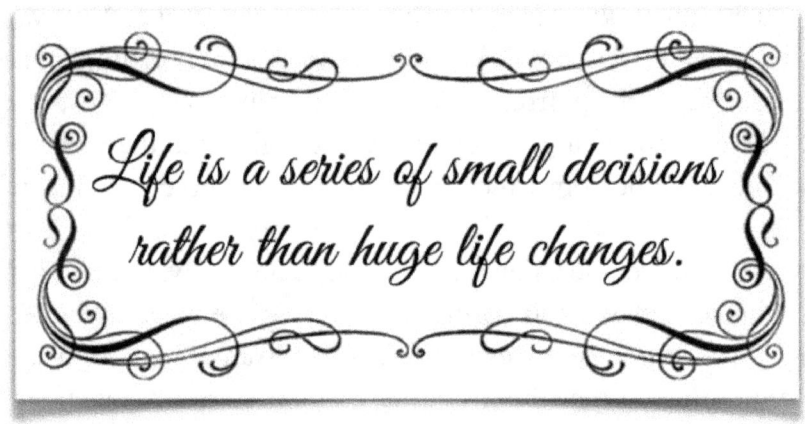

Life is a series of small decisions rather than huge life changes.

Acknowledging the decisions that are made throughout the day is an empowering way to build a 'Decision Bank'. This is a catalog of the choices you have made both big and small. When you have established a conscious catalog, you'll understand how good you are at making choices and approach decisions more confidently. Decision-making can be fun and easy or it can be fraught with fear and the difference between a right and wrong decision is the emotion. All choices have ups and downs with both wanted and unwanted aspects attached to them. When you get excited about a choice before it is made your focus is on what is wanted. The decision-making then becomes easy, as it 'feels right'.

Any decision is better than no decision as standing in the 'Waiting Place' is not much fun. Look at the choices you have available and imagine yourself moving down the path of each one. Which feels better, that one or the other? Make the decision based on which feels better, then back yourself and turn your attention to feeling great. Choose to move into a perspective of feeling great about any choice you have made, whether it is in the past or the present. Have fun making decisions as the Universe is on your side.

Finding Inspired Answers

"Positive thinking will let you do everything better than negative thinking will." Zig Ziglar

A positive attitude is a focused path towards what is wanted. When you have faith in your future, you have power in your present, so when you have something to look forward to and something to get excited about, a positive attitude is what turbo-charges the journey. Contrast is thought that opposes feeling good. It can be instigated by a situation, a person or a thought but you know when it arrives, as it feels angry, depressing, discouraging, critical or one of many other uncomfortable feelings. These are the emotions that keep your dreams distant. There is a positive purpose to contrast as the vehicle that creates clarity, because it helps to demarcate the wanted from the unwanted aspects of life. When you have decided what you do want because you have experienced what you don't want, a positive attitude makes the difference between manifesting or not. Choosing to focus on what is wanted is the basis of a positive attitude as it is consciously choosing thoughts that benefit your well-being.

A negative attitude comes from getting stuck in the contrast. When you feel wrongly accused of something it is common to tell people what has happened. You tell your story to seek support in feeling wronged. There may be a lot of support for you out there, but by regurgitating the story you keep it alive. It then becomes difficult to move your mood until your attitude changes as your story keeps you stuck. Life is a self-fulfilling prophecy, as the more you notice what is going wrong the more that goes wrong.

We all experience both positive and negative attitudes. People have asked me if I am a positive person. By that they mean, do I have a positive attitude? I must be honest and say not always, but I am aware enough to know when my mood has moved from Source, because it creates discomfort. I know that when I'm ready to stop telling the story of who or what wronged me, my attitude begins to change, and I create a new and improved reality.

It's probably helpful to know that famous people from every walk of life have experienced negative attitudes. They have sung the song of who wronged them, and the woe that has befallen them on a grand scale. It's only when they cease the complaining that they move into a positive attitude and gravitate towards finding a solution. Nothing great is ever achieved by discomfort, yet we build monuments to celebrate struggle and make heroes from hardship because we only hear the struggle part of the story. People don't want to accept that life is easy and supposed to be fun, as how would they be able to justify their discomfort?

The reason a positive attitude is so effective is that it aligns you with the synchronicity of the Universe. No matter how insurmountable a problem may seem, a positive attitude aligns you with the solution and a negative attitude aligns you with more problems. Solutions come into focus when you aren't fixated on what's wrong, as the problem and the solution are never in the same space. One is in a negative space, the other a positive. It's up to you to choose which attitude to align yourself with.

The good news is that you can find the attitude you need at any time by changing your perspective, as when your perception of a situation makes you unhappy there are only two choices, more of the same or something different. To move on to something different may seem as though you are avoiding the situation but this isn't the case. You are using the leverage of a better feeling, unrelated subject to move you to a different perspective and help you gain clarity on all subjects.

The question to ask yourself is "Do you want to feel better about this subject?" The answer may seem obvious, but when a mood has been practiced so that it is entrenched, moving onto something different may not be wanted just yet. When there is momentum around blaming someone else for a situation, then choosing another perspective means there is no one left to blame. Many people not only want someone to blame for what happens in their life, they only feel comfortable when blaming another. Not everyone is ready to let go of that fragile balloon string.

In any emotional discomfort, you will find:

- Answers are elusive when in a mood that matches the problem
- Telling your story of woe creates more situations that are similar

When you feel discomfort or tension, it is an indicator that your opinion does not match the opinion your Higher Self holds on the same subject. There is nothing you really want to achieve by experiencing a mood of blame or any other uncomfortable emotions. They will not take you to where you want to go. When the answers finally arrive, you have let go of blame and are allowing yourself to move towards your Higher Self. As struggle ceases, there is a natural flowing in the direction of well-being where the answers to all life's questions are found.

When you are not doing anything to push against a subject, a natural state of well-being will prevail. The advantage of moving into a mood of well-being is that everything you want is there. This is where all your hopes and dreams gather. It is like moving in your mind from a war-torn city ravaged by fear, to the tranquility of a country town where hope, love and opportunity abound.

Source Energy is always guiding the way, but the voice of Source is often mistaken. When you are afraid, the voice of Source can sound like fear. When you are angry it can sound like blame and when you are discouraged, doubt can be the voice of Source. The voice of Source doesn't always sound like angel wings and encouragement, because when you're depressed, you can't hear angels and you don't believe the encouragement.

Taking action without inspiration is living life the hard way, as instead of allowing the 90% to unfold and inspire you to action, you use the 10% action to try and move the 90% to where you want to go. This requires a tremendous amount of effort, as there is always another block to push against. Many books and seminars endorse taking action first, but unless your inspired mood is a match with the action you are taking, then life will be a struggle. It doesn't mean you won't get to the goal in the end. Many famous people have taken action when they weren't inspired and pushed against obstacles again and again. The reason they made it was because eventually they let go of the struggle by changing the subject and giving up on the effort. They inadvertently flowed with their well-being, which is the 90% of manifestation and eventually the inspiration came, easily and peacefully. Their choices were inspired; people and opportunities showed up; the timing was uncanny. It wasn't because of the ten years of struggle, but the year of letting go. As a society, we don't celebrate coming into alignment with the Higher Self, and the ease and flow that bring inspired creations; instead we focus on the struggle that led the way. The struggle wasn't necessary, as it only delayed the manifestation. The action to be taken is always about feeling good enough to be a mood match with your dreams and then taking the opportunities that present themselves.

Make peace with all your problems and allow the solutions to unfold.

Your Perspective is Important

Sandy was a client who found complaint with a cleaning contract that didn't pay very well. There was a lot of work involved, and the effort didn't seem to be worth it. This was her own business, so she knew the contract was a choice. After a thoughtful moment or two, she shrugged her shoulders and commented that her hips were getting smaller, and the job was a good workout, as she had worked up a sweat. The conclusion Sandy came to was that she was getting paid to 'work out', and this was cheaper than a gym membership. There were benefits. Sandy had created a new perspective, which changed her mood and created a new reality.

Looking at a situation one way and then changing how you look at it to affect a different mood, is consciously changing your perspective.

Perspective is much like looking at a narrated documentary. Being told the story through the eyes of another person, you are transported on a journey that is taken through the perspective of the storyteller. It's usually called an angle or agenda. If a storyteller's perspective is one of pity for the downtrodden, you will feel anger at the perpetrators of their injustices. It is their intention that you see the story from – their perspective. The same story could be narrated from the angle of saving the environment and you could have a completely different mood. You are being taken on a deliberate ride and only the storyteller knows the destination. The same story can be narrated with different perspectives and will evoke different moods. We each have our stories and we are the narrators in our own lives.

You will always find evidence of what you are searching for with any perspective. When you are feeling great, you will find evidence that the world is great. When you are feeling angry, you will find evidence of the same mood all around you. You haven't stepped into another world; you have aligned yourself through your perspective, with people that make you feel more of the same.

"It's not what you look at that matters, it's what you see."
Henry David Thoreau

Perspective is not only what you see, but also how you interpret what is in your view, and it is a method of automatic processing. Perspective is as unique and individual as you are. How you look at your life is a work in progress, and your perspective has been honed by the experiences in your life, and the choices you have made throughout your lifetime.

There are those who may have a similar mood to yours, but none can have the same perspective, as yours is born from your particular experiences. Your perspective changes as you grow, but you can determine the direction your growth takes. The way you feel about a situation is determined by the perspective you already have, so it makes sense that the way your immediate future unfolds is determined by your current perspective. When you look at something and decide that life doesn't work, and that the world is crumbling around you, you are choosing by your moods to process life in a way that throws more obstacles in your path.

As you are the creator of your own reality, the perspective used to process situations and observations makes a difference to your mood, and consequently to your future. Perspective is a way of looking at things, and when you change your mood, you influence your perspective, and see things differently. A new perspective creates a new reality.

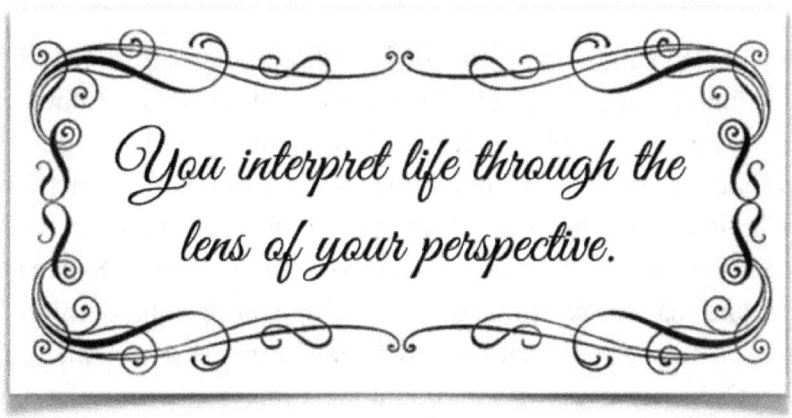

You interpret life through the lens of your perspective.

The way you perceive life can be a burden or a marvelous gift. Perspectives are soft and malleable, not written in stone. They want to be molded and used in a way that serves you in your highest venture, as they are your best allies. The great news is that all patterns are changeable if you don't like your perspective. Your perception of a situation is indicated by your mood, as when your perspective looks for what's not working, your mood is low on the Mood Map and you can feel the discomfort. There is nothing in this life you are burdened with, and by changing your perspective, you create a different future and change your life.

Ellen's Story

Ellen was having trouble moving beyond a situation in her life that had created bad feelings between her and her close friend. She knew there was no wrong and right in all of this, but still felt as though she had been betrayed. There were many feelings that would come up whenever she thought about the situation or her close friend, and so she avoided contact with the friend.

When I asked Ellen if she was ready to find a new perspective and let go of blaming her friend for the situation, there was hesitation. She felt, like many people, that to stop blaming and let go of the resentment somehow absolved the other from any wrongdoing. I asked Ellen how she wanted to feel about this situation, because, clearly, she didn't like the perspective she had now. She came to understand that her pain was due to having an opposing opinion to her Source on this subject, and not with the friend. Ellen wanted a new perspective, a new way of looking at the situation, because her current perspective was causing exhaustion. She realized that her longing to find peace with herself about the subject was more important to her than holding on to blame. She agreed to let go of trying to make it right in her mind and asked her Higher Self for another way of looking at this, one that made her feel better. It was a decision that helped her find peace with the subject.

There are many ways of looking at a situation and if the way you are looking at it causes you emotional pain, ask for another way until you find a perspective that is peaceful and right for you. If I am ever stuck and going around in my head over some situation or person, I tend to say with some conviction, "Show me another perspective. I don't like this one, so I must be wrong. Show me another way of looking at this." This method came from 'A Course in Miracles', (Schucman, 1976) and it works by stopping the chatter in the mind. The admission of being wrong interrupts the endless loop thoughts can take, enough to allow another perspective. The idea is not to look for another perspective but allow it to come. Similar to when you can't remember someone's name that you know, you just let it go and move on to something else, then the name comes when you least expect it. The reason a new perspective can be an advantage is that it makes you feel better and gives relief. A new perspective provides a new and improved mood.

Body Health

No matter which method you choose, changing your perspective on a subject can bring you into the frequency of the solution rather than the frequency of the problem. The problem and the solution are always on the opposite ends of the scale so when the problem is in focus, the solution is not. Moving thoughts off the subject is the key to finding yourself in alignment with a solution just as finding a new way of looking at any problem is moving towards what is wanted.

A healthy body depends on a balanced perspective, as the cells of your body eavesdrop on your self-talk. (Refer to *Physical* Dimension chapter.) When you choose to look at things in a way that makes you feel good, your perspective is enhancing your body's health. Changing perspective is the most effective method of healing you could choose, and can be used to enhance physical modalities, medication, alternative therapies and energy healing. You can't change your life without changing your perspective, so change your perspective and you change your life.

** Asking Source for another way of looking at things is just one method of changing perspective. Alternative methods are to be found in the Six Dimensions of Healing Workbook and on the website 6DimensionsofHealing.com

Become the Person you Love

Whether in your business or personal life, you have become the person you are through the experiences and beliefs adopted along the way. As you can't experience outside of your beliefs, you may want to look at the person you have become to notice if that is the person you are happy with. It is not necessary to change to a businessperson when conducting business. You are automatically a businessperson if you are in business. The values used in business will carry over into your friendships and family as there is no separation, so it makes sense to be the person you want to be rather than someone you don't admire. There is nothing more persuasive in business than an insightful, confident person and this can be achieved by aligning your mood with Source Energy. You will never be happy making dreams smaller to fit your beliefs, so expanding your expectations to fit your dreams is the key to unlocking a bountiful future.

Whenever you are unsure of which direction to choose, a visualization meditation can help you find clarity. Follow the relaxation techniques set out in the relaxation section (p97) and imagine it is the end of your life and you are looking down at your own funeral. You can hear what all the people are saying about you. What would you like to hear? What is the legacy you leave to your family and the world?

Are you on track to becoming the person this eulogy was about? If not, now is the time to change direction and become the person you really want to be. This is the clarification needed to create a new future.

Everything about your life is changeable including who you are, what values you have and what you stand for, as these are all attributes you adopted. The person you are now is most likely still a product of the environment in which you grew up, where, rather than conscious choices creating positive beliefs, reactions to experiences created default belief patterns. Now is a good time to refine who you are, by being aware of the moods you want to engage. Whatever you are feeling is a direct order to the universe for more of the same, as you don't ask with words but with dominant emotions. When you want to attract a particular type of person or people into your relationships, you must become those traits you are seeking. If you want loyalty in a relationship you must become loyal, if you are looking for fun, you must be a fun person and when you are seeking respect, you must respect yourself.

To redirect your path and clarify the person you want to be, make a choice as to how you want to feel, as soon as you awake.

Every morning is literally a brand-new day. As soon as you awake, you have the opportunity to choose how you want to respond as your day unfolds, and your response to that unfolding makes a big difference in the conscious creation of your reality. As Michael Bublé sings, "It's a new dawn, it's a new day, it's a new life for me and I'm feelin' good." from the hit single, *Feelin' Good.*

Desires, Goals and Dreams

Desires, goals and dreams are very different.
A *desire* is communication with the Universe through thought and focus. You are constantly having thoughts, ideas and emotional responses all of which create desire. Usually, you are unaware of the desires you have created until they manifest around you, and even then, most people are unaware that what has manifested is their desire. The Universe is constantly responding to desires, even when it seems nothing is happening, as the Universe is in a state of constant motion. Your life is a series of constantly manifesting desires. They can grow from what is wanted, or in response to something that isn't wanted, so it's easy to think that, because something has manifested in your life that you don't like, you couldn't have requested it. But manifestations aren't about luck or karma; they aren't because you have been a good person; and there is no need to qualify to deserve anything you ask for.

A desire is thought that becomes emphasized by your emotions. These focused emotions now set the Universe in motion to fulfill your request and when your dominant mood matches your desire, it paves the way for manifestation. Focusing on something wanted is creating a desire that is wanted, and focusing on something unwanted is creating a desire that is unwanted. Be aware of what you give your attention to, as we live in an inclusion-based Universe so when your focus remains on something you don't want, you are asking to include that which you don't want in your life. You become a conscious creator when you are aware of your thoughts and emotions, as you have the ability to consciously create a reality you love.

Goals encompass many desires. They have a time frame, because they're related to a collection of attractions. You may want to lose weight because you are excited about your sister's wedding, so the date for the goal is your sister's wedding. The goal also encompasses feeling good, having a wonderful time, feeling attractive, being able fit into your favorite dress, finding a wonderful partner and many more wonderful experiences. The expectation of this goal is to feel great and there will be many more desires that will manifest in the achievement. The expectation of a goal is probable, and an active goal needs a dominantly positive attitude, which determines a positive outcome. When you ask yourself what you want and why you want it, you can then focus upon how it will feel when it is achieved and as you start to feel at one with the outcome, the goal unfolds into a series of manifesting desires.

Dreams are much broader than goals, and have many components. A dream is life changing and created in the imagination, which plants the seed for many goals and desires. These desires may not seem to be related to the dream, but they are paving the way for your 'overnight success'. Dreams feel like possibilities for a grand future. They live in the imagination and feel wonderful as they grow and change, just as you do. They don't get closer to you, but grow with you as you move closer to the dream until you are a vibrational match. Eventually this changes the dream from a possible to a probable outcome, which will naturally transition into goals and desires.

Dreams exist to be enjoyed and, as the imagining becomes fun, growth is experienced. The expansion of humanity is created through dreams, and even though it may seem distant, a dream is never out of reach. If you have the ability to imagine the dream, you have the ability to achieve that dream. It's not a goal yet so be aware that you are inspired before taking action, as action without inspiration can lead to discouragement. Allow the dream to grow and expand with the understanding that every desire you have gets you closer and closer to the dream. Just as you can't stand on the other side of the world without traveling, neither can you manifest your dream without moving in that direction through goals and desires. Believing in your dream determines the path of your goals and desires and each step moves you in this direction. If there was no emotional gap that needed to close to achieve the dream, it would be a desire rather than a dream.

Recognizing a dream versus a goal is the key to joy. So many people are taught to put dates on their dreams and that is a recipe to squash your dream. Your job is to feel good as you are always moving in the direction of your dreams when you feel great. The way to know the difference between a dream and a goal is whether it feels probable or possible right now. Understanding that your dreams are always alive, and that they pave the way for all the goals and desires created will make you happy with life, no matter what it brings.

The expansion of who you are is the gentle calling of your desires. You are the dreamer and your Higher Self moves and expands into the fullness of the desire as soon as it is hatched. It is only when you doubt your own ability to realize the desires already created that you move in the opposite direction of the expanded you. This will only serve in creating tension, which will be felt as emotional, then physical, pain.

You have already become so much more than when you were born, as each desire expands who you are and this gives a new, broader vantage point from which to now dream. There will always be a dream, and there will always be a dreamer because if there wasn't, the Universe would not evolve and cease to exist. Your dreams are important not only to you, they are important to all that exists, both physical and non-physical.

Our Journey Spans Lifetimes

There are many people in this lifetime with which we have had relationships in other lifetimes. The reasons are many and varied, as there could be a higher purpose for two souls to connect for the greater good, or familiar souls may provide a support system for your growth this time around. Whatever the reason, there are no mistakes. You invited the influential people in your life, to assist your journey. Many people come into your life to assist your path of emotional growth. Even the scoundrels you don't like will pave your path, as growth is inevitable. Often you have made a choice in which direction your emotional growth will take before you enter this body. In this way, you have co-created with people to help along the way. Imagine if you wanted to grow in an area of compassion and your current path was focused in an opposite direction, because you haven't noticed the opportunities presented for compassion, along comes a nudge in the form of a scoundrel, a car accident, the loss of a job, or many other divergences that change the direction of your focus.

The byproduct of an unwanted situation is change, which creates permanent growth for the soul that is you. Opportunities for change are gentle at first, and become more dominant when ignored. When change has been ignored to the point of crisis, a situation will occur to change the direction. These are situations that recreate your life path.

It's easy to get stuck in the reality of a situation, but a situation only exists to change the emotional direction of your life path. When you understand all situations for the opportunity they present, you'll find yourself becoming aware of the indicators of emotional discomfort before they create havoc in your life.

If your life is starting to feel out of control, take a step back to observe the situation from the perspective of a third person. Rather than blaming others, the first step is to stop. Stop the chatter, the self-talk and the desperation. Don't talk about it or discuss the situation with others, and don't keep mulling it over in your head. Slow the pace of your thoughts, as you're looking for a solution when you're in the problem, and there is no solution to be found. Meditation will help to ease the momentum of thinking, and when you can distance yourself from the negative thoughts long enough to turn in the natural direction of relief, then you are turning in the direction of the solution. The problem and the solution are never in the same space. When you are in the frequency of sickness, you can't find health. When you are focused on unwanted thoughts, you can't find what is wanted. When you are focused on whom did you wrong, you can't find peace and you always deserve to feel peaceful.

Every experience creates growth for the soul.

We choose these nudges of realignment often before we arrive in this body, so that we can grow in a particular direction. Our personality moves through time with us, and the growth we experience stays with our soul forever. The emotional paths chosen are many and varied, but all place you in situations that create the best opportunity to grow into the oneness of that emotion. Opportunities will be uncomfortable situations as emotional buttons are pressed, but eventually you become accustomed to the new patterns, and your soul expands to incorporate the now peaceful emotion. This may happen quickly, or it may not happen at all in this lifetime. Because of the lack of understanding with opportunities, people tend to push against them by blaming others, or reacting in many ways, keeping focus on the situation and this serves to create louder and more dominant opportunities. Finding a way of making peace with agitation on any subject allows you to accept the opportunity of growth. The opportunities are gentle when we are younger, but they become more pronounced as we age, mostly because our patterns of thought become rigid. If you still don't grow in the direction as much as you wanted, you'll choose different circumstances next lifetime, but you will choose the same paths of growth in different situations until you incorporate with the emotional growth. You have already made your choices, and understanding them is the best ally you have. Your Higher Self already knows the emotional balance, and you will be uncomfortable each time that button is pressed until you catch up and know it too.

In reviewing your life after you pass over, you may see that you felt abhorrent towards a neighbor because of his color for instance, or you were annoyed with people in your life that you perceived were wrong. Even though there were opportunities to create in many directions, you will understand that your growth path was evident, through the situations you lived in. Your soul is never finished on its journey of evolution, so you would choose a different set of circumstances to give you varied opportunities next lifetime. The scoundrels that are causing you so much trouble are usually the ones that are giving you the best opportunity to grow in the direction of your intention. When you can change your attitude to perceive difficulties as opportunities for growth, change will flow easily and effortlessly into your life.

Changing your attitude to see life from a broader perspective is advantageous to smooth, easy growth. You aren't consciously aware of the bigger picture, so you just need to trust that someone who is guiding you does. Your Higher Self has your best interests at heart, and it is their job to let you know when you are closer to Source or further away, and for this communication they use the Mood Map. I was once waiting for someone in my car and was parked near the exit ramp of a large freeway. As I sat there watching, I noticed two accidents waiting to happen. The interesting thing was that something moved each car in a different direction at the last moment, and they weren't even aware that this action had probably saved their lives; yet I wonder how many were annoyed because of the last moment change of direction? That's the bigger picture.

It's easy to change your attitude about something by looking at it from a different perspective. This is pivotal in changing your reality. Whenever you feel physical or emotional pain, it is only because of your resistance and not your relationship with Source. Emotional pain is the tension felt between your opinion and the differing opinion of Source. Pain is never between you and another person, even if it seems that way and only you have the power to see it differently. When you do, you can transform pain into healing.

Sharing Energy

You may have noticed that you have an immense amount of energy when you feel excited. The emotions of love, joy, excitement, and fun all keep you buoyed up, as there is little need for sleep when you are in these moods. Tiredness or feeling drained is thinking in opposition to how your Higher Self thinks on the same subject. Offering a different opinion to your Higher Self will always make you feel emotionally drained, as you have moved farther away from Source. When this happens, two of the easiest ways to re-energize are either to sleep or to meditate. This helps to push the reset button and you can choose a new mood upon waking.

Darleen was a massage therapist who said she felt drained from giving. She had people around her all the time, and was convinced her job was wearing her out. She felt giving to people was draining and she didn't know what to do about it. Darleen's perspective was imbalanced, as she felt she was the giver, but we explained to her that she was a receiver, and not a giver. She could change her perspective, and tune in to Source as a receiver, and her ability to issue joy and healing would know no boundaries. Darleen didn't need to feel drained, as it was up to her to direct her mind and her mood to serve her and her clients beneficially.

Darleen didn't quite understand the receiving and sharing of energy so we explained it a little differently:

When you think you are giving endlessly, there is often the feeling of being drained, as you have not plugged yourself into Source Energy first. You are like a light bulb. The light bulb plugs into the energy source and it shines. This is often thought of as giving off light, but it isn't really giving anything. It is receiving from the energy source, which in the case of the bulb is electricity. People can benefit from the glow of the light, as their path is illuminated. It can light their way, but it doesn't give anything. It merely glows what it has received and so long as it is connected to a source of electricity, its glow is unlimited.

Just like the light bulb, you need to stay plugged in to your Source Energy to have an endless supply of love and healing energy. You emit your glow of energy, to which some are attracted, and of which others are afraid. Some may even try to turn your energy off, but your job is to plug yourself into your Energy Source and shine the glow of love. An unlimited number of people can receive your love, and you will always feel energized, as you are the receiver from an unlimited Source. When you disconnect yourself from the Energy Source, your love will not shine as brightly or last as long, as you have become the giver and your glow is limited. The more connected to Source you are, the brighter you shine.

Change Your Reality and You Change Your Life

Vibration Dimension

Six Dimensions of Healing

When to Take Action
"Nothing was ever created by a human being that was not first created in the imagination through desire." Napoleon Hill

There is a belief shared by many that when you want something, it is necessary to commence by taking action. The action referred to is physical and tangible. We would agree. When you are inspired, action is magnificent and empowering. You are moving in unison with the Universe, and the action taken is inspired and uplifting. However, inspiration is not usually the first step of creation. The first action to be taken is determining and refining within your own mind. When the physical action taken is not inspired action, it becomes counterproductive. This is how obstacles are created in the path. The Universe is patient and will wait until you've ceased pushing against your desire and only then, when you've shifted your mood, will unfold naturally. Taking action too soon is the single most common factor in defeat and discouragement. It's like pushing a loaded wheelbarrow uphill; you may still get there but you'll feel exhausted.

Creation is not supposed to feel that way. Life is not meant to be hard or tough. Everything you ever want is created in your imagination first. Thoughts mull around in a fertile breeding ground as they ignite passion in the imagination. The embryo of an idea is awaiting consent to grow by drawing more thoughts toward it to become an exciting concept. What you do next makes a difference. Your creation becomes similar to the novels where you choose your own ending from a multitude of options, so too do you choose the growth path of your burgeoning idea.

If you choose to tell someone about an idea before it has a chance to grow roots and they don't encourage your passion, there is a risk of killing the idea before it develops. When you keep the idea to yourself, developing and refining it in the mind, you allow the idea to establish before it is subjected to another's opinion. As the idea grows, it becomes stronger and gathers momentum. Even in your imaginings, the thought is forming into more than it was when you first had the idea. As you grow through experience, so does the constantly forming, organic idea, changing and developing with you. Because your mind doesn't know the difference between what's real and what's imagined, the thought grows and expands into fruition. This is the path that is lined with opportunities, such as a chance meeting leading to a step you had never thought of, allowing your idea to naturally manifest.

Resist the temptation to look for evidence that your idea has manifested into something tangible before it appears, as you'll probably be disappointed it hasn't done so. This is the singular most prominent obstacle people fall victim to, as noticing a manifestation hasn't occurred moves your attention to the lack of what you want. A subject is always two subjects, what *is* wanted and what *isn't* wanted. Noticing that a manifestation hasn't yet occurred is the subject of what isn't wanted and this changes your mood. It is a sure method of putting obstacles in your path, as what you want can't flow freely in your direction. If you have practiced this method, you aren't alone. It's a very common for people not to be a match with their desire and then blame something outside of them for it not manifesting. The solution is to move your imagination in the direction of what is wanted. Imagine what the idea, the thought; the dream is becoming, and how you will feel when it arrives. Keep your mood buoyant for as long as it takes.

The tendency when waiting for a desire to manifest is to take any action. Massive and physical action. It makes sense that if you take action when focused upon what hasn't arrived, the action taken will be in the form of impatience, doubt or desperation. The results will be situations with emphasized feelings of impatience, doubt, or desperation. Recognizing this mood and quickly changing it, is a natural process of refining.

Move into a mood of feeling excited and allow the idea to grow and inspire you to physical action. After all, the Universe is amassing all that you need for your dream to become a reality, and all you need do is stay excited until you feel inspired. This excitement spills over into your work, relationships and health and is a beneficial side effect of desire. It's when you're inspired that the phone rings with an obscure opportunity that is always different to the one expected. An offer comes out of nowhere, or a chance meeting becomes a stepping-stone to something bigger. You're inspired to go somewhere, or do something different from the usual. This method is known to us as 'coincidence', but is poignantly orchestrated by the idea that has taken shape and is eager to be born.

90% Rule

The workings of manifestation occur where you can't see the progress. In fact, as much as 90% of the progression takes place in the non-physical. Like an iceberg, what you see is small compared to what is hidden beneath the water. Thought is not only incredibly powerful, it's life giving. An idea starts with a small spark of thought, that thought becomes a thinker, which grows to a manifestation that can transform the world. By the time the manifestation of an idea occurs, it has become so much more than originally imagined, especially if the idea takes many years to manifest. Just like the iceberg, an idea may seem small, but there is much happening that is hidden below the surface. An idea is never dormant, but automatically gathers elements that enhance and grow as you do, so that when the idea becomes reality, it is hardly recognizable as the thought to which you once gave life. Much as a baby becomes an adult that has changed beyond recognition, so too does an idea mature and blossom. This thought and development is the process grows an idea into a dream.

A dream commences maturity by being nurtured in the non-physical, and gathering all the necessary ingredients in the advancement necessary for the rendezvous with you. This is the part of the iceberg you can't see, and yet it is still alive and vibrant, and when you are feeling great, the dream feels very close. When you aren't feeling great, it is easy to give up on the dream, because it hasn't arrived.

Never give up on your dreams because of the timing. Understand they are still in your vibration, real but unseen, forming into bigger and better versions. The timing of a manifestation has more to do with your emotional dimension being a match with your desire, than you taking action. This means, not only feeling great with your mood, but merging your imagination with your reality. It is in this merger that imagination becomes reality and you are a match with your desire. When something happens to make you diverge from the path of positive expectation, it is never wrong - only unwanted. During this time, it can be beneficial to understand that, because of the detour, you have expanded, and so has the dream. Stay routed in the imagination, as the key to keeping your dreams alive is getting excited about the idea as if it were still new and fresh. It is about to bloom into something truly wonderful and it's up to you to move into a mood of positive expectation about the imminent arrival.

The wonderful experience of having a dream you can believe in brings forth growth, so that you move in the direction of the desire. The dream doesn't move toward you, as it stays in the vibration of the joy in which it was created. Instead, you become the person to match the dream, so you move in the direction of the same joy in which the dream was created, and there lies the rendezvous. The dream doesn't come to you; you move toward the dream. There will always be dreams and desires that forge growth and joy in the hearts of all mankind.

Find your Direction by Feeling your Way

Some terms in the English language have now expanded to create ambiguous meanings. New Age, God, Love, Spiritual and Forgiveness have vastly different meanings across the broader population. As we create through emotions, these terms have become too ambivalent to use in communication. Loving someone because you are related is not the same as feeling appreciation and joy at the mention of their name. So, which love is love?

Desire is also one of those terms. To some it means knowing what you want, to others it is a wishing and hoping something wanted will happen. To many others, it is something they strive for with much effort. If desire conjures a feeling of excitement at having discovered a new direction on which to focus an exciting creation, then keep using the word. If it doesn't, change the word to something that does. 'Excitement' is a great alternative because it's easy to get excited about the word excitement. As many wonderful events have manifested in my life, I have been excited just thinking about them, and whilst the reality is good, the imagining, the creating, the mulling and the expectation is so much better. Not that the reality isn't wonderful, but the conjuring and developing of an idea to its peak has all the heights of excitement and none of the emotional pitfalls. Getting excited is so much more than a feeling and a manifestation; the feeling itself is a manifestation. If you can manifest the emotion, you can manifest the reality. Getting excited puts you on the same path as your desire, when you get excited; you are creating something wonderful that your Source is also excited about.

Expanding Vibration

Everyone in this world is a vibrational being, communicating through vibration. We are so natural at translating vibrational messages; we don't even realize we're doing so.

When I put my hands on and area of pain in a client's body, they often ask what I am doing, as the pain is relieved. The explanation offered is that as a healer I, like others of my kind, hold myself in a *high vibration*, a feel-good mood where all health and healing exists. When pain occurs whether emotional or physical, the vibration is compromised and a less vibrant mood is selected. Joy, love and excitement are the vibrations that facilitate optimum health and when the client removes their mind and relaxes, they too gently move towards this higher vibration. A healer acts as a bridge to a higher vibration.

You can understand vibration in different ways.

It can be like a grandfather clock that chimes seemingly to its own rhythm. If you put a line of grandfather clocks against the same wall, they will begin to swing their pendulums in unison. They have found synchronicity.

Have you ever gone to a party where all the guests are strangers? Some people you will instantly dislike and others seem like old friends. Translating vibration is conducted through your emotions. How you feel about anybody or anything is translation of vibration.

Why is this important to understand? Your vibration is a point of attraction, so how you feel right now is the indicator of what your vibration is communicating to the Universe; it is your vibrational request. Like the chiming of grandfather clocks, vibration attracts synchronicity, and your dominant vibration is what you are asking to receive. It is not words or thoughts that make up the request, but emotions. It isn't asking for material objects that form the substance of the request; it's an emotional request. If you are unsure of what your vibrational request has been, the people in your life will reflect your request. The reason it is important to understand is that you can change what you ask for, at any time.

Two vastly different examples of a vibrational request are:

1. Today, you are feeling great. Life is just wonderful; you can feel the effervescence of life bubbling within you. Noticing all the wonderful things in life seems automatic, and if someone cuts you off in traffic, you laugh and acknowledge they must be in a hurry, so you let them pass without a worry in the world. You never even notice how wonderful the people who surround you are, as everyone who comes into your life seems happy. Your order to the Universe is for more experiences of joy and appreciation.

2. You are feeling a bit ordinary today. The kids start fighting over breakfast, and they are going to be late for school. You tell them to hurry up, and a frown passes over your forehead at the realization that you're running late for a big day ahead. Now everything is a rush. Somebody cuts you off in traffic, so you yell at them and turn on the radio to keep you company. Listening to the news, you notice only negativity, and you have an opinion on each story. The frown is now etched on your forehead, and the day tends to find more unhappy people. Your order to the Universe is for anger and frustration.

Both of these scenarios are vibrational circumstances. They are attracting completely different situations because of the mood that is evoked. Through a vibration, you are connected to more situations that evoke the same mood. The Universe never discerns what is good for you and what is not; it just provides more of what you are asking and respects all of your choices. Remember, as a vibrational being you don't communicate with words. Take a moment to establish your vibrational request, which is reflected by your mood. When the mood is frustration, you are asking for more frustration to show up in your life. When the mood is one of anger, you're asking vibration is anger, and the Universe will gladly oblige. Similarly, when your mood is hopefulness, the asking vibration is one of hopefulness. You may not be able to control everything that happens in your life but you can certainly control how you feel, and determining your own mood will create a better future reality.

That is why when you're sick and the dominant emotion is one of noticing sickness, the illness will linger. When you are ill, there is a tendency to sleep, doze, or zone out, which removes thoughts from the equation and ceases the disallowing of health. This allows the body to heal in its most efficient manner, without interruption. The Universe is consistent and will always give you more of what you are asking for with your vibration. An emotion attracts itself like a magnet, which is why your mood connects with more of the same.

Confusion sometimes occurs when trying to interpret your own vibrational requests, as feeling angry does not necessarily attract angry people. Instead, it will attract situations that feed the feeling of anger. Someone may spill a drink in your lap or a passenger bumps you and you lose your ticket for the train. Your mood will determine your response, and if this emotion remains to become your dominant emotion, it becomes a vibrational request. Unwanted emotions that are allowed to roam freely in your life gather momentum and everything that has momentum is much more difficult to change. Snow falls with a few flakes that can easily be thrown over the shoulder. By the time it becomes an avalanche you don't want to be are standing at the bottom of the hill.

The great news is that you have control over your own vibration. This means that you can change your mood, which is the most empowering position you could ever be in. You have the power to choose how you want to feel, and when you change your mood, you are asking the Universe for something different.

Most peoples' moods are determined by what they observe. This causes happiness when things are going well around them but frustration mounts when it isn't, as nobody has control over that which is happening outside of them. Watching television, listening to kids fight, hearing about people at work, or being told what happened to someone in the next town are all outside influences on the mood. Explosions on the other side of the world, famine in third world countries, or drought in California are all situations you have no control over. You can't control droughts, war, or even a friend's terminal illness. What you do have control over is your mood, the vibrational response to what you hear, see or talk about.

Vibrating in the emotions of joy, love and appreciation no opinion is ever necessary as clarity determines that all is very well with the world. Waiver from these emotional connections with Source and you can find yourself having opinions. When you have an opinion, you have connected to a subject that has now commenced to influence your mood. You have about one minute to notice what is happening and change the mood; otherwise, more thoughts and feelings that are similar will connect. And just like the snowflake that became an avalanche, the more thoughts that are attracted, the more momentum is gained. So, toss the snowflake over your shoulder quickly and choose a new mood.

One of the most worthwhile habit patterns that can be created is the practice of being aware of your mood. It doesn't even matter if you can't recognize your emotions, as there can still be an awareness of what you are thinking. The thoughts that make you smile or frown are an indicator of your vibration, from which you can consciously choose a preferred mood. And when the inner signs aren't visible to you, the immediate environment will reflect how you are feeling about what is happening, as it is always a vibrational match with your dominant emotions.

So, to clarify, how you feel about what or who is in your life right now is a vibrational match with what you have been emotionally requesting from the Universe. Remember, everything you think becomes an emotion, which creates an order to the Universe from the menu of emotions. Your most dominant emotions become the vibration emitted, so if you think and feel fit and healthy sixty percent of the time, that will be most dominant vibration. The Universe responds to how you feel, and gives you more of the same. Life becomes simpler when the guesswork is removed. There is no 'luck' involved. There is nobody more worthy than you are.

Your vibration is all about you. Two people can be looking at the same situation, and have differing opinions. How each person sees something is based on their perspective and mood in that moment, as nobody can perceive outside of their beliefs. Each of us is the attractor in our own physical and emotional worlds. Your vibration is based on how you feel and because of that, what is manifested in your life is a direct reflection of you.

The Five Steps of Manifestation

There are five simple steps to manifesting any desire.

1. *Ask for what you want.* Your request is delivered to the Universe through vibration and not your words. Sometimes speaking out loud will help you to clarify what you want, but your request to the

Universe is always through vibration, and your dominant mood is where you vibrate. Asking is sometimes conscious but doesn't always come with awareness. Often, clarity comes in response to an uncomfortable situation. When you know what you don't want, you really know what you do want, even if it isn't verbalized. How you feel about a situation or person is your vibration, and the most dominant vibrations are called a request.

2. *The Universe responds to your request*, and begins to attract components. You don't need to take part consciously in this step, as it happens automatically. Remember, the Universe does not judge if what you have asked for is good for you or not; it merely delivers what you have asked for by your dominant mood. Manifesting what you don't want is just as easy (and common) as manifesting what you do want. Awareness is the key to change.

3. *Move into a space of allowing* what you want to come. The key to manifestation is allowing, and this is finding a focus that feels good, as when you're feeling great you are allowing all the joy that has been requested over a lifetime. Allowing all that you want to come to you is having belief in the process, 90% of which is unseen. Allowing the Universe to deliver your manifestation is sometimes the most difficult of all steps as the unseen part of the manifestation is confused with complacency.

4. *The fourth step is to remain excited* about your Desire, which keeps doubt from getting in the way. Because there is a delay in manifesting whilst the process is in motion, it is easy to undermine yourself, and negate the hard work you have done to create an excited focus. Undermining can be as simple as feeling unworthy

or having desire remorse, which is not keeping up with the same vibration as the one in which you desired.

5. *The fifth step is to let go.* When you really want something, the yearning can cause resistance. Move on to the next desire, the next project, and find a fun distraction.

There is no lack. When you want prosperity, it is not taking money from someone else and leaving them empty. Just as when you desire health, you aren't taking health from someone else and leaving them sick. There is so much more abundance in the world than there was 2000 or even 200 years ago. There is no end to creation. Desires and creations keep the Universe expanding and the world evolving.

Refining your Manifestation

A good cup of coffee is about so much more than the beans; it's also about the process. Starting with coffee beans, you grind them to the correct degree of fineness. After a firm tamp at thirty pounds of pressure, you clean the edge of the filter basket and place it tightly into the fitting on the coffee machine. One press of the button and 'Hey Presto', coffee comes out with a lovely caramel crema. But a simple change in the grind or tamping pressure and the coffee could be watery sludge. It's no use blaming the beans as they don't grind themselves. You need to refine the process.

Making a cup of coffee is much like manifesting in life. By the time a manifestation occurs, it is a matter of the next logical step. There are no bells and whistles, as you have been feeling the excitement of the desire for quite a while. The dream has been with you a long time and the imagining and expectation has created excitement. However, just like a cup of coffee, sometimes the outcome is not as expected. You need to refine the process to get the perfect caramel crema. It's as simple as saying to yourself, "I thought I wanted *this*, but I really want more of *that*." Refining is the ongoing work of manifestation.

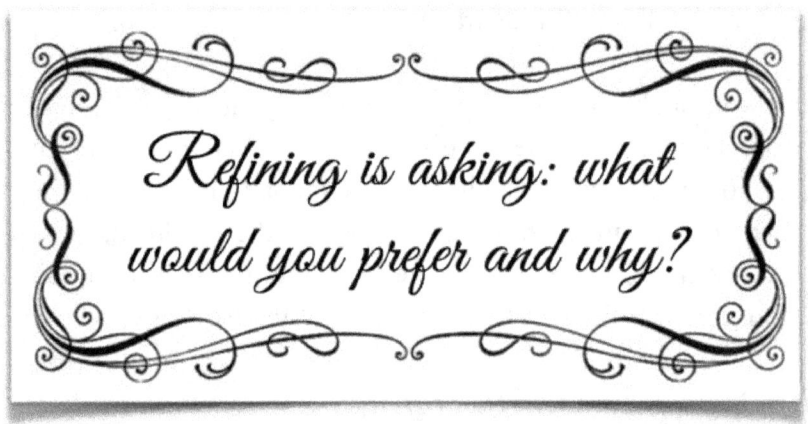

Refining is asking: what would you prefer and why?

When something in life comes your way that isn't quite what you wanted, there is no use blaming someone or thinking it's bad luck. This is the opportunity needed to adjust the grind or the tamp of the coffee. Nothing has gone wrong; it's just time to ask yourself what you would prefer and why? The process of refinement is about acknowledging what you want. The Universe responds to your order constantly, by giving more of your dominant moods, whether you want them or not. That's why you need to believe it before you see it, to imagine and feel the emotion of the experience as it is created. When people create a manifestation that isn't agreeable there can be a misunderstanding of the process of ordering and so they complain that it's not what they wanted. As a result, they get more of what they don't like because the focus has been on complaining. Something to complain about becomes the new order to the Universe.

Ninety percent of any creation occurs before any evidence is noticed in the physical world. The desire has manifested as a thought and a feeling long before it shows up in your life. When you feel a desire, it becomes a thought-form, which your imagination develops and expands. It is felt as though it already exists, and excitement is paramount as there is a knowing and sureness about what's to come. This excitement creates a benchmark, which becomes the new platform for imagining what is to come. Don't be concerned about the 'when' as the desire remains with you, and will grow and expand as you do, so when there is a convergence, it can be bigger and better than you ever imagined.

Master your Mood Changes

When you desire something in your physical life, whether it is a great body, health, or even a new car, your mood is the key to unlocking all you want from life. Regular use of these exercises will make your mood easier to direct, increasing your ability to master your mood changes.

4 Exercises for Changing your Mood

When you change your emotions, you change your vibration. This determines the mood in which your future is created; so changing your mood is desirable for a fun future. Sometimes changing your mood can be as simple as noticing the mood that is current, and deciding on a better feeling mood. Whatever the mood you are experiencing, these exercises can uplift your mood to a feeling of connection where everything is possible.

Consider the following to be less like exercises, and more like fun things to do. We call them exercises, purely because they're creating a new habit pattern, which is what an exercise is, a physical pattern to improve your health.

It's important to be comfortable and effortless in these. Take the effort out and just relax. You can't get it wrong.

1. Space between the thoughts 15 minutes

- A simple method of getting your mind out of the way, especially if you have thoughts running rampant, is to lie (or sit down), close your eyes, and focus on the space between your thoughts. In doing this, the space becomes longer and the thoughts fewer. Focus on your breathing as though watching yourself from above, watching the breath go in and out. Your breath is amazing. It gives you life. If you didn't breathe, you would cease to exist in this physical realm. "Here I am; therefore, I breathe." Focus on the breath. In and out.

- When you're ready, say to yourself, "I wonder what my next thought will be?" You can repeat this statement occasionally, when a thought comes up. You merely 'wonder' and that allows the mind to let go. It doesn't need to find a solution or be in control. 'I wonder' is a non-intrusive statement to make. The aim of the exercise is to get your mind out of the way.

- Don't be concerned if you have thoughts running through your mind, just let yourself be the observer and watch them pass. Allow them to come and go with a simple statement of 'That's interesting'. They will eventually subside naturally. If they are great feeling thoughts, follow them, as they will not interfere with your body's health but actually enhance it. There is no better path to optimum health than the path of joy, fun, appreciation and excitement.

- I have photos on my screen saver that are from our holidays in Disneyland. Whenever I look at these, I remember the wonderful times we had, and my mood softens immediately. I have interrupted the old patterns. It's up to me to look for new things that will make me feel good and build a momentum, but the interruption these photos provides, serves as a space between the thoughts.

2. The Spiral

Each morning, take a sheet of paper and draw a spiral like the shell of a snail. Begin with the edge of the page and end with a small circle in the center. Starting from the outside, write small statements about the things you like doing or being, or people you like having fun with. Keep writing different statements all the way along the line of the snail shell until the statements reach the middle. Then write the title of the emotion in the center that best described the statements, for instance 'fun' or 'joy' or 'love'. You can find examples on 6DimensionsofHealing.com or in the Six Dimensions of Healing Workbook.

Starting your day with this exercise can change how you feel and help you find a new, more connected vibrational request, creating a new improved reality.

3. Refining your Desires

- Draw a line down the middle of a page. Choose a topic and on one side and write all the things you like admire or appreciate about it.

- On the other side of the paper, write one of your desires. Describe what you want and more importantly, why you want this. Remember to include emotions in this list.

- This will improve your focus by changing the mood to one of expectation, as all things are possible.

4. Meditation

- Meditation is the art of stilling the mind. This allows the mind to let go of past anxieties and thoughts. When you let go of thought, there is a movement of the mood to a space of solution as the problem ceases to exist. It also helps to align and balance your thoughts and emotions.

- Meditations can be as simple as focusing on your breath or traveling through the Cosmos. They are many and varied. If you are looking for guided meditations, go to sixDimensionsofHealing.com and download the written or MP3 versions. Guided meditations are wonderful as it is much easier to have some thought than no thought.

Note: There are wonderful exercises for changing your mood documented in Ask & It Is Given by Esther & Jerry Hicks. (2005)

The Importance of Clarity

Clarity is an 'aha' moment. It is like the passing of early morning fog to reveal a sunny day. An ease and flow is created, and a burden lifted. It's such a small word, yet with a powerful meaning. So, don't get frustrated looking for answers, as they are elusive, when you are focused on a problem. Elaborate on the question instead. When the question is defined in a way that is clear and precise, the answer will also be clear and precise, and will come quickly.

When next posing a question, ask yourself whether you are ready for a solution or if you still want to dwell on the problem. If you are ready for a solution, either write the question or find someone to assist in reflecting, so you can define the key question clearly. This is clarity. Clarity helps you really know and understand the question in order to allow an answer to become clear. Understanding whether you want a solution or are content focusing on the problem will allow you to skip the frustration. Sometimes complaining is the place of temporary satisfaction, but don't dwell there for too long as it builds momentum.

I have witnessed how clarity works with my kids many times over. When they want something, but aren't clear, they don't know how to ask for it. In fact, they focus on the problem. Their frustration is obvious, so the next question is whether they want to refine. If they do, we muse together about what they want, based on what they have experienced. Like most people, there is an understanding and a strong opinion of what they don't want. The focus then becomes to clarify the question to reflect exactly what they would prefer. This technique becomes a pointed focus rather than a scattered one. Within days of clarifying, the solution becomes a reality, as it seems the Universe was just waiting for their change of mood and focus. It's truly amazing how fast this works.

On one occasion, whilst I was driving Ben the hour-long route back to the airport, we were talking about what kind of companion he wanted.

"I don't really want a girlfriend," he said. "I want someone I can tour with on the weekends, go out for dinner with occasionally and have fun when we want to get together. I don't want that complicated girlfriend stuff. It needs to be easy and freeing." Within two days of that conversation, he had connected with a girl who was happy in that role, and displayed all the traits he had clarified.

Morgan, aged twenty-six, decided he didn't want to be a worker on a road gang anymore. It was hard work, and he knew he couldn't do it for the rest of his life. As he had consciously manifested the position, he felt frustrated, thinking that this was what he had asked for. Morgan didn't know about 'refining' his desire, so I asked him what he preferred. He wanted a job that was secure with a wage and holidays, and that he could be a 'boss' of some kind, as wanted to feel better about himself. Within a few weeks, he was foreman on a job out of town. Within a few months, he had a permanent contract that gave him the security he had clarified.

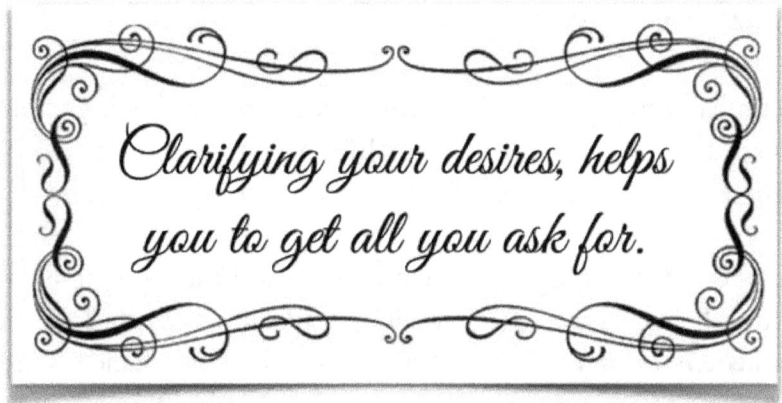

Clarifying your desires, helps you to get all you ask for.

The only thing these boys did to bring about change in their lives was to clarify their question. They didn't need to know how it was going to come about. There was no physical action taken, only action within the mind to define clearly what they wanted. Once there was clarity, it provided a focus and peace in which they could let go of frustration. This allowed their desires to unfold. What they received wasn't everything they wanted; it was everything they asked for. They will be refining for a long time to come, as we all do.

Six Dimensions of Healing is about empowering people to find their own solutions. When counseling, we have always helped people become clear about what they want. In this way, they can define their question much more easily and powerfully. It can help to understand that when you know what you don't want, there is an inner clarity of what you desire, and when this is born your Source moves to the expanded version of your desire, so that when you dwell in what isn't working it creates pain. The pain doesn't exist because of the problem; it exists because you haven't moved your mood towards the solution.

Vibrational Awareness

Sometimes you don't realize what you are requesting from the Universe until it manifests in your life. No matter how much pain is felt, sometimes you are completely oblivious to the indicators.

Dave was always coming up with the new best cure. If he wasn't inventing them, he was experimenting with the ones other people had suggested. Everything from headache alleviators to cancer cures, he experimented with them all. Dave even went to visit a man at the bar of the local hotel, because he was told this man had a cure for gout. However, Dave didn't have gout. Or anything else for that matter as Dave wasn't ill. When he made his potions, or told me about the cure he was trying that someone told him about, I would ask him what he was trying to fix. "Nothing", was his reply; he just wanted to see if it worked.

There was a flawed premise in Dave's thinking. If you are looking for cures, what are you focused upon? You may think it's on getting better, but in reality, it's on something to fix and to fix something there needs to be something wrong. This is where he was coming unstuck, as Dave started getting heart palpitations. He visited the hospital several times as they thought he might be having a heart attack, but found his heart was strong. The mystery illness he had spent so long focusing his cures on fixing had now manifested itself in his body.

There is a difference between focusing on fixing an illness and focusing on health and fitness. They are at opposite ends of the sword. When your focus is on fixing something, the vibration is that of needing to be fixed. When your focus is on being fit and healthy, the vibration is that of health.

Your vibrational request has no relevance to what's in your reality at present. When excuses are made that what has happened is a lesson, you create more lessons. There is no need to set up lessons for yourself, as growth and expansion are assured for the whole of this lifetime. A request to the Universe is made by the balance of your emotions so when you feel happy most of the day, you are asking for happiness. When you spend most of your day worrying, you are requesting situations to worry about. If you look for answers to problems, you will create more problems. Either way, they will all arrive at your request.

Whatever is happening in your life comes about because of the vibrational requests you have made, either consciously or without realizing. When there is no awareness of how you are feeling and what your dominant mood has been or is being, there is no awareness of what the request to the Universe is either. It's always simple to blame others, but it's much more fulfilling to be aware, and change your future yourself.

How we attract people

When you choose the wrong partner for a third time, you can start to feel pretty unlucky, just like having to work with that annoying person on a daily basis. Believe it or not, this isn't a matter of luck playing games with you. There really is a personal sign you display that says, "Pick Me". It's not a piece of paper on your back, nor is it visible or tangible. Rather, it's a vibrational sign available to everyone, and it advertises as vibrantly as any neon display in Las

Vegas. This works like a homing device that draws people on the same vibration as you, right to your doorstep.

The people attracted to this flashing vibrational beacon can be so diverse that you may think you have nothing in common with them. After all, 'annoying' or 'aggressive' isn't in your résumé. However, nothing is ever attracted into your life that you aren't a vibrational match with. This match may be completely different to what you want, but it isn't different to the mood you frequently emit.

So, let's go back to how vibration works. You can meet someone for the first time, and instantly like or dislike the person as there is a familiarity; it's as if you've known them before. You can either love them or instantly mistrust them. Instinct or gut feeling is what this hunch is usually described as and this is accurate, but it's more than that. What you're doing is instinctively translating vibration. As vibrational beings, this comes automatically. Elucidating vibration is so natural that you don't even notice yourself translating.

Responding to vibration is a natural response of this translation, whether you're aware of it or not. Most people will notice when someone is angry or upset, even when the obvious signs aren't available. Vibrational translation was innate when you were born, and has been with you ever since. The sensitivity you feel towards a child, partner or close friend's feelings is the translation of vibration.

When you're feeling low, you're a vibrational match to other people and situations that match this low mood. The neon sign around you is flashing to others who are also emitting similar beacons. These could be people you wouldn't normally cross paths with when feeling good, but as you are now on their frequency, they come into your vicinity.

People aren't the only emitters of vibration; beacons don't signal only to people, but also to every living organism and situation. When you are feeling low, you're more susceptible to viruses and illness, as this is the vibration they also keep company with. Noticing you are feeling ill or low will keep you in the same vibration, but it can just take a shift in mood to feeling good, and now your neon light is flashing to all those who have higher intentions and are uplifting. Viruses and illness move elsewhere, as your cells are emitting a well-being frequency.

When you are in an unwanted mood, it doesn't matter how much you try to protect yourself by a 'bubble' or surrounding yourself with 'light'. These are symbols of fear, and if this method of 'protection' doesn't change the mood you are currently emitting, you will attract unwanted people and situations like moths to a flame. The only way to 'protect' yourself from unwanted emotions is to change your frequency by practicing a good feeling mood. Change the thoughts and change your mood. Change your mood and allow a different perspective. Allow a different perspective and you've created a new life. Keep changing your thoughts until the mood is so practiced that it's an easy shift from feeling low to feeling good. This simple understanding can help change your reality from being in the wrong place at the wrong time, to being in the right place at the perfect time.

The vibrational translation of your mood gives an indicator of the path on which you are traveling. When the mood experienced is excitement, the translational vibration is a space that is aligned with your Higher Self. If your mood is frustration, the mood is moving in an opposite direction to your Higher Self and tension is felt. Whatever mood you're experiencing becomes the indicator for vibrational attraction. When you feel angry, you will attract situations and people that exemplify the anger. When you're discouraged, more situations will come into your life that amplifies discouragement. If laughter and having fun dominate your mood, people and events show up in your life that create more fun and laughter. How you feel about the people who come into your life is vibrationally translated by your mood.

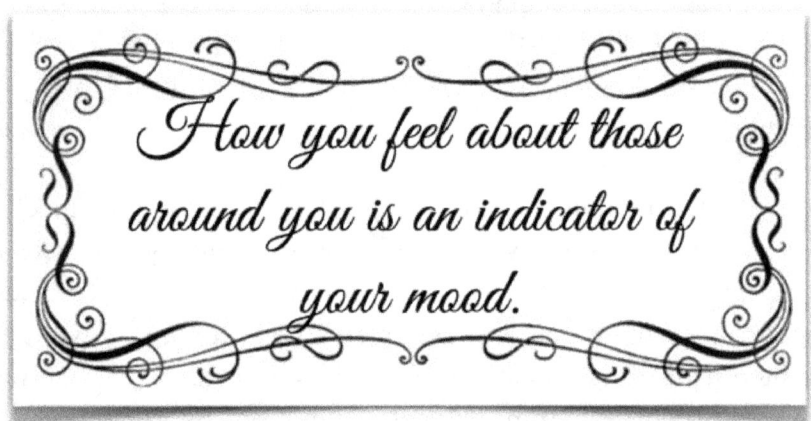

If you want to know the vibration you're emitting, just notice the people around you. How you feel about these people is the indictor of your mood. When you are frustrated in long lines at the supermarket or worrying about the train being late, this emotion is your vibration. Your vibrations create your reality. The difference between humans and other creatures that translate vibration is our unique ability to choose a different mood. The reality of your life right now is the reflection of where you stand vibrationally and if your mood remains the same, is what you can look forward to more of in the future. Use this reflection as an indicator to change your mood if the present is not one you want repeated.

The only reason this knowledge is not common is that when indicators of emotional pain were felt at a young age, for most people, the adults in their lives decided they needed to provide a reason for their child's emotional pain. As they were unaware of any understanding about creating your own reality, and could not experience outside their own beliefs, the child was taught not to not trust their own vibrational indicators. Instead, it was encouraged to blame others for any emotional discomfort. This led to a misconception that controlling our emotions equated to controlling the people around us. In society, this false method worked so well that there are very few people who understand they control their own reality. Now that you know, you can teach your children differently by guiding them to take notice of how they feel. Show them by example, how to change their emotions and notice how situations reflect the new mood. They will be aware that when they feel good, life gets better and when they feel bad, life seems worse and they are the ones with the power to change this. With this personal power, they will never need to hold anyone to ransom for their emotions and their relationships will blossom. They'll have a whole new set of beliefs and a different springboard, from which to bounce the desires and dreams they were born to live.

The only reason anything comes into reality is because it's invited. It's invited by your attention and not your words. Giving attention to what's desired invites wonderful experiences into your reality, and giving attention to what isn't wanted invites undesired experiences into your reality. The choice is always which end of the subject to give your attention, as this is a vibrational invitation to create the future of your dreams.

A New Understanding of Communication

We all communicate vibrationally. When someone speaks, it can affect the way others feel, as any mood you feel can also become vibration. Have you ever been in a meeting with someone and the conversation starts to spiral in a direction you don't want it to go? If you are aware, there is a slide in vibrational movement within you, indicated by mood changes. If you aren't aware of the mood changes quickly, you can end up feeling much worse by the time the conversation is exhausted. Some people seem to drain the life energy out of others just by their words.

Try to cheer a depressed person and you can end up feeling down yourself. This isn't because they drain your life energy but because the strongest vibration will always dominate. A happy mood is not always the strongest vibration; it is the mood that has been practiced the longest until it's chronic. A practiced mood of joy will dominate, but it's unlikely you will find yourself in a conversation with a chronically depressed person when you're in this mood. However, there is something you can do to prevent feeling drained, and that's by understanding how vibration works when we communicate.

When communication occurs between two people of different moods, one of three things happens.

- One person's mood will be higher and the other will be lower and to meet in the middle so that they may communicate, one must move upward towards the higher and the other will move down towards the lower; or
- If two people aren't near the same vibration, they'll move apart as they won't understand each other as their frequencies are tuned differently; or
- If the moods of the people in the conversation are of a similar vibration and fairly high, each will lift the other to an even

higher mood and all will leave the conversation feeling great. The gain in clarity will be exponential.

Another way of understanding this is by observing that when two people choose to communicate who have a difference in mood, they will move towards each other vibrationally. This means one will move up the mood map and the other will usually move down. They will move closer to each other to merge their energies to a vibration where communication can occur — a similar frequency, so they may understand each other. The one moving up the mood map will feel uplifted, as they have turned in the direction of their Source Energy. The other may feel a little deflated, as they have moved down the mood map and further from Source, to communicate. If you're the one that feels good when you commence a conversation, then you understand why it could feel as though others can suck the energy away from you. However, this isn't what's happening.

It's important to realize that no one can take or suck any energy from you. You're the only person responsible for how you feel, and nobody can change that unless you allow them to coax your mood in their direction. Contrary to how it feels sometimes, you actually make a choice to move vibrationally closer to a person to communicate. Often a default pattern occurs because of the game you play.

(Have a look at the *Relationship Triangle* in the *Emotional Dimension* in this handbook. Choosing to move out of the triangle is essential in maintaining an uplifting vibration. If you've read that subject and decided you couldn't leave the game, maybe it's time to make a decision about the reality you are creating.)

There is a preferable scenario to feeling drained, with the key being awareness. This is the *fourth method of communication* and is uplifting for all. The feeling of joy and excitement is the most dominant vibration. It's the vibration of the Universe and is one with Source. When you have an awareness to hold your vibration in the best possible mood you can muster, the other person moves towards your vibration, but in no way is your mood diminished. Your mood is maintained, even though the other is also lifted. The vibration you're keeping becomes the most dominant guiding light and because of your newfound awareness, the physical signs of how you feel in the conversation will let you know if you are straying from this path. If there signifies a change further from Source, gently correct your intentions in your mind to stay feeling great.

This following pattern will take a little practice but gets easier, and will reward you with an awareness that keeps your mood at its elevated state in all your interactions.

1. Move your mood into a place where you can feel the best you can. The closer to joy and excitement, the better.
2. Set your intentions to 'feel good, no matter what'
3. Monitor how you're feeling
4. Be ready to pivot the conversation if you recognize the mood shift from your intentions
5. Look only for things to feel good about

This may seem a little heavy in rules. However, with a little practice they all roll in together and become seamless. As you practice one and then another, they become a part of who you are. It is fun to be conscious in a conversation and practice, as there is nothing to lose.

We have used these guidelines in our healing practice for years. It's the technique used to avoid getting burnt out. Burning out doesn't happen because of giving too much, but because of the strain from moving in the emotional direction toward your client's mood. When you choose to maintain the mood of joy you've practiced, the difference will be visible. Not only will your friends feel good around you, but you will also feel uplifted.

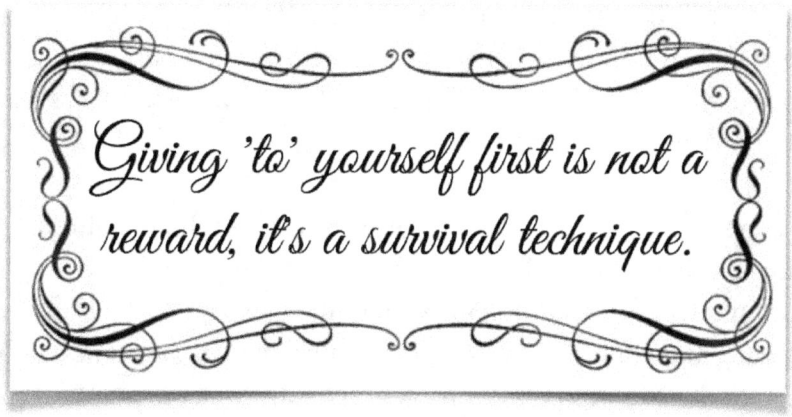

Giving 'to' yourself first is not a reward, it's a survival technique.

Giving 'to' yourself is a pre-requisite to giving 'of' yourself. It's like cleaning the house before your guests arrive; similarly, you want to prepare your mind and intentions before they arrive too. When you don't give to yourself you have nothing left to give others, as your energy is depleted, and you rely on others to make you feel good. Making it a priority to give to yourself first, by regular meditation, good feeling thoughts, sleep, exercise and anything that makes your heart sing, energizes the whole body and spirit. If you are a parent your child deserves the best of you, and not the worst so giving to yourself first allows you to feel your best, which makes parenting so much easier. The whole family benefits from your good feeling mood. Try it and see.

There are also things you can do to allow others to move in to the same state. Focus on the best in the person you are giving attention to. In that way, you'll remove all blocks between the two of you, and allow them to move towards their natural state of being, which is what you are now holding for them. This does not diminish their choice, as how they feel is always their choice; nor does it diminish your good feeling mood, as there is room on this platform of joy for everyone. It's probably a good time to note that even though you don't see direct evidence of the results you are looking for immediately; don't be fooled into thinking nothing is happening. Just as you can't see vibration, you also can't see change until it has manifested, as the first 90% of any change is internal.

There are times as a Healer I have been asked when healing if I can visualize the problem. In response, I ask the client which is more important, seeing the problem or helping them heal. As by now you are aware, the solution and the problem are not in the same vibration. When you focus upon the problem you become a match with the problem. The effectiveness of healing is the ability to see a person healed and hold that vibration. A healer acts as a bridge, allowing the client to move towards their innate healing ability, which is the vibration of Source Energy.

If you're going to use the technique of holding your vibration when visiting family (and it works), you might want to practice on others first to create a chronically joyous vibration. It's so much easier to practice any technique on a stranger than on people who have learnt how to 'press your buttons' over a long time. Politicians and their campaign parties have mastered the art of redirecting the focus of a subject by using this same technique. Some call it being a spin-doctor. You are looking to change the angle of the conversation into something that's uplifting. The Spin Doctor technique is beneficial to practice, as the more you do it the better you feel and the more chronic it becomes.

(For more information on the Spin Doctor technique and how it can help you feel good, refer to 6DimensionsofHealing.com or the *Six Dimensions of Healing Workbook.)*

Giving the best of you is your gift to the world and it doesn't come from you, it comes through you.

Vibrational Platform

As you are now aware, you invite whatever you focus upon into your vibration. This invitation is called an attraction. It is not something you need to believe in for this to occur. Rather, it is happening all around you anyway, to everyone and everything. The Universal Law of Attraction is a natural process of matching vibrations that are similar across the Universe. For humans, this means when a vibration of abundance is achieved, more abundance is directed to the vibration at the rate of intensity in which the vibration occurs. We call this vibrational intensity an asking or a request to the Universe. This law can't be manipulated or controlled; however, you can choose what is requested by changing your focus. In this way, you can steer vibrational attraction down a pathway that is to your liking.

Animals act on instinct and their vibrational attraction is clear and simple — food or survival. Their focus is singular. You are sifting through situations all day, making decisions that are much more diverse than the simple choices of food and survival. Each choice and observation creates moods and emotions that become a dominant vibration, which then attracts more of the same. Most people are oblivious of the affect situations and thoughts they experience have on their future reality. There is a tendency to blame others for feeling drained or something that happened during the day. This method of vibrational request is creating your reality by default.

If you are one of these people, you will understand how disempowering being at the mercy of another person's opinions, comments or actions can be. Remember, you are the person who has your best interests at heart. People give advice and make decisions based on their own beliefs. Only you know best what your dreams and aspirations are, so if you are unsure of whether to follow your own dreams, or to believe another's dreams for you, believe in your own guidance. Many a time, when someone is saying they know what's best for you, what they are really saying is "If you do this, it will make me more comfortable." We were taught from an early age to please others. To take our feet off the couch, sit up straight, wear good clothes when we go out, and be polite to people. Now I'm not saying these social graces are bad things; however, they are a pattern of teaching people how to act for the benefit of others. It's social training. The downside of this conditioning is that we override our innate sense of what is pleasing to us, and think that when we are pleasing others, or doing what we were taught is right, that we are pleasing ourselves. This is hollow gratification and doesn't lead to a fulfilling life.

It is not your role in life to make others happy. The way you know if something is pleasing for you and not something you are doing to please others out of a learned behavior is by how you feel. If your intention is to feel good, you are pleasing yourself. If your intention is to make someone happy, you are pleasing others.

These two intentions are not the same, as you can't control what another thinks and feels. You can't even control their mood. So, if you are expecting a behavior as a particular response from someone to something you are doing, and it doesn't come, your mood is affected. You cannot bend over backwards in enough ways to please people all the time, as what pleased someone once may not please them again. Those who try to please people will understand how emotionally draining it can be. There will always be difficulty trying to please people when there is an expectation from another. If they don't respond accordingly, then you aren't happy either.

The only time you can have a positive effect on another's mood is when you are feeling great and they can be inspired by your mood. It is the difference between trying to affect another's behavior and allowing your joy to blossom.

Rule 1. Firstly, choose to feel great. Each day set your intentions to feel the best you can. Practice this intention moment by moment at first, until this pattern becomes a new groove on the record. *Look for things in your life that you can feel good about.* Choose to see events and people in a way that is pleasing.

Rule 2. Secondly, when not feeling great, refer to rule number 1.

When you decide that nothing is more important than how you feel or what your mood is, everything changes. Your life moves in a direction towards what you want in comparison to moving to what is unwanted. There is no dependency on someone else's moods to affect yours, as your mood becomes independent of events occurring around you and what others are thinking. Opportunities begin opening up in a way that you never thought possible. People who leaned on you start looking for others to lean on, as you are no longer a match with their vibration. Relationships transform, and you begin attracting people that you are happy to be with.

When your mood is mostly happy, the vibrational attraction is happiness. You are ordering from the catalogue of the Universe more situations to feel happy about. When you are laughing, you're asking for more situations to come into your life to laugh about. When you are appreciative of what's around you, you are requesting more of the same. Being happy and finding things to laugh about is key to steering your vibrational asking to a direction that is preferred.

You choose every emotion that you experience. This is not usually a conscious choice, but instead a response to what you observe. It may not seem that you can change the feeling of worry to another mood, but being aware of your thoughts and emotions is the key to change and imperative for consciously creating your joyous life. When you have practiced feeling worried, a knot in the pit of your stomach can be an indicator of worry gathering momentum. When you learn to heed the early warning signs, it is an indicator to change your mood to a new waterfall. Early warning signs become more pronounced with momentum, as compounding a feeling of worry will attract more situations that are similar. This is just the next indicator for change, and when you know what you don't want, you have clarity.

Don't expect your mood to stay buoyant. Sometimes you will fall, as moods change often. Just become conscious of moving your mood in the direction of Source by choosing better-feeling thoughts that are in alignment with who you really are, until you once again reach the platform of joy and excitement. The more often you practice, the quicker the journey to joy.

Practicing the emotion of excitement or joy, creates a platform of higher wisdom that is balanced and strong. Paying attention to how you feel exudes clarity, and inspires ideas that are empowering. They unfold easily and lovingly, which other like-minded souls are drawn to. Your joy is of great value to people who observe you, as it can inspire them also.

The Power in Your Present Moment

The present moment is not all of today, but right now. There is a common saying that your power is in the present moment. Not ten minutes ago and not in an hour, but right now. The present is but a moment in time. Reality is made up of a series of present moments. As those moments are observed they become the past, as the unique ability of a present moment is to transform itself immediately from the present into the past. The present is a paradox, it lasts forever yet is momentary. Whatever the focus is upon in the present moment is where attention is directed. Where attention is directed, energy is gathered. Between the past, present and future, the present is the most powerful place to focus. Attention directed to any subject becomes an observation and forms a dominant mood, which becomes your vibrational request.

Whatever has happened before this moment is in the past. Whilst the present is pivotal, the past has no bearing on what is becoming in your life. It doesn't create your reality, the only time the past can affect your future is if you bring the emotional memories from the past into this present moment. Then it is no longer a past memory but a current observation. As you observe in your present moment, emotion is created. Build some momentum with this mood and you create more of the same emotions for your future. This is how the past is repeated.

It doesn't mean that it is what is wanted, but you attract more of the same emotions. Your current mood is a request to the Universe that you would like more of the same emotions as how you are currently feeling.

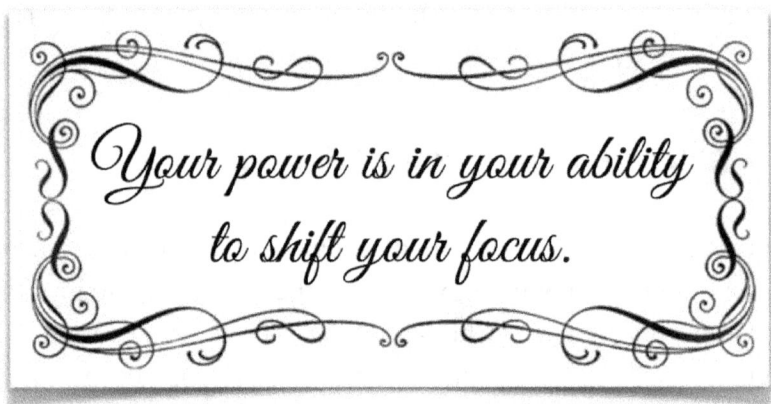

Your power is in your ability to shift your focus.

If something hurtful has happened in the past to put you in a position of feeling unworthy and unwanted, a realization begins to come into focus about what you do want. In response to this new request for self-empowerment, joy, security and love, the Higher Self automatically moves to that expanded place of empowerment and remains there, shining the light and waiting for you to move your focus in this enlightened direction. This is the Soul calling you forth and because it is so far away from where you are still standing, this calling can feel like pain. When you look for reasons to feel unworthy no matter the situation, it brings past moods into the present and this creates more of what you don't want in your future. That is the reason so many hurtful relationships are repeated. Nobody wants them, but giving attention to that which is unwanted creates a vibrational request to the Universe for more unwanted. This means not only do you wear a sign on your back but also carry a neon light to attract those who will help you attain the vibration you are requesting.

The true power in the present moment is in your ability to choose how you want to feel right now. When a past memory rises to the fore, you need to find a way of changing your focus to something more pleasant and thus, make the unpleasant thoughts less dominant. You will never rid yourself of bad memories. You can cleanse and absolve all you like but if you practice changing your mood to feeling better and better, the memories will become less dominant. Knowing that what you focus on you create more of, it would be beneficial to move the focus to a direction that feels good as often as you can.

Being unaware of your moods allows default opinions to form when observing situations both close and afar. For instance, you could be feeling relatively good and decide to watch the news and after observing death and destruction for a short time, your mood could quickly plummet. If you stay in this altered and not-so-good feeling mood for even as little as a minute, you will then start to vibrate in that mood which will accumulate more thoughts that are similar. Before you know it, you could be feeling agitated without even stepping out of the lounge room.

Moods can be influenced easily. Your good mood can go awry quickly when you listen to others complaining. If you aren't aware of the change in mood within, you may start participating in the subject, which adds momentum in a direction you would prefer not to be the creative vibration for your future. Of course, it can be changed and it is never too late, but moods are much easier to change when there is less momentum. By using the power of this present moment and choosing what you observe and the conversations you participate with people, you can catch any changing mood early. When finding yourself in a conversation that is deprecating, change the subject. This is a good habit to practice, particularly if you can 'spin' the subject to advantage for yourself. You can become so good at 'spinning' a subject that people don't even notice. It is very empowering to be in control of your own conversations so practicing being a good Spin Doctor is a coveted tool in creating your own reality.

I remember Marie, a lady who practiced spinning the subject so that she could enter any conversation and leave it with everyone feeling uplifted. She practiced this habit for herself and was so enamored with feeling good that she wouldn't allow anyone or anything to encroach upon this mood. When she visited her family, it came in handy, as her mother was good at 'spinning' in the opposite direction. Because Marie was aware of her mother's habits and had set her own intentions, she spun the conversation in the direction of a good feeling again and again. Marie admitted she could see the frustration on her Mother's face at first, when the mother wasn't allowed to devalue the conversation, but by the end of the evening Marie noticed that her Mother appeared to be feeling better than she had seen her in a long time. Everyone innately wants to feel good, but not everyone is practiced in achieving happiness.

Being aware of your mood in the present moment is the key to change. It's no use beating yourself up about the mood you were in yesterday or the day before as your power is in the present. It can take as little as ten minutes to change your mood, if it is one you aren't happy with. Each day is made up of many new present moments so you get to choose your mood over and over, commencing at the beginning of the day. If you don't make a conscious choice each morning, the default mood will continue from the previous day. It is only the present that creates your future, not the past.

Nothing remains in the present forever. The power you have now is the ability to consciously choose the mood you want in your present moment, and in doing so, create your own reality. You and only you, have the power to change your future. If this present moment is wonderful and you are feeling great, then enjoy it. Expand the wonderful feeling to the next moment and the next as this is the future you are creating. However, if your present moment is not feeling as good as you want it to, then change your focus and change your mood. Right now, you have the power.

It's not the opportunities in life that define you, but your ability to change your mood. As you look back over the years, the good times will stand out as those of joy and happiness. These were the times of success when you moved your mood to a place of heightened awareness and love. We would just like you to have more of those moments, for when a good feeling mood is practiced in the present moment as often as possible, it is creating a future that will be joyfully remembered from the past.

New Patterns for the Future

When planning your new reality, look back at the dreams you had as a child, and see if they're still relevant. If they are, refine them and create a list of Joyous Becomings. Sometimes, becoming a fireman is not as enticing at sixty as it was at age six, and traveling the world may seem tiresome with grandchildren to factor into the equation. This isn't a bucket list; it's a redefined dream list of what you would like to become a reality. The difference is that you're not looking to do these sometime before you die, but formulating and growing the desires now, to create a better present reality, and a very exciting life.

A client came to see me who felt lost and out of his depth in emotional family divisions. He had recently finished work in the mines, and wanted to spend time with a twelve-year-old daughter he hardly knew. When I asked him what he had always wanted to do when he was younger, his reply took me by surprise. He had always dreamed of writing the musical score for a Hollywood movie. This was a small country town in Australia and Hollywood seemed a fantastical dream, so I asked him if he could play an instrument. He could, and had started writing a score years ago, but put it away. He also had a friend in Hollywood, and felt this was a connection. From the change in his mood I could tell that simply speaking about it had reignited his dream. His friend in Hollywood was the link that made him feel this dream was more probable than possible. It's rewarding to share the excitement of someone who has reignited their hopes and dreams after years of dormancy. Moods are contagious, so excitement is of benefit to everyone. The Universe will always support your dreams. You just need to continue believing in them.

The only time people let go of their dreams is when achieving them seems unrealistic. This is entirely self-defeating as you can't see the bigger picture and don't know the capabilities of the Universe. When traveling to the other side of the world, you purchase a ticket for an airplane but you don't ask the pilot to turn around after eight hours, because you can't see how far you have to go. You just know the pilot knows his job. Whenever you want to get somewhere that you don't know the path to, it's your job to keep the dream alive by feeling good. If you can imagine the fullness of the desire, the Universe will gather the necessary elements and provide what you refer to as coincidences and chance meetings to unfold the dreams in ways you haven't imagined.

The timing of the manifestation of a dream is always perfect and to keep a dream alive is to know it will come. There is an element of faith involved, but not blind faith. When you've practiced dreams by imagining what your life is like today and tomorrow as if they have already arrived, you are building a pattern of faith or knowing. This patterning is similar to how the body builds immunity to a disease. When you have been sick, the blood cells learn how to fight the disease and build immunity so that next time, when the symptoms of the disease arise they immediately know what to do. This is similar to mind patterning.

When you have consciously changed your mood in a time of discomfort, these become successes. Those successes form a pattern, which creates a steady platform for the faith needed to keep your dreams alive. Instead of patterns like "I don't have enough money", they become "Things work out for me". Patterns of self-talk form a self-fulfilling prophecy, and are pivotal when planning your new reality.

To plan your Reality, take a moment to write down your current dreams.

1. Write down your dreams. What you do want, even if you don't know how they will come about.
2. Why do you want these?

Patterning can occur from wanted and unwanted situations. If you aren't aware of the patterns you've created that hinder well-being, then it's more difficult to understand why things don't work out the way you feel they should. The key is listening to your verbiage. Your words speak your beliefs, and you can't move beyond your beliefs. If you've developed patterns of understanding that you never win prizes; you can enter all the raffles and lotto's you wish but you've already established that you won't win. I've witnessed people buying raffle tickets with the preface, "I never win these things." You've created the pattern that sustains Murphy's Law. How you feel about everything in your life creates a self-fulfilling prophecy, which determines your reality. Sometimes it can be difficult to understand what the patterns created are, but this comes with practice of awareness. Listen to your self-talk, as well as the way you communicate with others. These will give you an indicator of what reality is being created in your future.

My introduction to patterns came through an old acquaintance. We were talking one afternoon and he asked me what I would like to do in the future. After I told him I concluded with, 'but I probably won't be able to do it.'

He said to me "Do you realize you just undermined yourself?"

As soon as he made the comment, I realized that I undermined myself all the time. When I imagined my desires in the shape of a tall building with one hand, I would pull them down with the other. It was a pattern I'd been using for over forty years and from that day onward I decided I wouldn't do it anymore. I really appreciated his pointing this out. Most patterns are blindingly obvious to others, even if they don't know what they represent. There is a saying, "When the Student is ready the teacher will come," Well, I was ready to hear what he had to say that day, and it changed my life.

When you use the situations in your life that have helped create a mood of excitement, you can build a habit of optimism. This becomes the pattern you perceive life with, the steady platform from where you choose what comes next.
Next on your plan is to:

3. Be aware of thought-patterns that are managing your life, whether consciously or subconsciously. Write them down as they present themselves, then make a choice. To keep them or change them.
4. Notice the objections you have to other people's suggestions. These form your beliefs. Ask yourself if these are for your highest benefit?

Our daughter Katie was twenty-three when she decided life was supposed to work for her and not against her. She wanted a small upright freezer in her apartment and a particular model of car that was her dream. It wasn't a big stretch. She knew what she wanted and how she would feel when these items came into her possession. Katie often imagined herself with these items. It became very real for her and it was exciting. Firstly, she found the freezer advertised and it was at a house only three doors down. Within a week of finding the freezer, the particular car she wanted came into her life. Katie had saved enough money for half and could finance the other half. She was so excited she drove her new car all over town.

What Katie came to realize was that she was building a pattern of optimism. As a few things she wanted came into reality, she was now developing a pattern of things working out. By acknowledging she had created smaller manifestations, she had brought new habits into her life. Katie was optimistic about what was to come. No dream was too big. She knew that when manifesting it's as easy to create a castle as a button. It just depends whether it's easier to believe you own a castle as a button.

What patterns of optimism have you created?

Build a pattern of optimism and congratulate yourself on achieving a good feeling mood. It's a manifestation and you did it.

Another benefit of building a pattern of optimism is that people can't knock you off your platform, because your happiness isn't dependent upon theirs. It is common for people to want others to feel good. We all want our loved ones to be happy. However, when the feelings of others affect your mood, you are handing over control of your moods to circumstance. In this way, you feel good when everything is going well, and you feel bad when it's not. This is not freedom; its claustrophobia. Set people free and allow them to feel the way they want, when they want. Let them have their bad day, but mind your own mood. The only way you can teach is by example so be the best you can be. That's freedom.

Practice:
Look for things to feel good about constantly and know you are the creator of your own happiness.

Sometimes allowing the mind to wander on thoughts that are detrimental to our well-being sidetracks us. That's where meditation can be of benefit as it allows the mind to gently subside. You can then press the reset button as you get to choose the track it travels along. If you are aware, there will always be indicators that show the direction in which you are heading.

I remember one day, on my usual morning walk, I decided to look for things to appreciate along the way. On my way down a hill, I could hear my guidance telling me I had so much abundance that if I were to lean forward down the hill, it would hold me up and stop me from falling. I could imagine the huge wave of steady abundance pushing towards me and holding my body upright. It was one of the many defining moments in my life, as the realization that my focus had shifted from what wasn't in my life to what was.

Create a daily list to focus on the abundance you already have, real or imagined.

Notice your abundance in each moment and write it down in the form of appreciation at the end of the day. It's a great way to end the day as when you sleep with the feeling of appreciation, you wake with the feeling of appreciation.

Six Dimensions of Healing

Change Your Reality and You Change Your Life

Intentional Dimension

Six Dimensions of Healing

Set your intentions!
"Make it your dominant intent to look for things that feel good."
Abraham with Esther Hicks

An elderly friend was 95, and whilst she had lived a long life she tended to gravitate towards the negative side of experiences. When she spoke, it seemed to be an opportunity to complain but that's what kept her going. She wasn't happy, as happiness seemed to be dependent on everything being perfect, and her perception of perfect changed constantly. When we went shopping or spent time together at an event, I would reach the end of the day feeling a little washed out for having been in her company. One day I decided on the way to the shopping center with Edna that I wanted to feel good no matter what. That was my intention.

(I have found the 'no matter what' part important when I'm not sure what I will encounter, as it covers everything.)

What occurred was really remarkable. Not only did we have fun together, but I didn't notice her complain once. I introduced her to an old friend we met by chance, and they exchanged interesting stories over lunch. They were both pioneers of the area and fun stories of history unraveled. This was a side to Edna I rarely saw. Her favorite lunch place was a café I didn't usually frequent, as I didn't particularly like the experiences I'd had with their food or coffee. This day though, my coffee tasted delicious, and the salad I ordered was scrumptious. I enjoyed every mouthful. Because I had set my intentions and was determined to stay there, I had moved myself into a place of being a vibrational match with food that tasted great, coffee I enjoyed and conversation that was uplifting. Edna 'came along for the ride', as my mood was dominate and it helped us both. This is an example of how to bring out the best in people.

You can change your life and the life of those who are inspired by your optimism by consciously setting your intentions. It isn't possible to change other people, but they do respond differently around you when you have chosen to be joyful. It's empowering to know that you can enhance life's experiences by changing your perception.

When our children were at high school, they would come home and I would always ask them how their day had been. If it were any less than great, I would ask them if they had set their intentions in the morning. Invariably they would say they hadn't, so what they were experiencing were default intentions. They came to learn this very quickly, as there were direct consequences for their laziness in not setting intentions. If you are unsure of what default your intentions are set at, it is the balance of your mood during the day. You can't experience anything other than your intentions.

The simplicity of changing their experience was to consciously tell themselves they were going to have a great day, and believe it as they left for school. The Universe was obliging, as when they moved into the space of a 'great day', their experiences changed. It sounds so simple, and yet is a very effective method. As a parent, I never got involved in the situation of what had happened if they had not set their intentions, as they knew the whole situation could have been avoided had they set up their day intentionally. The irritable teacher may still be the same, I pointed out, but you are no longer in her sights as you aren't her vibrational match. You can't change other people but you can certainly change how *you* feel about someone. As you feel differently, you perceive your environment differently. This creates a new path that matches how you feel.

A friend of mine would conduct seminars internationally, and spent much time intentionally setting out the ground rules at the beginning of his seminars. He would go to great lengths to tell the participants what he expected from them, how he wanted them to act and behave. The more ground rules he set out, the more he needed as he was attracting participants who seemed to want to break his ground rules. His is an example of being focused on what you don't want rather than what you do. All he needed to do was set his own intentions by spending the time before the seminar to know what *he* wanted. In this place of clarity, he would have attracted a match with his intentions, rather than a vibrational match with what he didn't want.

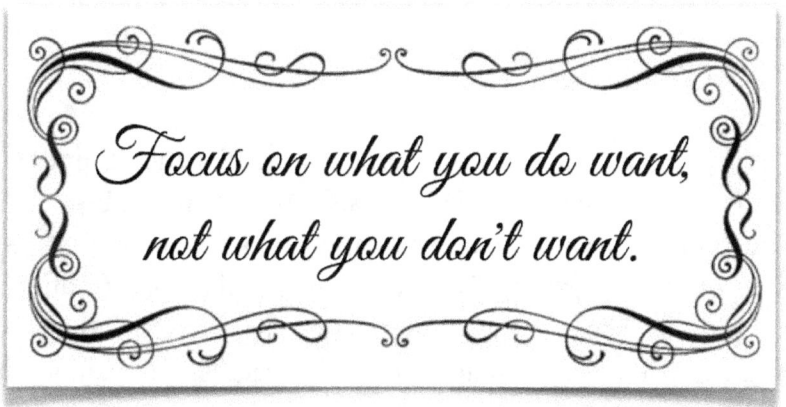

Many people are very aware of what they don't want, and the focus of this awareness brings attention, which creates default intentions for what you don't want. In your awareness of the unwanted you are requesting from the Universe more of what you don't want. To change the request, you need to be aware of what you do want. This is an intentional path where it is unnecessary to set ground rules or boundaries for others as you are attracting those who share your intentions. When you do the work before you step out the door you are guided by the intentions you've set. Just take a moment to breathe and reset them if needed, during the day. It is worth the conscious focus to gain the reward of feeling great during the day.

Intentions are rather like a menu. The waiter takes your order and the meal arrives in a little while. You know you are going to receive Chicken Kiev, if that's what you ordered, but if you wait until the meal arrives on a buffet table and then decide to make a choice, you may or may not get what you want. In this case, the best you can do is to decide intentionally that you are going to enjoy whatever is on offer, no matter what. A menu of emotions helps you to decide now what you want to create for the future. Consciously choosing your intentions determines the path along which you will travel.

The Parent Trap

Like many teenagers, I gave my parents a really difficult time through my formative teen years. There was always an endless struggle between what I wanted and what my parents wanted for me. The thinking of many parents of that era was that they had to direct their children's lives, because the children were incapable of doing so. The pushing against authority that occurs then installs buttons that may be pressed for the rest of our lives. When we became parents, and our children were growing, I came to understand a lot of things my parents had no idea about.

Such as:
- Children are born selfish, which is a normal and healthy trait. It just means they're interested in their own well-being rather than anyone else's. They are keen to make themselves happy.
- When kids feel resistance from someone, they push back harder. In response, adults move into defense mode, which puts up barriers and hinders communication.
- Love is where children come from, and they expect to be loved. This remains true unless they are taught the opposite.
- Every child starts out believing they can do anything. Usually by the time they become teenagers, they're not so sure about the 'anything' part so it's up to parents to believe in them.
- Kids are like sponges. They soak up the environment around them and mold themselves to respond to people they live with in a way that allows them to fit in.
- All children have their own innate guidance. This keeps them safe unless it is overridden by someone who thinks they know better and convinces the children accordingly.
- Every child is born with its own inner mood map. They naturally learn how to use it from their emotional responses, but it does help if someone can explain the correlation between how they feel and what's happing in their life.
- Every child born has the seeds of brilliance within. No exceptions. It's a parent's job to help this blossom.

Parents often comment on how difficult parenting can be. This is often because parents are attempting to influence the direction of their kid to one that suits them, and not necessarily the child. Kids push their parents to give them the tools they need. Innately, the kids know what they need to move in the direction of their dreams. Many times, they don't have the tools, and the obvious and safest place to discover these tools is in a home environment. The tools needed are always about perspective, as when a child is in pain they want to know how to change the situation. This can sometimes translate to conflict, as the parents fail to recognize the request as that of growth. Life is fluid, and changing around us all the time. Nothing ever stays the same. Death and change are the only two certainties. Even though they are certain, they peak at the top of the list of human fears. Change is inevitable, and all children push parents down the path of change, which is inevitably growth for everyone.

As a parent, you can set your intentions about what you want, so that you can change perspective and gain the tools needed. Moving in the direction of your Source will help you gain clarity, and allow you to find the solution you are seeking. Understand that your children are already whole and complete human beings that are here to guide you rather than learn from you. They have their own Inner being and their own guidance. Of course, they'll make what you call mistakes, and so did you. Their knowledge will expand because of this just like yours did. Your children are supposed to grow beyond your beliefs, so encourage their dreams, whether you believe in them or not.

Your children weren't put on this earth to make you happy, they're in this life to create what interests them and whilst they gain tools from you, these are only a platform for what's to come.

All children will push you to gather the skills they need the most. They are usually expressed in frustration, as they don't know what they need and you don't have these skills yet yourself. Pushing against their frustration is not the solution. Obtaining the skills they need is the road to harmony. You teach by example, not by your words, so kids are molded by their environment and will emulate your behaviors and beliefs.

Parents can be Role Models or Anti-Role Models, as not everyone likes or respects their parents. As a parent, you get to choose which you would like to be. Your intentions can be inspiring or inhibiting.

There is so much to be gained by encouraging your children. For example:
- ☐ *Expanding and growing with them.* Gaining skills the kids need also enhances your journey.
- ☐ *Being proud* of who you have become as a parent and an individual.
- ☐ *Respecting yourself* means you teach your kids to respect themselves.
- ☐ *Finding joy* in watching your kids use the tools you provided to manage their lives.
- ☐ *Developing strong relationships.* When you have strong balanced relationships, your kids are likely to attract balanced relationships in their lives.
- ☐ *Encouraging them* when they falter, rather than picking them up when they fall.
- ☐ *Having confidence* in them to make their own choices so they can feel self-empowered.

When I chose to work through some issues that were holding me back with my parents, a particular self-help book was recommended to me. The instructions in one section were to write down everything my parents had done that caused lingering emotions of anger and resentment. I wrote and wrote with tears pouring down my cheeks for hours. It seemed much more important to acknowledge how I felt than what the situations were, but I extracted pages and pages of memories. Next I carefully folded the pages of my soul's outpouring and stored them away. The book suggested that I confront the people with what I had written, but I didn't want to, as I didn't feel the need, so I just put them away. My realization, was that how I felt wasn't about other people, it was only about me. I finally burnt the pages, as it was freeing and they weren't for any other eyes. This was my therapy.

By the next time I got together with my parents, I had burnt the pages. There was no indication in the book of what was to happen next, and so I didn't have any expectations but there was a weight lifted from my shoulders. It was emotionally freeing. But the real surprise was that the relationship had changed, and my parents treated me quite differently from then on. They weren't aware of my self-therapy, but there was a new beginning with a clean slate; they were respectful and friendly. We had interesting conversations and we all left the visit feeling uplifted. Acknowledging how I felt about what had happened was freeing; I was ready to move forward. My parents hadn't changed; yet they treated me differently, as my intentions had changed. I wasn't coming to the table with emotional baggage, and I had removed the buttons.

I was at a restaurant twenty years ago, and I met some lovely people in their mid-thirties. We must have been talking about parents and they acknowledged how your relationship changes as you get older. I had this amazing moment of clarity and added,

"You don't change it." I said with new wisdom. "You finish the relationship you had and then start a new one. If you want to."

I'm not sure they understood what I said, but it was clarity for me and I understood relationships clearly for the first time. Sometimes relationships need a line drawn under them. They would benefit greatly from ending rather than fixing. You can fix a smashed bicycle all you like, but if the chassis has been bent it will still be wobbly. The solution is a new bicycle. You can decide who you want to have relationships with, and who you don't, but you are entering the communion with a clean slate and a new perspective. It's important to understand that your relationships are all about how you feel and don't reflect the other person. As you finalize a relationship your intentions are to make peace with your emotions and let them go. It doesn't make the other person right or wrong, but releases you from the bondage of old patterns. As you create the intention to release all that has gone before, your path changes.

Not all relationships are worth renewing but they are always worth making peace with. This isn't something you do with another person; it's done inside your own head. There is nobody that can object to what you think as thoughts belong to you. A common belief is that others need to change for your situation to improve but that isn't ever true. You are the creator of your own reality, so you get to make the decisions about how you feel and that changes everything.

Nobody has to change for my life to be harmonious, fun or easy.

When you no longer need to blame another for not getting what you want, your life changes direction. Waiting for someone to change is a fruitless pursuit; so set your intentions for what you want knowing you are the one in control. Making peace with yourself about any relationship on any subject creates freedom. It's not about what other people think or what others expect. Your freedom is created and experienced by you.

Parenting is a delicate balance of guidance and love and when we set out intentions to provide both for ourselves it's automatically passed on to our children.

Relationships

Our intentions don't always seem clear when we find ourselves in relationships, but it is the way we feel about a relationship that reveals our intentions, initially at any rate. Relationships can be fleeting or eternal, as we co-create with many people throughout a lifetime. Some will be close and others distant. Some relationships can even be detrimental to our health, as we allow others to eat away at our well-being, causing us to feeling undeserving or unworthy. It is not for punishment or karma that we feel this way, nor for lessons or drama. We have merely forgotten our path.

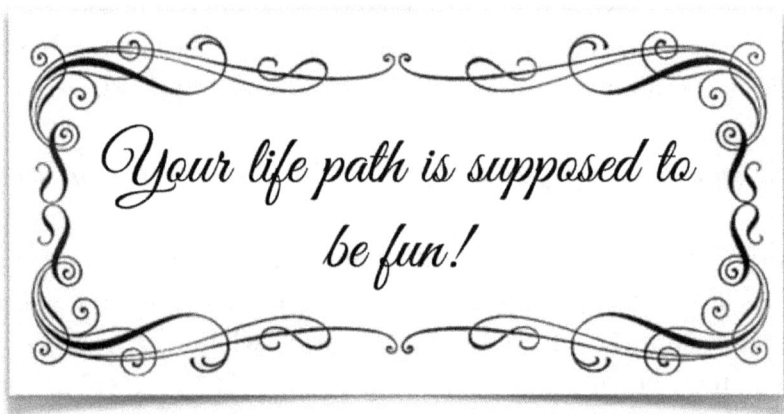

Growth is inevitable, but the path of your life is supposed to be fun. The journey is through joy. Many have forgotten this understanding, yet all that is needed as a reminder, is the connection to Source which we all have available. Meditation, being present in the fun, playing with the dog and immersing yourself in nature are pursuits that can lead you back to the relationship you desire most, which is the relationship between your physical and your spiritual self. Along this journey your Mood Map will be a valuable GPS guiding you along the winding path of life.

When your intentions are to feel good, you can find yourself smiling as you feel happy and perceive life as just wonderful. You've also experienced that life seems unfair when you've been cheated, a situation that changes your perspective of life. Emotions guide you through the pitfalls of relationships and there are many things you can do to make this more fun.

Here are some common traps to avoid:

- ☐ *Don't try to change people.* People are the way they are, and it is right for them at a given time. The only reason anyone wants to change another is because they think they will feel better if the other changes. As you let go of judging right and wrong and accept people as they are, you will find peace. Unless someone has asked for your help and you are able to give the help they need, let them be. It's not your place to say that the decisions someone has made are not good enough. You don't need to have an opinion on how you think they should be living, as their change does not need to affect your life.

- ☐ *Reflections.* How you see people is all about you, not them. If you see people as angry, you are a vibrational match with anger at the moment. Everyone has positive and negative moods, just as some people bring out the best or the worst in others. Instead of going with the anger, change your intentions and look for things to feel good about. When you keep the best of them in your focus, they can move towards the best in you. Hold their light and not their darkness.

- ☐ *Accept others the way they are.* When you accept yourself as you are, you're likely to accept others as they are. This allows you to find joy in life, as happy people attract happy people. You won't always attract happy people in your life, but just understand that the acceptance is an indicator that your mood has changed, and you have the opportunity to set intentions for the mood you want.

- ☐ *Minding your own business.* If you have an opinion on a subject that doesn't please you then you are inviting what you don't want into your vibration and into your life. When that opinion isn't uplifting, you're not going to be pleased with the outcome you are creating, as you ask for what you want by your vibration, not your words. The words you speak or listen to can change how you feel, for better or worse, so discern wisely and choose the thoughts you think consciously.

- ☐ *Be fussy about who you hang around with.* If the people who come into your life are not the people you want to share your life with, choose your own company. It's sometimes difficult to avoid certain people, especially if you work for them, or are married to them, but you can set your intentions so that you are ready to feel good 'no matter what'. In this way, you can change the frequency of the conversation to an uplifting channel.

☐ *Enjoy your own company.* It's difficult to escape people altogether in this day and age of technology, but finding some alone time is important for nurturing the Soul. Being on your own gives you the time and space to re-gather through meditation, sleep, and fine-tuning your vibration, which helps you move into the feeling-great mood you are really wanting. When you can't find a mood of peace in your own head, it's difficult to find it in other people, as they only serve to emphasize your current mood, which is where you are and not where you want to be. By allocating 'alone time' you can find a mood of joy and love where you are connected with Source.

A neighbor wanted to know what she could do about a person she didn't like, who often attended the same social functions as she did. It was a common theme, as there are many people who have in their social circles, work colleagues or family that makes their lives a misery, and these people can sometimes be unavoidable. If you know you are going to be in the company of someone like this, set your intentions before you leave the house. "I am going to feel good, no matter what". Then go and enjoy yourself. If you feel that you are being drawn into conversations that are not pleasing, extract yourself, change the subject or repeat to yourself a mantra.

It would be difficult for me to describe to you the miracles that setting your intentions can create in your reality. If you set your intentions each day to 'feel good' (and repeat the intention regularly throughout the day if things go awry), you would need do nothing else, as your life would unfold beautifully.

Your journey may be shared with others but your life is all about you. People around you can influence it, but it is you who makes the decisions that affect your life. The universe really does revolve around you. It responds to your moods, creates in response to your vibration, and attracts people and situations that match your vibration. This is called your reality, and no two realities in this Universe are the same. It is a personal journey of growth, and how you live this life is your choice. The Universe doesn't judge what is right or wrong for you to create, or judge you for what you should and shouldn't have created; it respects your choices.

From your experiences, new desires are born in an ever-expanding, abundant Universe. You knew when you came into this life that it was all about choosing through experience and having fun in the process. All roads lead to Rome, as the saying goes, so you can't ever get it wrong because you are eternal, and the desires are never finished.

Transforming Your Relationships

As people are attracted to one another through vibration, it makes sense that the ideal time to find a life partner is when you are feeling great, as the person who is attracted will reflect those emotions. It is a joining of two like-minded people who know they create their own happiness, and that the one won't hold the other responsible for their moods. They will see that this is the basis of a strong, joyous relationship. Many people also find a partner when they are needy or emotionally unstable, and the very best the Universe can provide for them is a vibrational match with the way they are feeling. An insecure person attracts one who will fulfill his or her needs. This works for a while, but eventually one of the partners gets tired of playing a role and wants to find their own power. This occurrence threatens the emotional side of the partnership, because when one person in the relationship expects the other to act in a certain manner, there is emotional instability when it doesn't happen. The next step is blame and resentment for the way the one partner feels. It may be difficult to notice what needs changing in a relationship, but it can be empowering to understand that you are the only one who can please you.

A friend of mine wanted to know why she kept being drawn into the kinds of conversations with her daughter which ended in both parties feeling frustrated. We discovered it was because she had learned from her mother that when you heard someone's problems you needed to offer a solution. She knew that what her daughter was looking for was not solutions but someone who would listen to her problems. It was the mother's need to make things better that was getting in the way. The solution was to have a clear set of intentions ready, so as soon as her daughter called, she could move into a feeling of optimism and well-being rather than dread. She could change the tone of her voice, and become focused on listening rather than fixing. Her past behaviors were patterns she had learned as a child, and they had been passed down for generations. Mothers to their babies communicate many unspoken beliefs and fears even before they are born. The child grows not realizing the beliefs adopted are pivotal in creating their reality. When these patterns no longer work, as exhibited in relationships with others, their beliefs are challenged. Powerful, conscious choices of setting your intentions can transform your life.

Jody's Mother

Jody was having trouble with her mother. They used to be close when her father was alive. Jody always stood up for her mother and became the protector when there was an argument between her parents. She loved her father dearly, but admitted he was a tyrant towards her mother who, in turn, was convinced her unhappiness hinged on the behavior of her husband.

Jody's father became ill and passed away. After the initial upset, Jody's mother became jubilant, as she realized she was free. A burden had been lifted, and people commented on how good she looked. Jody's mother always said she loved her own company, and now she had as much as she wanted of it, but the vibrant mood didn't last. The feeling of freedom that had given her so much relief gave way to fear. She began to suffer from anxiety, dreaded being on her own, and was afraid her new male friend wasn't attracted to her anymore.

Like so many people who blame another for the way they feel, Jody's mother was realizing that it wasn't Jody's father who was the reason for her unhappiness. The patterns of thought that created the unhappiness when Jody's father was alive were still the same thoughts that existed in her life now. It was a pattern she wasn't keen to release, so she looked for a substitute. Jody was expected to fill the role of perpetrator. Since Jody noticed what was happening, she was upset about the behavior and came to see how she could alleviate the cycle but still share her mother's love.

It is often difficult to understand that the person who annoys you the most in your life isn't the problem. How you perceive someone is always a reflection of your emotions and the expectations you have of another is a learned behavior. Self-talk determines the patterns of thought that create your perspective of the world. If this is how someone you care for is feeling and they are only willing to blame others, don't worry as there will come a time when they are ready to see things differently. This is their journey and you only have control of your own path. When Jody understood what was happening, and why her mother needed to play this game, she made sure her intentions of staying in a buoyant mood were paramount when she was around her mother.

Transforming your life is a matter of knowing what you want. When you are in an unharmonious relationship, you automatically know you want a harmonious one. Your Higher Self automatically moves to this new and improved version of your life calling you forth. This is a natural process that takes place often. Your only job now is to focus on a harmonious relationship even if it isn't yet your reality, by changing your self-talk.

Pretending to be Polite

As we age, there is a tendency to lose inhibitions once needed to fit into society. Both older people and young children will describe the way they feel about a person in candid terms, and the description can sometimes seem brutally honest, as they have removed the 'politeness' filter. The rest of us are conditioned by society to be 'careful' what we say. As Cathy's father had dementia, he lived in a nursing home. She was always embarrassed when a woman walked past them, as he stated quite loudly their imperfections, for all to hear. She 'had a big ass", was his favorite expression. When a child points at someone in a shopping center and announces they are fat, they speak their observation without malice. In a little while, that child will learn about 'politeness' filters. He will be taught to be mindful of what he says in case it hurts someone's feelings. This is the beginning of learning a false premise, that it's his fault if someone feels bad. Of course, it's never going to be acceptable that people walk around

Six Dimensions of Healing

calling others fat, but the point is that nobody can hurt your feelings except you. A million people can share the same opinion, but as long as it doesn't affect your opinion, it doesn't affect you. Their opinions affect their world and your opinion affects yours.

Set your intentions to be a conscious creator, and be aware of these six things:

- *What you're thinking.* Thoughts are tangible and are the beginning of any creation.
- *Who is coming into your life?* The people in your life are a reflection of how *you* feel.
- *How you feel.* Choose your thoughts and choose your emotions, don't leave it to somebody else. How do you want to feel?
- *What you're holding on to.* Remembering your past guilts, become your present projections.
- *Who you're blaming.* Let go of the blame game. Whether you're right or not is irrelevant as it's just not worth your peace of mind.
- *What you're observing and the opinions you hold.* If what you're observing is making you feel uncomfortable, look elsewhere and choose opinions that make you feel good.

It would be wonderful to be happy and joyous all the time, but that's just not going to happen. This is not only OK, it's necessary for your growth. If you are feeling agitated or angry, so be it. Just understand that your life will be reflected to you the way you are feeling. Not as a punishment or a lesson and not because of karma, but as an indicator of what you are creating.

Manifesting Negative or Positive

Many people ask, "How is it that negative things come into my life faster than positive things? I can be feeling great for a long time and then my mood changes and, before I know it, bad things happen."

When you have a well-practiced pattern of thought, which becomes a belief, (a belief is a thought you think over and over again) you create momentum in the direction of those thoughts. If each subject is a waterfall, then the thoughts you give most attention to will flow with more water. The waterfall may trickle on some subjects and be a raging torrent on others. You have many waterfalls flowing at the one time and the direction of your thoughts determines the amount of water flowing. When you are excited about a project, involved in the aspects that please you, and feel that life is working well, the waterfall of well-being is flowing freely. The more time spent in the feeling of well-being, then the more the momentum over the waterfall. Just as thoughts diminish rather than disappear, these waterfalls only diminish but never disappear, so when you have been frustrated for any length of time, the waterfall that is frustration begins to flow. The more time spent in thoughts of frustration, the more momentum is created, and the waterfall of frustration becomes a raging torrent. This is your path of manifestation. The only way to change the momentum of a waterfall is by creating momentum in a different waterfall. In this way, the momentum in another diminishes. You can't clear a subject, as both positive and negative thoughts add momentum. When your thoughts of frustration seem to be in control, the only way to change the momentum is to gain momentum on a better feeling subject.

Because each subject has its own momentum, it is important for your well-being to set your intentions each day to determine the emotions in which you'll gain momentum. It is much easier to stop a trickle than a raging torrent; just as it is much easier to change your thoughts when you are first aware they are not serving you, than to wait until momentum is gathered.

You have many waterfalls of emotion all flowing at different rates, and it is of value to you to focus on the thoughts that create the emotional waterfall you want to flow. That is always your choice. When you aren't aware of the thoughts you are thinking or how you feel when you are observing a situation, then default observations will move you in a direction most common. The longer you spend complaining about what you don't like or don't want, the more momentum you create in patterns that manifest more situations you don't like.

The only reason negative situations manifest more quickly than pleasing ones is that you have added to a negative waterfall over the years. It will lie there as a trickle or even remain dormant, but as soon as you add thoughts to the subject, momentum will commence a raging waterfall which manifests situations that reflect those emotions. It is worthwhile being aware of your mood as then you can choose your thoughts wisely.

Choose your Master wisely

"When you are standing on a higher hill there is so much more of the landscape of opportunities that are visible".
(Gayle Maree, 2008)

There is always an emotional gravitational pull towards a default mood. This mood like most other patterns is a learned behavior. When feeling good is a mood you love, but can't seem to maintain, it is usually because of the default mood that has been practiced over many years. If the practiced mood is one of boredom, frustration, impatience or maybe blame, this becomes the place you hang around in and it is the mood from which you create. The more often you keep the company of undesirable moods, the more likely you are to manifest unwanted situations in your life. As all emotions that are dominant create your reality, it makes sense to move towards changing your default mood.

Creating any new default vibration is similar to etching a new song on a record. You experience the emotions over and over again; until you create a deep groove that your thoughts can move to directly. When your intention is to create an uplifting default mood then awareness is your best ally, as looking for things to feel good about will change the direction of your thoughts and your mood. This may not seem important, as you can change your mood at any time but a default mood is the place where your mind rests. It can become the master of your reality, the platform from which the next thought is created, and a mood from which you respond to the world. Joy, fun, excitement, enthusiasm and passion are much better emotional masters than fear, hatred and blame. As emotions are your constant companion and lead the way down the path of life, changing your master can change your life.

Resentment is a poor master. Everyone has felt wrongly done by at some time, but only you can determine whether this feeling will shape your future or not.

Many years ago, I conducted Personal Development seminars for long-term unemployed. When I asked a group of men how many had been wronged in their life, to my surprise everyone raised their hand. There wasn't one person in that room who hadn't had cause to feel resentment, for an experience that was no fault of their own. One man asked me after the class if I remembered a particular hit song from the 80's, which I did. He told me he had been part of a well-known band and had written the song. When the group broke up, two of the other band members put their names to his song and gave it to someone to sing, who made it into a hit. He got no credit for it. I could understand his disappointment, but more than twenty years later he was still allowing resentment to be his master.

We crossed paths a few times over the next year, and I came to understand that his fame was in telling people his hard luck story. The people who surrounded him helped him play the victim, a role he continued to maintain. Self-pity is a very poor master, and the only place he found solace was in a bottle. He left this physical plane not long afterwards, and I'm sure he now has a more enlightened vantage point.

Practicing a mood of resentment creates a default mood of resentment. This becomes the way you perceive the world and is what is attracted into your reality. It is beneficial to your well-being to be aware of how you are feeling, as it is just as easy to create default moods of optimism as it is of resentment. They are both learned behaviors.

Making a conscious choice to move into a good-feeling mood creates an uplifted default mood. When your intentions have been set to feel good before you even walk out the door, there is a conscious awareness to raise the default mood to a higher vibration. This won't guarantee a vibration of joy, but will move your default mood closer to that of Source, which is where everything you want to manifest exists. When there is a temptation to slide down the slippery slope of emotions, you can reset the intentions to feel good. These are all practiced emotions, and the more often you set these intentions, the quicker your mood changes.

The forming of a new default mood pattern will not only make you feel better, but also give you a new perspective from which to create your future. It makes a lot more sense to jump out of a plane with a parachute than doing so without one, hoping it will appear mid-air; and taking control of your mood is ensuring the parachute is in good working condition.

As it takes twenty-one days of consciously moving your mood to create a new default pattern, take up the challenge to change your reality. It only takes ten minutes of self-talk to change how you feel now and twenty-one days to change the pattern.

Look Where You Are Going

Jane was a friend who wanted much from life, but was very aware of what was missing in her quest for fulfillment. She was aware of the lack of money, desires that weren't manifesting and the feeling of depletion. All this added up to a mood of resentment, which wasn't directed towards anyone in particular but towards the Universe in general, and she resented that she'd missed out on the joy of life.

Jane was going through life looking for the evidence of what she wanted, but was noticing the absence of her desires, which is otherwise known as reality. Reality shows only the evidence of what has been created in the past. The more Jane noticed what was missing, the more she resented what others had achieved. It's not that she didn't want them to have their abundance but she couldn't see from her reality how the improvements she was seeking were going to manifest.

Jane was asked if she could look ahead and imagine a better future, but the patterns she had practiced were entrenched and she could only see what was. By focusing on her reality Jane was creating more of the same, and this is only good if your reality is what you want in abundance. For Jane to get what she wanted there needed to be a shift in her intentions and a focus toward her desires.

Jane commenced a program of breathing exercises to hone her focus, and it helped her to think less. By decreasing her thoughts, she was putting fewer obstacles in her path and, because there is a stream of well-being, it meant she was beginning to allow this stream to flow. She began to let her imagination wander and create an image of what an abundant future might look like, which included what she was doing, where she was, and who she was doing it with. Her instructions were to really immerse herself in this imagining and feel it, touch it, and use her senses to become immersed in this vision. When she had practiced these visions until they felt real, the activity created an excitement about her future.

At first the old patterns were intrusive and her visions felt scattered, as the imagination ran rampant searching for something she was comfortable imagining, eventually to settle on an image that wasn't a big stretch for her imagination. It is important to create something that feels real, so Jane imagined a scenario that felt real. Using images the mind will argue about is self-defeating, so there is no point imagining you are going to change the world, if you can't grasp the vision, and your mind keeps telling you that you can't do it. It's much simpler to start by imagining something you *can* resonate with. You certainly can change the world but your thinking needs to support your dreams, so starting simple is a matter of believing in yourself, then you can grow your visions and the beliefs move with you. Life is made of a series of small confidence steps, not one giant leap-off the cliff.

Jane found that she could imagine finishing her manuscript and building a following. She could see herself developing a center where people would be interested in what she had to say and it became easier for her to immerse herself in this dream the more she practiced. Jane became aware of the underlying mood that usually defeated her, which was a feeling of impatience. Time seemed a factor as she wanted to achieve more in this lifetime than she felt there was time for, so the more she noticed things weren't moving fast enough the more they slowed down.

Eventually Jane came to understand she had plenty of time to get the next thing done, and the next. We are Eternal Beings and even though we will achieve much in this lifetime, there will always be things left undone. She knew she needed to let go and allow her life to unfold.

Most of us are guilty of wanting something specific, and then being afraid of missing out, so we try to make things happen more quickly. Effort goes into pushing against opposition and by doing this we create more opposition. What needs to be done is getting into a good-feeling mood as often as possible, imagining what you want, and allowing the next step to unfold. Your work is to find a way of staying in a good mood as often as you can. There is nothing you 'should' do.

There will always be things we want that don't appear in this lifetime. It doesn't mean they won't come. Our souls are eternal. We create forever, not just for one lifetime. There are thousands of manifestations we are living now that were the desires of those before us. We are not the only ones to have created this lifetime, as our ancestors have created before us, through the hardships they encountered. Their desires have become our reality. Your desires are not only enhancing your life, but also paving the way for generations to come. That's evolution.

Changing Patterns of Behavior

There are many patterns of behavior you have adopted from those you grew up with. Some support you and others can be debilitating. Opportunities to let go of old patterns and create new ones present themselves until the day we die. Often they aren't recognized, as a person who is abrasive presents them. It can be difficult to understand that the scoundrels who come into your life do so for your benefit.

There is always an opportunity to respond differently and when you respond favorably you create a harmonious reality.

Children are also aware of this understanding. When our eldest daughter was thirteen she was having trouble with a girl in her dancing class. I stopped the car to drop her off one evening and noticed she was hesitant about going, so I said, "You don't have to go, you know."
She turned and looked at me and said,
"Yes I do Mum. Otherwise it will get worse as I get older."
I was shocked at this display of wisdom from one so young. I also knew she was right.

Often, we think the elderly should be peaceful and happy towards the end of their lives. Some are, but many elderly people aren't feeling the joy of wisdom. This has a lot to do with how they have perceived opportunities that have presented themselves as pebbles when they were younger, only to become boulders as they got older.

Throughout our lives, we are all presented with opportunities to move beyond any limiting patterns we have held, as we are always moving toward the Source Energy within us. This is the expansion that happens over many lifetimes. You may expect a shining angel to light the way, but not all angels shine a light; there are times when a light is invisible, when all you can hear is frustration. If we feel angry the opportunities present themselves as anger. When we are depressed we only hear depression. Opportunities for growth are often ignored, because of the one who delivers them. When you are feeling angry, all you hear from the messenger is anger. It can be difficult to see these angry people as messengers, but these scoundrels that come into your life are an integral part of your growth and expansion, as there always lays an opportunity to move beyond your limiting beliefs.

Opportunities to rid yourself of limiting beliefs commence as a whisper when you are younger, but become more pronounced, as you get older so that you can hear them. If you hear the whisper and change the pattern as Leonie did when she was dancing, you have developed a new pattern that serves you and is no longer limiting, so there are no more whispers or messengers for that belief. In other words, once you have changed the pattern, it is eternal. You have the opportunity to move beliefs beyond these limiting patterns to the day you die.

There are no lessons in life, but many opportunities to change your perspective. A wise friend once said to me, "Avoid saying it's a lesson, as you only keep setting up lessons for yourself." You're not here to learn, you're here to grow and expand by having fun. The reason lessons sound appealing is that feeling of unworthiness, which suggests you are not in control of your life. When you feel worthy, life is for living, not learning.

Old Habit Patterns

Old habit patterns are like friends who come to visit. Sometimes they are wanted and sometimes they aren't, but all eventually wear out their welcome.

You can have a wonderful perspective flowing in your reality. Then someone comes along and provides some unwanted news that affects your health, relationships or financial status and you react with old habit patterns. There is a guarantee you will get the same results as the last time you responded with the same patterns. That bully you thought you were rid of just poked their head around your door and asked if they could help. It's tempting to accept the help, but better to tell them you don't need them anymore. You have a new uplifting friend who may be unfamiliar, but you want to walk with them.

A friend of mine goes so far as to give her old inner voice a name. Some call it the ego and some even the devil. She calls it Freddy F***wit. She can be walking alongside the lake as she does most mornings, and here she finds Freddy running along in front of her. She promptly tells him to get lost in no uncertain terms as she doesn't need him anymore. She is very aware that when Freddy plays with her, she always gets the same results and they are never pleasing.

You will always find that the use of humor will help to release tension, and sometimes it is the tension that keeps you in a stranglehold. When you start to believe what others say about you, it is time to release the stranglehold.

There is an old saying that goes, "It's none of your business what others say or think about you". It should go on to say that it *is* your business, however, what you say and think about them. How you respond to a situation is your mood, and your mood creates your reality. It is none of your business what others think of you and it has no effect on you if you don't allow it into your thoughts. If you can laugh it off and feel good your life will unfold in ways beyond your imagining.

Freeing Yourself From Fear, Anxiety, Stress & Tension

When something happens that wasn't planned, it's easy to move into a spiral of fear. In just a few short minutes you have concluded that you aren't in control of your life, but that someone or something else is calling the shots, and there seems to be nothing you can do about it. The feeling of fear is the feeling of being out of control. You have an urge to put your foot on the brake of life so that it will slow down and give you time to think. Fear is not a feeling that is close to your Source's opinion on any subject, and that is why it feels so uncomfortable. This emotion is the opposite of freedom, which is the natural state of well-being.

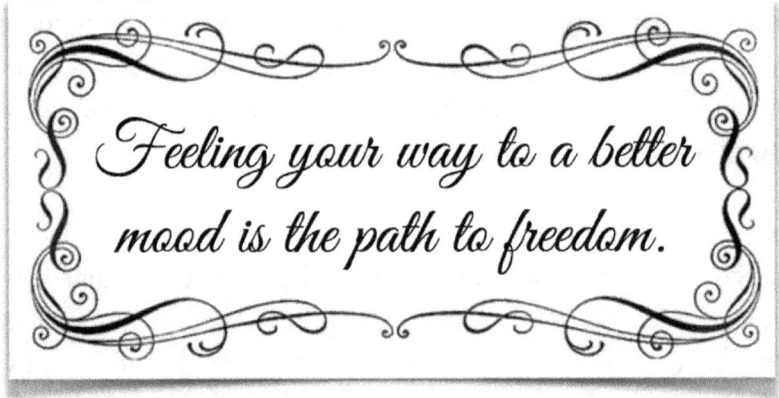

Feeling your way to a better mood is the path to freedom.

It's quite common to justify or blame others for the situation you find yourself in, but this keeps you from taking back control. When you attempt to think yourself out of the black hole of thought, you find yourself getting deeper and deeper as no amount of digging can get you out of any hole. The more you try not to think about the subject that has you worried you, the more you focus on what isn't wanted. Feeling your way to a better mood is your only path to freedom.

Any method to move beyond an unwanted pattern takes discipline. That may be a dirty word but the alternative is to keep doing what you don't want and get what you don't like. Whether the pattern is fear, worry, anger, stress or anxiety. If you would like to move beyond any debilitating moods, you can. It took practice to create them, and it will take practice to create something different. It doesn't mean that you will never again feel a negative mood, but it does mean you will have developed a method of handling these, and with practice, they will affect you less and less.

You haven't failed because you have been feeling great, then move into diminishing thoughts and emotions that are negative. Everyone in the world experiences a fall from the feel-good train intermittently. You really don't want to keep thoughts that are diminishing as they have a negative impact on your life, so it is beneficial to catch the mood early and move your attention elsewhere. In this way, you will be changing your future to something exciting.

- *Notice how you are feeling.* Be aware of what mood you are feeling, and observe your thoughts as they move through your mind.

- *Acknowledge* that these thoughts aren't working for you. Your thoughts are making things worse and, although your mind has you convinced thinking is the only path, no solution can be found in this space. Problems are on a different frequency than solutions, and if you are thinking, you are on the same frequency as the problem. The aim is to move into the frequency of the solution.

- *Using the method of self-talk,* convince yourself there are many paths to handling this situation. There is even one you will enjoy and get results. Your self-talk will undermine you if you aren't determined to move in another direction as we have been taught from a young age to think our way to a solution. Solutions are found when we can get off the subject and not tangle it with thinking. The key here is self-talk and not talking with others. Sometimes people can be helpful, but most of your friends have no idea how you feel, or that you are aiming to move into the frequency of a solution. When you share the 'poor me' story, you can easily fall into the trap of feeling victimized. This is a trap that can be difficult to extract yourself from, so if you want a harmonious solution for yourself then move to the next step.

- *Choose a simple thought.* Halting the momentum of what isn't working can be as simple as being present in nature, patting the dog, drinking a clean glass of water, breathing in fresh air, or smelling a scented rose. Keep the subject simple and give it your full attention. Then notice another simple thing and another. Within a couple of minutes, you will have changed how you feel. There will be ease and some relief.

- *Look around for another simple observation.* Because your focus may gravitate towards noticing what is wrong with everything, make it your intention to look for things that are working in your life. There can be a hundred things that aren't working and only one thing that is. Give your attention to the one thing that is working. Perpetuate the momentum of what is working by acknowledging how you are feeling. When you are feeling a mood of relief, no matter what it is from, acknowledge you have created this relief as it becomes self-empowering.

- *Make a conscious choice.* As fear, anxiety, stress and tension are based on not believing the Universe is supporting you (which of course your Source does not agree with) set your intentions first thing in the morning. Before you set foot out of bed say some affirmations that have no resistance. You will need to feel your way through this path as it may change from day to day. As you start each day on a new footing with a new mood and a clean slate, the affirmations you choose create a new path. Each morning you have a choice as to how you want to commence your day.

Depending on the circumstances, there may be a need to recommence some of the steps in this method. Use the steps that resonate. Resist the temptation to evaluate early by looking for evidence of what is absent. Instead, use your Mood Map as a guide, and see the way you feel as evidence that you have moved direction.

When you are in alignment with your Source you will feel great. It is the only direction that will ever sustain and fulfill you. It isn't religious, but it is connection.

Releasing Pain Through Acknowledgment

Most people usually find their comfortable place in the world by the end of a lifetime. There is comfort in knowing someone loves you, and feeling loved is acknowledgment that you must be doing something right. But what happens when a life is cut short by war or trauma before a person finds their place of belonging? Then an imbalance comes about in the form of yearning. Balance is important to each body, mind and soul, so an imbalance always seeks to be balanced.

Although the corrections for an imbalance can be found in your current life, it is sometimes beneficial to acknowledge what memorable events have gone before. There are many statistics that point towards the value of Past Life Therapy and whether you understand past lives, or acknowledge that we have a connection with what has gone before us, it can be valuable to acknowledge some events of the past. In acknowledging a traumatic event whether in this life or another, there can be a release of the physical symptom held on into the present that achieves balance. Balancing the body is what we call healing.

Some years ago, our hairdresser had a congenital back problem. Specialists predicted she would be in a wheelchair by the age of fifty. Pauline was already in her forties and suffering much pain. Experiencing Past Life Regression for the first time she remembered* that she had been killed in several previous lifetimes due to having a broken back from a rock slide, a horse accident, a sword wound, and a few more similar traumatic endings. Within a week of the regression, her pain had reduced and for months afterwards the symptoms slowly cleared. The acknowledgment had changed the need for symptoms from the emotional trauma. There is no wheelchair in her immediate future.
(* Remembered by the client through Past Life Regression hypnosis.)

Many people die alone. Some aren't missed and others aren't recognized as having been part of a war, a titanic event or even a holocaust. It's as if they didn't ever exist, and these spirits tend to hang around until they are acknowledged. Their life did have a purpose, and they will keep pointing people toward their demise until it is acknowledged. That's what Rest in Peace means. It's an acknowledgment at the funeral of one's life. Our journey, participation and contribution to the world, no matter how large or seemingly insignificant, is important to each and every one of us.

As connection to Source is through emotions, it makes sense that we also connect with ourselves through emotions. Past memories link like a cord to emotions that changed the course of our journey whether in the immediate or distant past. When you remember circumstances from your childhood, it won't be the events that create memories but the emotions; and if an event is significant, it is because the emotions were strong. Strong joyous emotions become a solid grounding for more joyful emotions. That is fertile ground from which many wonderful memories grow. If the emotions are painful, they will also remain strong until they are acknowledged by you or for you. You hear of deceased murder victims helping the police through those who can connect with them, to find the murderer and uncover the true circumstances of their murder, as they need to have this acknowledged.

Acknowledgment of pain can lead to acceptance of self. This has nothing to do with forgiving another. Making peace with any situation is always for the benefit of self. When traumatic situations are experienced, the emotions can be stored for many years and sometimes lifetimes. This deep-rooted pain can mold the personality and physically manifest itself through the body. In fact, behaviors in reaction to pain can become so entrenched in our current lives that we can't recognize the patterns that created them. Fortunately, all the moods and patterns we are unaware of, are also reflected in the people around us. That's the reason 'blame' has become such a social addiction. It's much easier to blame another for their behavior than to admit what we feel about someone is a reflection of ourselves.

We are so closely connected to one another by emotions that one person can acknowledge for another. If someone has died and it comes to light they were mistreated as a child, the acknowledgment of the event is still important. It is never too late to acknowledge another's worthiness. When they die, they may be non-physical, but they are very much present. In a healing session, it would sometimes become apparent that a person's pain was related to a traumatic 'past life' memory. The therapist could acknowledge this trauma as it was presented and the pain in the client would immediately start to dissipate, which demonstrates how closely people can be linked.

Acknowledgment is not something you can prove but it is a calmness you can feel. When a person's trauma is acknowledged because they are ready to release emotions from the past, peace and harmony can be the result. Acknowledgment of another is an integral part of compassion. It is finding that peace amongst the chaos.

How Unconditional is your Giving?

How many times have you heard or felt the statements "I give and give and receive nothing in return" or "I need more from this relationship"? These statements are examples of conditional giving, which is giving when a return is expected for what you are giving. Giving is a two-way street, but sometimes the intentions are singular. Giving is very personal and quite selfish, as the giving is created to make you feel good. Unconditional love is giving because it is uplifting.

When your intentions are to get something in return, even if that return is a mood or a smile, then the giving is conditional. If you find yourself in a situation where you feel obliged to contribute, then change how you feel about it. Change your mood. Give not from resentment but from joy, as it will bring you joy in return, rather than resentment.

Repeated actions and emotions create beliefs.

It is not wrong to expect another to make you feel good, but it will not give you much joy, as you are building the belief that another holds the key to your happiness. That's a mountainous vocation for anyone to excel at, and they won't be able to exceed in this role forever. When the focus of another changes and their sole purpose isn't on pleasing you anymore, the feelings of unworthiness come to the fore and you look for another to fill the role. You will also become an Anti-Role Model for your children, as you teach them your habits of being dependent on someone else for their happiness. This isn't communicated verbally, as words don't teach, but your repeated actions and emotions create their beliefs. Just as you were influenced by the people around you, so too will your children adopt the habit patterns they grow up with, whether you want them to or not. The only influence you have over another is by your example. How you think and how you feel is passed down your lineage.

A forty-six-year-old man came into the clinic and stated that he had Bipolar Disorder. He said it had been diagnosed and there was nothing he could do about the illness. He was quite proud that his mother and his grandmother had both had 'Bipolar' and it was inevitable that he would also suffer. When it was suggested that maybe he could do something about the symptoms, as he had adopted the habit patterns of his mother who had adopted them from her grandmother, he nearly ran out of the clinic. You see he wasn't ready to find a solution; he only wanted to have an excuse to be ill.

When you are in a situation and giving for the sheer joy of giving, you won't even describe this experience as giving. It will be described as uplifting, fun, joy and certainly fulfilling. As another can never fulfill you, it seems futile to look for another to give to you, as what you are really seeking is your own connection, not connection with another. The connection you are seeking is between you and you — the physical you, and the non-physical you who holds the light. There is no separation. There are not two entities. The only pain you ever feel is the pulling away from the part of you who holds the light. If you were to sever a body part, it would hurt, and so does moving in the opposite direction of your own light.

There was a spirited ninety-six-year-old lady who lived alone down the end of our street. I would pass by in the mornings and pick up her paper and place it on a table. Sometimes she was awake, and so we would sit and chat a while. She had three children. (You don't think of children being in their seventies.) One son lived on the other side of the world in Canada, one an hour away, and she had a daughter she didn't communicate with. People had taken advantage of her, and I lived close, so I would see if she needed a hand now and again. We would go to the doctors, go shopping and have lunch together. A friendship developed and I was happy to accompany her where she needed to go. Sometimes it was for necessities and at other times it was to attend a function. If she needed me to steal the papaya from over the fence, I could do that too.

One year, I met her son at a Christmas party. He thanked me and asked what I got out of helping his mother. I told him she was giving me the opportunity to experience unconditional giving. If there were nobody to receive, then giving would become obsolete. Unconditional giving and receiving is balanced by the intentions with which you give or receive, as who you give to will not always be the same person you receive from. It's a global phenomenon, as we're all in this together.

The Benefits of Feeling Great!

This handbook talks a lot about feeling great, as it is the connection with Source Energy that you seek. Whilst you aren't ever going to stay in a place of feeling great continuously, the aim is to know the feeling of excitement and joy that becomes so well-practiced that it is chronic; the more often you visit the mood of joy, excitement, love, enthusiasm and passion the quicker you will bounce back towards these moods.

The advantages these buoyant moods create are endless. Not only will you feel amazing but also you'll look and feel younger with eyes that sparkle with life-energy. Your metabolism will increase, and the body will balance itself. You will feel free and unburdened, understanding your abundant nature and knowing your true self. Clarity and confidence in life will abound. You will attract uplifting people where the frequency of ideas and opportunities will increase.

Feeling great is your natural state of being. It is the corner stone of health and well-being. It doesn't matter if you can't remember how to feel great. The intentions are that you *want* to find relief, as everything in your life can be changed.

Joy can be created by anyone.

- Situations don't have to change.
- People don't need to do anything for you.
- The environment doesn't need to be different.
- Luck doesn't play a part.
- You don't have to be deserving in the eyes of others.
- There isn't a better time than now.

There is only a stream of joy and health, so when you aren't feeling this way it is you who is impeding the flow. It can be helpful to remember these injunctions:

- Stop beating up on yourself.
- No more undermining.
- No need to feel insecure.
- It's nobody's fault so there is no need to blame.
- Feeling sorry for yourself doesn't get you to where you want to go.
- Don't dwell in doubt.

When you can change these six obstacles, you will transform your life, as you are allowing the stream of well-being into your life by not impeding the flow with thoughts and opinions.

We've provided a multitude of tools in this handbook on how to move from where you are now standing to where you want to be, and none of them require you to buy a new car or mortgage your soul. Whether you are religious or not, you can move into your stream of well-being at any time and do it by yourself, simply by changing your mood.

Motivational Tapes

It was a popular trend to listen to 'motivational' tapes in the eighties. These were intended to help you get what you wanted in life by emphasizing how big you should dream, how much to put yourself in debt, and what other actions to take. Lastly but certainly not least, was the strong message that nothing could be achieved without sacrifice. They used big goals for motivation, with the thinking that if you would choose to buy an expensive car that was out of your reach, you would work really hard to make the payments. For some this was motivation enough to achieve in a big way, and others handed the car back to the finance companies when they were drowning in debt, which lost them money and self-confidence. It was an era of huge personal debt, which created problems for society that had previously been unrecognized. The 'eighties was a decade when many, rich and poor alike, discovered the silent killer of stress.

What all of those people had in common was the desire to change their circumstances. How they differed was in their moods, thoughts and emotional backgrounds. What was offered to them was a blanket solution for an individual problem and that will only ever work for some. Motivational tapes were all about physically taking action, and they didn't take into consideration the consequences of emotional opposition. Taking action when not inspired and excited, becomes a self-defeating challenge.

When your emotions are in opposition to what you are telling yourself, there is disbelief which manifests in the form of resistance*. This doesn't mean you settle for mediocrity, and it doesn't mean you can't have the expensive car you desire, but going out and buying the car just to take action will cause a mountain of stress and effort that will not have a happy ending until you can make peace with your emotions. So, make peace with your emotions, and then feel inspired to get the car, as this method will bypass the stress and effort.

(* See *Resistance* in the *Emotional* Dimension chapter.)

You could want the luxury car and have a glossy photo on your wall. You can imagine the details of the car. When you allow the time factor to become irrelevant, you can enjoy imagining being the driver of that wonderful car. Then as you sit in your present vehicle you could be imagining that beautiful sleek car with the new smell of luxury leather upholstery and enjoying the steering as it hugs the road. You can imagine everything about the new car. Just imagining your new car would feel so good that it wouldn't even matter when the car showed up. When you imagine your life as you want it to be, without the resistance of opposition thoughts, you are in the same frequency as your desires. These desires will manifest — whether tomorrow, next year, or even decade, but the timing will be perfect. It will be easy and effortless with no stress involved. Anything desired, needs to be believed in your mind before it is seen in your reality. Dr Wayne Dyer (1940-2015) wrote a book on this subject. He called this; "You'll See It When You Believe It."

If the only intention you ever had was to feel good, your life would unfold beautifully.

Change Your Reality and You Change Your Life

You and Your Purpose in Life

Six Dimensions of Healing

Enjoy the Journey

Life is neither a marathon nor a sprint; it's a journey. Most people focus on the destination, when it's really the hard work and effort to get there that counts. It's all about the journey and not the destination. Destinations change. Goals and dreams change over time and become more refined. The real purpose of the destination is to excite you so that you have life energy coursing through your veins.

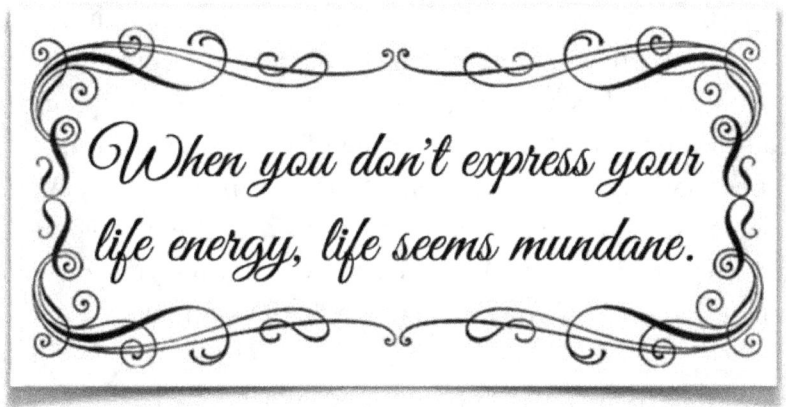

When you don't express your life energy, life seems mundane.

Your life energy determines the direction of your life as it excites you into taking opportunities and making choices. This journey is your life. Imagine if you didn't have a dream you were excited about. It would then be difficult to enjoy the mundane job you are working in, your partner's success, or even discover your children's fun. Life would seem flat and lacking in purpose. Not because of who you are, but because of who you aren't. You aren't expressing your life energy, and it has become a trickle, a mere shadow of who you could be. If you have a dream that is exciting, and it ticks all the boxes, and you can feel it, taste it smell it and touch it, then your life takes on new meaning. Everything you do is enjoyable and everyone you meet is inspiring.

There is nothing in particular in this life that you're supposed to do, only that which you are inspired to do.

In Conclusion - Keep It Simple

There are many words of advice and many methods for living a spiritual life. However, you are a spiritual being by your very existence, and you don't need to be taught how to be one. Be guided by your own Mood Map and follow your inspiration. That is the key. Your purpose is joy. Growth is inevitable. The only time you feel unhappy is when you have pinched yourself off from that which is Source — Your Inner Being, your Higher Self. Unhappiness is the indicator to move back into that space of joy, excitement, inspiration, and appreciation. There isn't something you need to achieve. There isn't someone you need to be. Take it easy and enjoy your life, no matter what it brings, knowing that it will always get you to where you are going, even if you don't know where that may be.

The Universe is always unfolding and expanding beautifully and it can be beneficial for you to take a step back to see the bigger picture on everything in your life. There is a place for you in this world, and your magnificence enhances everything around you. There is a broader perspective your Source uses to see the bigger picture, which is called clarity, and it is a valuable tool. Seeing your life through the eyes of Source gives you an appreciation of how things unfold the way they do, for everyone.

Journey through Time

Many relationships transcend time. Here is an excerpt of a Past Life Regression conducted a few years back that changed my perception of life, relationships and premature death.

"Where are you now?"
"I don't know. I can't see. It's tight around my eyes and my legs seem to be stuck. I can't move. It's all black. I can't see anything."
"Can you look down at your feet?"
"I can't see them."
"Are you inside or outside?"
"I don't know."
"Is there a window?"
"I can't see one."
"Can you move to another place?"
"No."
"OK, try and move ahead five years down the track. What's happening?"
"I can't see anything. I have something around my eyes. I can't move."
"Is there anyone there with you?"
A pause. "I can't tell."
"Can you move anywhere?"
"No."
"OK. Take a deep breath and let go of that lifetime. Move into the space of love and light where you feel safe and gain clarity. "
A long pause.
"Do you know what was going on?"
"Oh yes. I can see now. My mother was giving birth. I was in the birth canal and got stuck. That's why my legs and arms felt restricted and it felt tight around my eyes. We both died."

"What was the purpose of that life?" said the therapist.
"It was for my father," she said matter-of-factly. "I had a brother and my father needed the chance to be the father he always wanted to be. So, we gave him that opportunity."

Change Your Reality and You Change Your Life

Interview:

Why create this Handbook?
We've acquired some experience and knowledge over the years in Fitness, Health and Natural Healing and felt it might help some people to integrate an holistic approach to their body, mind and spirit.

What is healing?
It's about bringing your life back into balance. When you cut your finger, you're not quite in balance. Balance is what is required to live a happy and healthy life. It's not just in the body. Balance is for the whole Six Dimensions of your life.

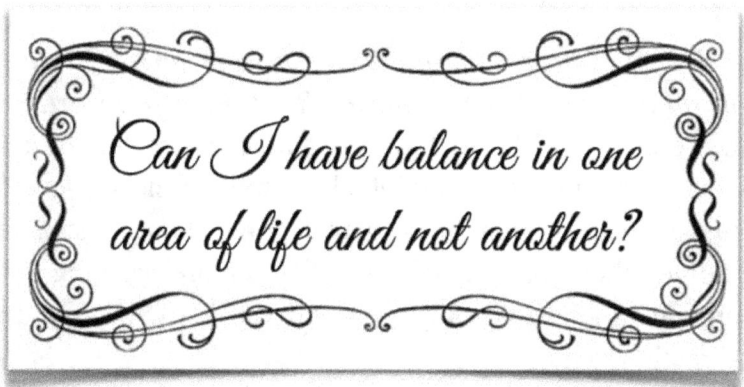

Can you have balance in one area but not another, or are you just completely out of balance in that case?
You can have balance in more than one area and not others. For instance, you may be in hospital after having suffered a heart attack and yet you are optimistic that things are going to work out well. So, your outlook is calm and peaceful, your attitude one of knowing that all is well. Therefore, your body may be undergoing some work, but the rest of you has already moved on. You need to remember that

what you are going through now is because of an imbalance in the past. We don't manifest illness immediately. It takes time. It came about by an attitude, but this may well have changed by the time the manifestation occurs. Illness is really a time of evaluation. Situations of physical imbalance really get our attention as they cause pain or disease. They call for clarity. When you know what you don't want, you certainly are clear what you do want.

How do we know how balanced we are in all these areas of our life?
It's really not necessary to monitor where you were before now. It's only important to keep moving in the direction of what feels good. Life continually changes and so do your moods. You will always attract opportunities to move your focus in the direction of your connection to your Higher Self.

How do I know which area of my life to work on? My relationship might be on the rocks but so is my health. Where do I start?
The first thing would be to figure out how you're feeling and then look for something neutral to think about to stop the self-talk torture. Then find something, anything to feel good about. Just a little bit better. Some relief from the noise is what you are reaching for. Some peace amongst the chaos. Only then will you know beyond doubt, in which direction to move.

How can this change my relationship?
All relationships are about the relationship you have with yourself. There really is only one relationship. Get that one right, and the others follow effortlessly.

What about the cancer in my body though? How does changing the way I feel fix that?
I know of surgeons that won't perform potentially life-threatening surgery, such as for cancer, without the patient having a positive outlook and loving support from a relationship, whether from a spouse, family or friends. They have come to understand that the outcome of the surgery is heavily influenced by their patient's emotional and attitudinal health.

How do I stay thinking positive when the people around me are doing my head in?
The only power you have in your life is the power to choose your own thoughts. If you were standing with a million dollars in your hand, you wouldn't let someone come and take it from you, would you? So too you should be conscious of the value of your own happiness. The best thing you can do is to get away from the people who are not thinking as you are. If you can't do that, then you need to put things into place to make sure you stay in the space you want to be in. These are called intentions. Setting your intentions makes a huge difference in your daily life.

I can't seem to maintain a good feeling place, especially when I am in emotional pain.
The more you practice a feeling good space, the easier and quicker it will be to get back into the mood you want to be in. There will be times when you are not feeling how you want, for many reasons and these times are important as contrasting experiences and emotions. They help you to define and refine what you want. They point you towards clarity and give you a richer experience. If you didn't know the pain of not having something you wanted, you wouldn't focus

your imagination on the joy of having of it. Focusing on what is working is pivotal for maintaining that good feeling place.

Can you imagine a blue butterfly? *A beautiful big blue butterfly that is fluttering around you, flitting around looking for a place to land. See in your mind's eye the vibrancy of the blues as they range from deep azure to turquoise. Picture the veins of the butterfly's wings and almost feel the breeze as it flaps so close to your face that it tickles your nose. It is so close, that you close your eyes so as not to scare the butterfly as it lands on the tip of your nose. You feel the tiny feet as they fleetingly dance on your skin, the gentle wings as they flutter upward and around you, then slowly toward the trees.*

For that moment of imagining the butterfly, you are in the present moment of joy and have joined your Higher Self in clarity and balance. For that moment, you felt no pain, no heartache, but experienced the freedom of love. *Your power in the present moment is in the ability to shift your focus from pain to distraction at any time you wish, no matter what is happening around you.*

Glossary

Terms that are interchangeable:
To give you a better understanding of the descriptions used in this Handbook, here are some terms that are interchangeable with words you may already know and use.

Higher Self, Your Source, God, Inner Being, Wisdom Universe, Source Energy
Vibration, Feeling
Mood, Emotions, Space
Balance, Connection
Joy, Love, Excitement, Clarity
Energy, Flow
Reality, Life, Present, Now, Vibration
Resistance, Contradiction, Pain, Pushing Against
Into Being, Reality
Faith, Knowing
Becoming, I Am, Wholeness, Oneness
Well-being, a state of being comfortable, healthy or happy

Six Dimensions of Healing

Bibliography

Bricusse, Leslie (1965)   Feelin' Good (song – cover by Michael Bublé, & Newley Antony 2005)

Campbell, Joseph (1988)   Joseph Campbell and the Power of Myth, with Bill Moyers, ed. Betty Sue Flowers. Doubleday and Co., N.Y.

Clemens, Samuel Langhorne (Mark Twain) (1889)A Connecticut Yankee in King Arthur's Court

Dyer, Wayne (2001)   You'll See It When You Believe It, Harper Collins, N.Y.

Dyer, Wayne (2006)   *The Power of Intention: Learning to Co-create Your World Your Way*, Hay House, Inc., USA.

Geizel, Theodor (Dr. Seuss) (1990)Oh the Places You'll Go, Random House, N.Y.

Harvard Medical School (2009)   Exercise and aging Can you walk away from Father Time.htm

	Retrieved from http://www.health.harvard.edu/newsweek/ Exercise_and_aging_Can_you_walk_away_from_Father_Time.htm
Healthstatus.Com (n.d.)	*"How Is Anxiety Different from Stress?"* Retrieved from https://www.healthstatus.com/health_blog/depression-stress-anxiety/how-is-anxiety-different-from-stress/
Hicks, Esther, and Jerry (2006)	The Law of Attraction: The Basics of the Teachings of Abraham, Hay House, Inc. p.b.

Hicks, Esther, and Jerry (2005)Ask and It Is Given, Hay House, Inc. p.b.

Hill, Napoleon (1937)*Think and Grow Rich,*

Lipton, Bruce H. (2006)	Wisdom of Your Cells – How Your Beliefs Control Your Biology Sounds True, Louisville, Colorado

Markets and Markets. com (2011)　　　Global Weight Loss & Gain
　　　　　　　　　　　　　　　　　　Markets 2009-2010
Retrieved from http://www.marketsandmarkets.com/four

Mayo Clinic (2007)　　　　　　　　The "NEAT" defect in
　　　　　　　　　　　　　　　　　　Human Obesity:
　　　　　　　　　　　　　　　　　　Endocrinology Update
　　　　　　　　　　　　　　　　　　Volume 1
　　　　　　　　　　　　　　　　　　Retrieved from
　　　　　　　　　　　　　　　　　　http://www.mayoclinic.or
　　　　　　　　　　　　　　　　　　g/documents/mc5810-
　　　　　　　　　　　　　　　　　　0307-pdf/doc-20079082

Schucman, Helen (1976)　　　　　　*A Course in*
　　　　　　　　　　　　　　　　　　Miracles, Viking, N.Y.
& Thetford, William

Thoreau, Henry David (1854　　　　)Walden

Watts, Fraser (1988):
& Williams, Mark　　　　　　　　　Cambridge

Weiss, Brian (1988)　　　　　　　　Many Lives, Many
　　　　　　　　　　　　　　　　　　Masters, Only Love Is
　　　　　　　　　　　　　　　　　　Real, Sinai Hospital,
　　　　　　　　　　　　　　　　　　Florida in USA.

Ziglar, Hilary ('Zig') (n.d.)　　　　　*"You cannot tailor make*
　　　　　　　　　　　　　　　　　　the situations in life, but
　　　　　　　　　　　　　　　　　　you can tailor make the
　　　　　　　　　　　　　　　　　　attitudes to fit those

situations before they arise."
Retrieved from http://www.planetmotivation.com/zigziglar.html
"Positive thinking will let you do everything better than negative thinking will."
Retrieved from https://www.ziglar.com/quotes

Change Your Reality and You Change Your Life

Six Dimensions of Healing

www.ingramcontent.com/pod-product-compliance
Lightning Source LLC
Chambersburg PA
CBHW071856290426
44110CB00013B/1165